FEMINIST EXPERIENCES

Northwestern University
Studies in Phenomenology
and
Existential Philosophy

FEMINIST EXPERIENCES

Foucauldian and Phenomenological Investigations

Johanna Oksala

Northwestern University Press
Evanston, Illinois

Northwestern University Press
www.nupress.northwestern.edu

Printed in the United States of America

10 9 8 7 6 5 4 3 2 1

Library of Congress Cataloging-in-Publication Data

Names: Oksala, Johanna, 1966–
Title: Feminist experiences : Foucauldian and phenomenological investigations / Johanna Oksala.
Other titles: Northwestern University studies in phenomenology & existential philosophy.
Description: Evanston, Illinois : Northwestern University Press, 2016. |
  Series: Northwestern University studies in phenomenology and existential
  philosophy | Includes bibliographical references and index.
Identifiers: LCCN 2015041154| ISBN 9780810132412 (cloth : alk. paper) | ISBN
  9780810132405 (pbk. : alk. paper) | ISBN 9780810132429 (e-book)
Subjects: LCSH: Feminist theory. | Phenomenology. | Neoliberalism.
Classification: LCC HQ1190 .O37 2016 | DDC 305.4201—dc23 LC record
  available at http://lccn.loc.gov/2015041154

Contents

Acknowledgments

As a student, feminist philosophy first drew me to philosophy, and this book is the result of many years of reading, writing, and thinking about it, but also, importantly, of discussing it with a number of great feminist thinkers—too many to thank here by name. I have had the honor and the pleasure to meet in person many of the philosophers whose work I discuss, comment on, and criticize in this book, and I am extremely grateful to them for their seminal and inspiring work. The book itself is hopefully the best acknowledgment of how important their work has been for me. Special thanks must nevertheless go here to my former teacher and current colleague and friend, Sara Heinämaa, who has shaped my thinking to an exceptional extent. I might be doing other interesting and worthwhile things now, but without her, I would not have become a feminist philosopher.

Many of the chapters in this book draw on previously published articles. An earlier version of chapter 1 appeared as "How Is Feminist Metaphysics Possible?" *Feminist Theory Journal*, vol. 12, no. 3 (2011): 281–96. Chapter 2 was originally published as "In Defense of Experience," *Hypatia: A Journal of Feminist Philosophy*, vol. 28, no. 4 (2014): 388–403. An earlier version chapter 3 appeared as "Experience: Foucault, Phenomenology and Feminist Theory," *Hypatia: A Journal of Feminist Philosophy*, vol. 26, no. 1 (2011): 207–23. An earlier version of chapter 5 was originally published as "What Is Feminist Phenomenology? Thinking Birth Philosophically," *Radical Philosophy*, no. 126 (2004): 16–22. Chapter 6 was published as "A Phenomenology of Gender," *Continental Philosophy Review*, vol. 39, no. 3 (2007): 229–44. An earlier version of chapter 7 was published as "The Neoliberal Subject of Feminism," *Journal of the British Society for Phenomenology*, vol. 42, no. 1 (2011): 104–20. An earlier version of chapter 8 was published as "Foucault, Feminism, and Neoliberal Governmentality," *Foucault Studies*, special issue on feminist theory, no. 16 (2013): 32–53.

FEMINIST EXPERIENCES

What Is Feminist Philosophy?

The purpose of this book is to provide a sustained defense of feminist philosophy. I use the term *feminist philosophy* here in a specific sense, distinct from a "philosophy of sex and gender" and "feminism in philosophy," for example. While a philosophy of sex and gender denotes a philosophical investigation of issues related to sex and gender, and feminism in philosophy can be understood to refer to a study of the ways in which feminist orientation has been able to reveal male biases and omissions in the methods and the canon of philosophy, both are essentially apolitical endeavors in the sense that their primary aim is to make philosophy—or forms of knowledge more generally—more comprehensive and objective. By feminist philosophy, in contrast, I refer to a form of social critique that aims not just for better forms of knowledge, but also for better forms of society. It is my contention that a key objective of feminist philosophy is to expose, analyze, criticize, and ultimately change the power relations that produce and organize society, or more fundamentally reality, in a way that makes it unequal or unjust for beings who are constructed and classified as women. In other words, I advocate an understanding of feminist philosophy that is first and foremost a form of *social critique* attempting to undertake a philosophical and critical analysis of the world we live in.

Such an understanding of feminist philosophy raises a host of theoretical problems and paradoxes, and my contention is that feminist philosophy has not responded as well as it could and should. The term "feminist philosophy" itself is a contested notion because of the tension it seems to harbor between pure philosophical contemplation, on the one hand, and the political aims of social change, on the other hand. Those of us who call ourselves feminist philosophers have no doubt had the experience of being told by a colleague that feminist philosophy is in fact an oxymoron: it refers to a political ideology which is the very antithesis of critical philosophical inquiry. The situation is often not much better in those women's studies and gender studies departments dominated by social sciences. There the accusations tend toward the opposite direction: the problem with feminist philosophy is not that the purity of philosophical contemplation has been compromised, but the fact that it has not been. The deeply rooted prejudice against philosophy, even feminist philosophy, is that it has nothing to do with social reality. The standing joke is that women could be reduced to slavery and philosophers would still continue to debate the same problems they have pondered for the last two thousand years totally undisturbed.

My aim is thus not just to defend the importance of feminist philosophy in the above sense, but also to identify a series of fundamental questions and challenges that such an understanding implies and that feminist philosophers have to face down. I insist that we have to provide some kind of satisfactory answers, even if these answers are necessarily preliminary, incomplete, and contested, if feminist philosophy is to continue as a viable form of social critique.

The first set of essential questions concerns the need for and the possibility of metaphysical inquiry. I contend that a certain kind of metaphysical inquiry is vital for feminist theory: it is crucial that we expose and criticize the taken-for-granted background beliefs and conceptual frameworks that produce and organize reality. A purely empirical study of women's lives or of the social facts affecting them is not enough. We need also to understand what kinds of beings these women are and how the facts about them are conceptualized, organized, and legitimized. In short, we need a feminist philosophy that is capable of exposing, analyzing, and criticizing the *metaphysical schemas* that organize both our experience of reality and the empirical sciences that produce facts about it.

The difficult question that such an understanding of feminist philosophy implies is methodological: How is such a philosophical analysis possible? How can we analyze in thought that which makes our thought possible? If a theory which is critical of society is to remain consistent, and if that theory also assumes that reality is, at least to some extent, socially constituted, then it cannot proceed from a standpoint that purports to lie outside its own social context. Rather, it must view itself as being embedded within, or even as being constituted by, this context. In other words, such a theory must be *immanent* social critique: there exists no place outside language, power, society, and history from which one could construct a theory of these things. We cannot take a position extrinsic to the reality that we are investigating, but must regard the very notion of a decontextualized, Archimedean standpoint as impossible.

It is my contention that this paradoxical predicament of immanent social critique implies that our approach must be transcendental: it has to take the form of transcendental philosophy. While most philosophers agree that transcendental philosophy was inaugurated by Immanuel Kant's Copernican turn, many thinkers focus on his search for universal structures of cognition as its defining character. In their view transcendental philosophy becomes more or less a synonym for what is understood as traditional metaphysics: an attempt to identify the most universal structures of everything. It is my contention that such an understanding completely misses the point about what is specific about transcendental investigation as a distinct philosophical approach. A more fruitful way to understand it is to see it essentially as antinaturalism: transcendental philosophy presents a sustained attempt to problematize natural realism as our taken-for-granted view of reality. While natural realists hold that we must attempt to remove the contribution of subjectivity from our perception of reality in order to achieve the best grasp of that reality, transcendental philosophers insist that reality cannot be understood independent of the historical and cultural community of experiencing subjects (Zahavi 2002a).

While we obviously have to start from our naive, precritical experience of the world, the philosophical, transcendental step that immanent social critique requires means questioning the appearance of things and asking what kinds of conditions or structures make them possible. What do we have to assume in order to be able to account for our experience of them? What I propose here—similar to most poststructuralists and many phenomenologists—is that these transcendental, constitutive conditions have to be understood as intersubjective: historical, cultural, and, not least, political.

Hence, if the tradition of "continental philosophy" is said to begin with Kant, what characterizes this tradition are the varying attempts to historicize the transcendental conditions of experience and to understand them as a set of historical and cultural presuppositions that mediate the way reality appears to us. Such historicized, transcendental inquiry is what must distinguish feminist philosophy from empirical sciences, on the one hand, and from logical or purely conceptual analysis of language, on the other hand.

To be able to argue that our experience and understanding of gender is not a simple fact that empirical science can discover, describe, and refer to objectively, but rather the effect of specific power relations, social practices, and deeply rooted patterns of prejudice requires a profound denaturalization of metaphysics. As feminist philosophers, we cannot simply accept reality at face value and assume that our experience of the world could ever be direct and unmediated. Rather, we have to ask how we have come to understand the world around us as hierarchically gendered, for example, and how genders and their relationship could be conceived otherwise.

I will show in this study that both phenomenology and Foucault's genealogy can be understood as engaging in transcendental philosophy in this historical and critical sense. In other words, they do not shun metaphysics when metaphysics is understood as a critical questioning of the historical conditions of possibility for our experience. I argue that they can therefore contribute important methodological insights and conceptual tools to the project of feminist philosophy.

I will mine Foucault's thought in particular in my attempt to sketch such a historically orientated metaphysical investigation here. My project could therefore be called *a feminist ontology of the present.* In his late writings, Foucault significantly emphasized the philosophical status of his work and introduced the idea of philosophy as an ontology of the present. It poses the questions: What is our present? What is the contemporary field of possible experiences?[1] Although Foucault linked such a project explicitly to Kant, he argued that the critical ontology of the present should not be practiced in the search for formal structures with universal value, but rather as a series of limited, historically specific analyses of contingent practices. Hence, although I read Foucault as following the tradition of metaphysics inaugurated by Kant—the idea that the structure of reality can only be comprehended by studying the conceptual schemas we impose on it—it is important to observe that he does not agree with Kant on the status enjoyed by these schemas. For Foucault, they are not constituted by universal structures of human reason, but rather by a field of historically changing practices and games of truth.

I will also emphasize the importance of phenomenology as a groundbreaking critique of naturalism. The key methodological procedure of phenomenology, *bracketing* or *reduction,* is intended precisely to break with our "natural attitude," the attitude in which the world simply consists of the various objects, events, and states of affairs as they appear around us, whether these be women, rain, or globalization. The aim of phenomenology is to problematize natural realism by asking how these objects or states of affairs are constituted in one's experience. Phenomenologists have typically applied the method of bracketing to perceptual experience: they bracket the "transparency" of experience—the way our attempts to describe or reflect on experience normally bring into view only the experienced world and not the experience itself. By contrast, in the phenomenological attitude, my experience or perception itself becomes the object of thought and awareness. For example, I am able to recognize the way that I can actually only perceive those aspects of things that are visible from my perspective, yet I experience a three-dimensional reality. The process by which reality is constituted in my perceptual experience—the way in which perceptual experience acquires world-presenting content—can thus be opened to philosophical investigation.

Analogously, to be able to engage in an ontology of the present and to investigate the way that contemporary reality is constituted as understandable and meaningful in political, historical, and cultural practices requires a form of bracketing, a stepping back from the taken-for-granted assumptions that we hold. An ontology of the present must thus also involve a methodological step that, for lack of a better word, I will call bracketing. Bracketing should be understood in the minimal, but essential sense as the capacity of the philosophizing subjects to take some critical distance from their experiences in order to study their constitutive conditions. We must be able to recognize as least some aspects of our metaphysical schemas not only as problematic, but also as radically historical and therefore potentially subject to political change. In short, to challenge the naturalness and objectivity of oppressive categories, we must be able to identify these categories and render them contingent.

While poststructuralists such as Foucault are often depicted as critics of all forms of transcendental philosophy through their denial of the possibility of such a step, on closer investigation this view does not hold true. Significantly, Foucault introduced the notion of *problematization*.[2] He explained that it refers to the way in which certain forms of behavior, practices, and actions can emerge as possible objects of politicization, redescription, and, ultimately, change. He acknowledged that for a practice, a domain of action, or behavior to become the object of problematization, it is necessary for certain historical, social, and political factors to have first made the practice uncertain and to have provoked a number of difficulties around it. This is the result of social, economic, and political processes, but their role is only one of instigation. Effective problematization must be accomplished by thought. When thought intervenes, it is not the direct and predictable result or the necessary expression of social, economic, or political difficulties. It is an original response, often taking many forms that are sometimes contradictory in their aspects (Foucault 1991b, 388–89). The notion of problematization can thus be understood as the possibility of contesting and transforming metaphysical schemas understood as the sedimented and normally taken-for-granted background beliefs. Thought is capable of problematizing itself, of taking a step back from the practices in which it is embedded and exposing at least some aspects of the hidden grammar, the rationality, that regulates them. In other words, through a kind of bracketing it is possible to take distance from forms of behavior and to reflect on these forms as a problem.

I will follow Foucault here in attempting to problematize some contemporary practices and forms of gendered behavior, particularly in chapters 7 and 8. I attempt to expose and analyze the historical ontology of neoliberalism from a feminist perspective—the new neoliberal organization of the social realm. I will investigate neoliberal governmentality and the corresponding form of the subject, which I claim this new technology of governing has produced during the last three or four decades. Despite my analyses of contemporary political issues such as economic globalization and neoliberal governmentality, my argument is decisively philosophical: it concerns ideas and conceptual presuppositions that make the world around us understandable. Hence, I will not engage in an empirical study of neoliberalism by relying on systematic review or analysis of empirical data. As a form of an ontology of the present, my analysis begins from personal experience. Foucault explains:

> The experience through which we grasp the intelligibility of certain mechanisms . . . and the way in which we are enabled to detach ourselves from them by perceiving them differently will be, at best, one and the same thing. This is really at the heart of what I do. What consequences or implications does that have? The first is that I don't depend on a continuous and systematic body of background data; the second is that I haven't written a single book that was not inspired, at least in part, by a direct personal experience. I've had a complex personal relationship with madness and with psychiatric institutions. I've had a certain relationship with illness and death. . . . The same is true of prison and sexuality, for different reasons. (Foucault 2000a, 244)

Engaging in a critical study of contemporary forms of governance and the shifting forms of the subject also means, of course, to engage in a study of one's self. This does not mean that one is required to produce confessional discourse, but it does require reflecting on the new kinds of demands and pressures that I, as a woman, a professional academic and a single mother, have experienced and have had to negotiate in today's academic environment and more generally in today's world. My reflections in part 3 on neoliberalism and feminist politics should be understood as stemming from personal experiences and concerns.

The emphasis on personal experience brings me to my next key topic, namely the role of experience in feminist theory. In addition to the thorny questions concerning the method of feminist philosophy, another decisive philosophical issue that I want to take up for reconsideration here concerns the relationship between experience and language. The significance of "experience" in contemporary feminist theory has swung like a pendulum, from one extreme to the other, during its fairly short history. In the 1970s, feminist theorists held experience to be one of the irreducible starting points for understanding the situation of women. The explicit aims of calling attention to experience was both to retrieve women's experiences, which for too long had remained invisible and marginal, and to validate these experiences in the face of scientific theories that had either discredited or ignored them. The pendulum reached the other extreme with Joan Scott's influential article "The Evidence of Experience" (1991), which argued against the idea of either appealing to experience as incontestable evidence or as a foundation upon which analysis of difference and social oppression was based.

The notion of experience thus became polarized as either a positive or a negative term in the feminist debate between postmodernism and modernism and, more specifically, between poststructuralism and phenomenology.[3] On one side were anti-essentialist, nominalist, or poststructuralist accounts, such as Scott's argument that experience is a discursive effect. On the other side, were phenomenological accounts that foregrounded experience, insisting that it must be explored from a first-person perspective and in terms of its affective and prelinguistic meaning.

It is my contention that this debate has been cast in simplistically binary and philosophically problematic terms. Accounting for the constitution of experience in feminist theory means no less than facing up to the metaphysical challenge that has occupied much of twentieth-century philosophical thought: trying to understand the relationship between experience and language. As many philosophers have argued, the major achievement of twentieth-century philosophy has been the paradigm shift that accords transcendental importance to language, the linguistic community, or both. Language has come to be understood as the condition of possibility for intersubjectively valid experience. Exactly what this insight means and what its consequences are in terms of philosophical reflection vary. Yet instead of studying this thorny metaphysical question about the relationship between experience and language, many feminist thinkers have discarded both metaphysics and experience as theoretically outdated notions.

I will critically examine the poststructuralist side of this debate on experience by taking a closer look at Joan Scott's article. I will investigate the phenomenological side by taking as my starting point Sonia Kruk's *Retrieving Experience: Subjectivity and Recognition in Feminist Politics* (2001). My aim is to show that both of these accounts rely on problematic ontological presuppositions concerning the relationship between experience and language and that this has dramatic consequences for their respective methods and conclusions. These positions represent two extremes, each of which is untenable. According to one extreme, experience is studied as a discursive effect; according to the other extreme, experience is considered to be independent of language. I will argue that rather than narrowing the scope of its claims to one side of this stalwart binary, a viable and philosophically interesting feminist account of experience should instead attempt to investigate the complex imbrication of language and experience.

I will show that on closer examination few poststructuralists or phenomenologists support the view that experience is either a discursive effect or independent of language. The so-called poststructuralist views on language include very different models for theorizing it, depending on whether we focus on the ideas of Foucault, Derrida, or Kristeva, for example. While the accounts that remain wedded in important respects to structuralism are in my view problematic, the ones that emphasize the pragmatic aspects of language, such as Foucault's genealogy, offer more fruitful possibilities: discourse is understood not as a deterministic and static symbolic system, but as a historically specific practice, a web of language games.[4] The constitution of sense thus cannot be understood through any system theory because language cannot be theorized independent of social practices and the subjects' actual use of it. The language users or speaking subjects are not the determined effects of linguistic structures, but they act in signifying practices or language games. They "do things with words," namely interact with each other and the world around them.

A similar metaphysical view concerning the relationship between experience and language can also be put forward from the phenomenological side. While Merleau-Ponty, for example, emphasized the importance of pre-predicative experiences, which can never be exhaustively articulated using ordinary language, he did not posit a pure realm of experience outside language, culture, and history. On the contrary, he emphasized the intersubjective constitution—social, cultural, and historical—of experience.[5] My focus, however, will be on Husserl's account of linguistic meaning. I want to show that, already in his thought we can find a sophisticated problematization of the question of language. I will also study how his most famous students, Eugen Fink and particularly Martin Heidegger, developed his account further by strongly emphasizing the personal or existential significance of phenomenological investigation. For young Heidegger, the return to lived experience meant an attempt to retain the original richness of experiential meaning without objectifying it and transforming it through theoretical and linguistic reflection. The methodological challenge that he had to face thus took the form of the following inquiries: How can the streaming experience of life become an object of reflection without being reified? How can we describe this experience in a way that does not inevitably distort, violate, and objectify it?

I will show how the same problem plagues those feminist phenomenologists who advocate a return to a prediscursive female experience.
Giving due attention to women's experiences of bodily pain and fear that
exceed discourse, for example, can only be done by somehow identifying
and articulating these experiences. How can we do this without turning
these experiences into descriptive accounts properly belonging to discursive analysis? In other words, if feminist phenomenology is understood as
a study of prediscursive, immediate experiences, then feminist phenomenologists, like young Heidegger, have to provide some kind of answer
to the methodological question of how this meaning can be theoretically
analyzed and communicated to others.

I will argue that the phenomenological emphasis on lived experience does not imply that this experience is prediscursive or immediate. There are different views within phenomenology itself on linguistic
meaning as well as on the relationship between experience and language. It is possible to argue, with the help of Husserl's thought, that the
meaning of the "felt or lived experience" is always, in principle, expressible in language and that, therefore, phenomenologically, it is equally an
experience to be explained.

The chapters of this book are grouped into three parts. While the
key arguments are developed across the parts, the chapters are themati-
cally more interlinked within each part.

In part 1, *Feminist Metaphysics*, traditional metaphysical questions
dominate. Chapter 1, "How Is Feminist Metaphysics Possible?," defends
the importance of metaphysical inquiry in feminist philosophy, but it also
raises the crucial questions of what feminist metaphysics means and how
it is even possible. A key aim is to question the possibility of revisionary
metaphysics as well as to emphasize the consequences of the linguistic
turn for any such project. I argue that before we can embark on any
metaphysical inquiry—feminist or otherwise—we are doomed to repeat
Immanuel Kant's monumental question, how is metaphysics possible?
I then ask how metaphysics is understood in feminist discussions and
focus on one contemporary effort to create feminist metaphysics, namely
Christine Battersby's *The Phenomenal Woman: Feminist Metaphysics and the
Patterns of Identity* (1998). Through a critical analysis of her position I
tease out the problems, paradoxes, and obstacles faced by the project
of feminist metaphysics. Finally, I explicate the politicized conception
of reality that I find in Michel Foucault's thought and conclude by considering its consequences for our understanding of feminist metaphysics
and politics.

Chapter 2, "In Defense of Experience," poses the question of our
philosophical understanding of experience in order to question the cur-

rent political and theoretical dismissal of experiential accounts in feminist theory. The focus is on Joan Scott's critique of experience, but the philosophical issues animating the discussion go beyond Scott's work and concern the future of feminist theory and politics more generally. I ask what it means for feminist theory to redefine experience as a linguistic event the way Scott suggests. I attempt to demonstrate that the consequences she draws from such a theoretical move are both philosophically and politically problematic. A critical study of the evidence of experience does not have to imply metaphysical or epistemological foundationalism as Scott claims; on the contrary, such a study is indispensable for challenging them. We must hold on to experience as an important resource for contesting sexist discourses and oppressive conceptual schemas.

Chapter 3, "Foucault and Experience," explicates Foucault's conception of experience and defends it as an important theoretical resource for feminist theory. I analyze Linda Alcoff's devastating critique of Foucault's account of sexuality and her reasons for advocating phenomenology as a more viable alternative. While I agree with Alcoff that a philosophically sophisticated understanding of experience must remain central to feminist theory, I attempt to show that her critique is based on a mistaken view of Foucault's philosophical position, as well as on a problematic understanding of phenomenology. I contend that Foucault does not hold experience and discourse to be ontologically coextensive as Alcoff claims, but that he makes a crucial theoretical distinction between experience as a subjective self-relation—having an experience—and its objective determinants and descriptions. Moreover, even if we accept that experiences are conceptual through and through, they can be conceptualized and rendered intelligible in multiple and competing discursive practices and conceptual frameworks. I emphasize both the epistemic and political importance of subjective experience in Foucault's thought and conclude by juxtaposing his account of experience with that of phenomenology.

In part 2, *Feminist Phenomenology*, I turn to a more detailed study of phenomenology as a theoretical framework for feminist philosophy. Phenomenology seems to present itself as the obvious candidate since it has not only provided an explicit and rigorous method of philosophical inquiry, but has also presented a powerful critique of naturalism—the argument defended in chapter 1—as well as foregrounding the methodological importance of first-person experience—the argument defended in chapters 2 and 3.

My investigation of phenomenology in part 2 is largely critical, however. While I attempt to highlight those aspects that I claim are useful or even indispensable for feminist philosophy, I also attempt to identify its problems and lacunas. I argue that phenomenology can provide a fruit-ful theoretical and methodological framework for feminist philosophy, but only if it is radically modified to the extent that it might no longer be recognized as phenomenology. In sum, my aim in part 2 is not pri-marily to engage in feminist phenomenology as such, but again to raise metalevel questions about what feminist phenomenology is and what it can accomplish.

Chapter 4, "The Problem of Language," problematizes an under-standing of feminist phenomenology as being able to account for the prediscursive, personal, or lived meaning of experience and therefore opposed to forms of feminist theorizing that focus on discourses and lin-guistic analyses. Instead, I want to propose an alternative understanding of feminist phenomenology as a sophisticated study of the constitution of linguistic meaning. I am in full agreement with feminist phenome-nologists such as Kruks and Alcoff who argue that feminist phenome-nology can provide important theoretical and methodological tools with which to challenge the narrow focus on discourse analysis and concep-tual history in feminist philosophy. However, in order to do this, fem-inist phenomenology should not identify itself too narrowly as a form of theorizing that examines experiences in terms of their prediscursive, grasped, or felt meaning. Rather, it should face up to the philosophical challenge posed by language and mine the rich heritage of phenomeno-logical thought on language and linguistic meaning for its own objec-tives. Hence, the chapter continues to explore the question of the rela-tionship between experience and language, only now it is investigated from the perspective of phenomenology.

Chapter 5, "A Phenomenology of Birth," continues to explore the question of how we should understand the project of feminist phenom-enology. I challenge another common understanding, which holds that feminist phenomenology complements phenomenology with accounts of female embodiment. By discussing an experience that is often under-stood as a feminist issue and relegated to the margins of phenomenol-ogy, namely giving birth, I raise the question of the consequences of the phenomenological study of this experience for the phenomenological project as a whole. The argument is that such study not only comple-ments phenomenology while leaving intact that which has previously been discovered, but forces us to question critically some of the central tenets of phenomenology. My key aim is to show that feminist phenome-nology is not a faithful assistant to the phenomenological project dealing with its marginal or regional subthemes. Rather, it should be understood as a critical current running through the whole body of phenomenologi-cal thinking.

Chapter 6, "A Phenomenology of Gender," asks how phenomenology, understood as a philosophical method of investigation, can account for gender. Despite the fact that phenomenology has provided useful tools for feminist inquiry, the question remains of how to study gender within the paradigm of the philosophy of a subject. I explicate four different understandings of phenomenology and assess their respective potential in terms of theorizing gender: a classical reading, a corporeal reading, an intersubjective reading, and a fourth interpretation, which I call a postphenomenological reading, which is where my sympathies lie. I argue that phenomenology can extend its analysis to the question of gender only if its method is radically revised. Phenomenology can help us understand how gendered experiences are constituted and how their constitution is tied not only to embodiment, but also to the normative cultural practices and structures of meaning. This can be accomplished by a subject who, through radical philosophical reflection, manages to take critical distance from certain forms of experience. At the same time, we have to accept that ontology can never be totally suspended, because it is irrevocably tied up with our language, our methods of reflection and our ways of seeing the world. This means accepting the always partial and preliminary character of any philosophical investigation that concerns ourselves. An analysis of experience that aims to be radical and transcendental can only be fragmentary and incomplete.

Part 3, *Feminist Politics*, moves from mainly studying the conditions of possibility for feminist critique to actually engaging in such critique. My focus will be on neoliberalism and the new challenges it presents for feminist theory and politics.

Chapter 7, "The Neoliberal Subject of Feminism," discusses the disciplinary production of the normative feminine body and analyses the shift that has taken place in the rationality underpinning our current techniques of gender. Foucault's studies of disciplinary technologies show how bodies are constructed as certain kinds of subjects through mundane, everyday habits and techniques. Similarly, feminist appropriations of Foucault's ideas, such as Sandra Bartky's influential work, have demonstrated how feminine subjects are constructed through patriarchal, disciplinary practices of beauty. My argument, however, is that there have been significant changes in the recent decades in the rationality underpinning these techniques of gender, changes that have emerged in tandem with the rise of the neoliberal, economic subject. I will appropriate Foucault's idea of governmentality, and particularly neoliberal governmentality, as an alternative framework to discipline for studying the contemporary construction of the feminine body. I will show that this idea provides us with a more comprehensive conceptual framework for understanding the construction of the feminine body in its current form.

Chapter 8, "Feminism and Neoliberal Governmentality," investigates the consequences for feminist politics of the neoliberal turn. Feminist scholars have analyzed the political changes in the situation of women that have been brought about by neoliberalism, but their assessments of neoliberalism's consequences for feminist theory and politics vary. Feminist thinkers such as Hester Eisenstein and Sylvia Walby have argued that feminism must now return its focus to socialist politics and foreground economic questions of redistribution in order to combat the hegemony of neoliberalism. Some have further identified poststructuralism and its dominance in feminist scholarship as being responsible for the debilitating move away from socialist or Marxist paradigms. I share their diagnosis to the extent that it is my contention that the rapid neoliberalization characterizing the last thirty years has put women and feminist thought in a completely new political situation. However, in contrast to those feminist thinkers who put the blame for the current impasse on the rise of poststructuralist modes of thought, I contend that the poststructuralist turn in feminist theory in the 1980s and 1990s continues to represent an important theoretical advance. Foucault's thought can provide a critical diagnostic framework for feminist theory as well as for prompting new feminist political responses to the spread and dominance of neoliberalism. I will also return to Nancy Fraser and Judith's Butler's seminal debate on feminist politics in the journal *Social Text* (1997) in order to demonstrate that a critical analysis of the economic/cultural distinction must be central when we consider feminist forms of resistance to neoliberalism.

Chapter 9, "Feminist Politics of Inheritance," raises the question of solidarity in feminist politics. Feminist political theory has moved decisively away from essentialist notions of identity to a purely strategic understanding of feminist political identity. My critical concern is that such a strategic approach to political identity in fact closely mirrors the current, neoliberal understanding of the subject dominant in our society and discussed in the previous chapters. I will investigate the possibility that history could provide a viable basis for feminist solidarity and the feminist political projects built on it. I begin by studying Wendy Brown's (1995) influential argument against any feminist attempt to turn to a shared history of suffering as a source of collective identity. Brown appropriates Nietzsche's idea of *ressentiment* to argue that feminist attachment to the injured identity of "woman" is predicated on and requires its sustained rejection by a hostile external world. Forms of solidarity built on it will therefore necessarily lead to political impotence and defeatism. I respond to Brown by turning to Walter Benjamin and Jacques Derrida to investigate critically the unacknowledged views of history and politics that underlie our feminist projects. I argue that instead of simply forgetting and letting go of "wounded attachments," feminism must rethink its relationship to historicity. The dispersal of history as a unified and linear narrative of progress signals a possibility of rethinking our past in a way that is able to redeem our politics against charges of *ressentiment.*

In sum, I endeavor to defend and develop a distinctive understanding of feminist philosophy as immanent social critique. I investigate the philosophical challenges that such a project faces and outline the ontological presuppositions and methodological innovations it requires. I defend the importance of the methodological procedure of bracketing, understood as a problematization of our present, and I highlight the role of personal experience for feminist theory and politics. I will also engage in a study of language and linguistic meaning and advocate the fundamental importance of such a study. Finally, I attempt to engage in a feminist ontology of the present by critically investigating neoliberalism and the challenges it presents to feminism.

It should be noted that my aim in defending a distinctive understanding of feminist philosophy is not to close down the field of feminist philosophy.[6] Rather, I want to respond precisely to its openness and diversity by seeking to determine what feminist philosophy means for me. The question of how feminist philosophy is defined and understood has to be open to deliberate and *personal* scrutiny if we want feminist philosophy to be more than an empty label.

Finally, we have to consider the objection that any defense of feminist philosophy is simply going to be outdated and conservative: feminist theory is a remarkably interdisciplinary field resistant to traditional academic classifications. Its appeal and exceptional creativity must be attributed to a large extent to its agility in crossing established boundaries. So why should feminists have any fidelity to philosophy in particular, especially considering how hostile the canon of philosophy is to women and how deep its masculinist bias runs?[7] Influential feminist theorists such as Rosi Braidotti, for example, have consciously positioned themselves outside of the academic discipline of philosophy and openly criticized not only its content, but crucially its style and methods too. Braidotti (2002, 9) describes her choice of a nomadic style as a deliberate gesture of rejection of "the competitive, judgmental, moralizing tone" that characterizes traditional philosophy. She acknowledges that her style may strike some as allusive or associative, but her hope is that "what appears to be lost in terms of coherence can be compensated for by inspirational

force and an energizing pull away from binary schemes, judgmental pos-
tures and the temptation of nostalgia" (ibid.).

I personally find the coherence and lucidity of philosophical argu-
mentation inspirational and energizing, but I also hope to demonstrate
that feminist philosophy, as a specific approach to philosophical inquiry
is able to provide a distinctive, critical level of analysis that is indispensable for feminist theorizing.

Investigating philosophically issues such as female experience, feminist metaphysics, consciousness-raising practices, and feminist history
also means reopening questions that were central to the second-wave
feminism in 1970, but which many feminist thinkers today assume to
have become outdated. Women's liberation movement of the 1970s was
a unique political phenomenon: it created a new conception of politics
that built on personal experience and lived practice. My aim here is not
a nostalgic return to the feminism of a bygone era. I strongly believe
that such a return is impossible and even undesirable. Rather, it is my
contention that the corpus of feminist philosophy is in many ways like
a boomtown that was built rapidly with contagious energy and enthusi-
asm. It is now necessary to do some backtracking and strengthening of
its structural elements if feminist philosophy is going to withstand and
face up to the political challenges of our rapidly changing world. At the
risk of seeming unadventurous, I nevertheless believe it is what needs to
be done.

Part 1

Feminist Metaphysics

1

How Is Feminist Metaphysics Possible?

The starting point of my reflections on feminist metaphysics is a curious development in gender equality in my native country, Finland. In Finland and other Scandinavian countries, often held as forerunners in gender equality, women have enjoyed equal opportunities for education for a relatively long period. Consequently the level of their education has surpassed that of men. In 2003 already, for example, 71 percent of all M.A. degrees and 58 percent of all Ph.D.s were granted to women in Finland.[1] This means that in professions requiring higher education and academic qualification—such as doctors, lawyers, and university staff—the majority of employees are, or soon will be women.

This is a laudable achievement and a formidable victory for the feminist movement. One might assume that it inevitably meant the social privileges that traditionally have been connected with education would now also have been transferred to women: corresponding to their level of education their salaries would also surpass men's, for example. This has not happened, however. Instead, the salaries in the fields that have recently become dominated by women—such as medicine—have started to lag behind. Similarly, the social status and respect enjoyed by these professionals has diminished.

The example of Finland thus strongly suggests that the creation of equal opportunities through education is not enough to change deeply rooted patterns of thought. The underlying values and conceptual structures—what I call metaphysical schemas in this book—which link women and their work to inferiority and supplementarity still remain effective.

It is my contention that it is therefore important for feminist theory to expose and criticize these schemas: feminist metaphysics is vital. Metaphysics is not a popular field in feminist theorizing, however. As Sally Haslanger (2000, 107) notes, "academic feminists, for the most part, view metaphysics as a dubious intellectual project, certainly irrelevant and probably worse." The *scienticism* characterizing our culture is evident also in academia where many people simply hold that questions concerning the nature and structure of reality must be answered by natural sciences such as physics, not by armchair philosophical speculation, and the metaphysical presuppositions of natural sciences are simply taken for granted.[2] Feminists also have their own particular reasons for being critical of metaphysics. While criticizing metaphysics for being completely irrelevant, feminists have also, paradoxically, based their anti-metaphysical stance on the argument that it is politically pernicious. A lot of poststructuralist feminist theory in particular has attacked metaphysics as being essentializing and foundationalist.[3] Metaphysics should be resisted because it masks an effective ideology of oppression. As numerous feminist thinkers have demonstrated, the devalued side of such ontological oppositions as mind/body, nature/culture, reason/emotion, and animal/human, for example, has been attached to femininity and this has led to and upheld oppressive practices and conceptions about women.[4]

Accepting this argument means, however, that feminist theory cannot respond to the sexism of metaphysics by adopting a position of hypocrisy. Not mentioning the word "metaphysics" does not mean that feminist problems concerning it will disappear. Rather, it means that we have to acknowledge the profound connection between metaphysics and politics and the need to critically study it. Metaphysics forms the framework that functions to constrain our political theorizing and action, and all political orders as well as theoretical reflections therefore presuppose metaphysics. As my example of Finland shows, metaphysics forms a fundamental limit for our efforts to change social reality. Struggles for political change cannot be reduced to the rewriting of legislation or to the redistribution of resources. We must question the metaphysical schemas and ontological categories on the basis of which our political claims are made.[5] If feminist philosophy does not contribute anything to metaphysical inquiry, it is hard to see how it could contribute anything significant to political change either.[6]

My discussion of feminist metaphysics will proceed in three stages. It is my contention that before we can embark on any metaphysical inquiry—feminist or otherwise—we are doomed to repeating Kant's monumental question, How is metaphysics possible? I will ask how metaphysics is understood in feminist discussions and focus on one contemporary effort to create feminist metaphysics, namely Christine Battersby's project, *The Phenomenal Woman: Feminist Metaphysics and the Patterns of Identity*. It is one of the most explicit and extended attempts to create a new feminist metaphysics and as such, symptomatic of the problems that the project of feminist metaphysics faces. My contention is that the critical questions raised by Battersby's project could also be directed at several other feminist attempts to revise metaphysics and to understand it as more dynamic and processual.[7] Through a critical analysis of her position I attempt to tease out more explicitly the problems, paradoxes, and obstacles that the project of feminist metaphysics faces. I will then explicate the politicized conception of reality that I find in Foucault's thought. I will conclude by considering its consequences for our understanding of feminist metaphysics.

In sum, my objective in this chapter is, on the one hand, to pose a question about the very possibility of feminist metaphysics. While many important feminist thinkers such as Irigaray, Butler, Braidotti, and Grosz have dealt with questions of time, space, being, and identity in their writings, my aim is not to analyze or contrast any specific metaphysical positions in the field of feminist thought, but to ask a more fundamental question about the possibility and limits of metaphysical inquiry. A key aim of this chapter is to question the possibility of revisionary metaphysics as well as to emphasize the consequences of the linguistic turn for any such project. On the other hand, I also want to put forward a specific, politicized understanding of ontology with the help of Foucault's thought. I will do this in order to be able to advocate an understanding of feminist metaphysics that is politically relevant.

What Is Feminist Metaphysics?

Metaphysics was traditionally understood as a study of essences, the necessary elements that are common to all members of a natural kind or species. This conception formed the basis of our metaphysical tradition in philosophy for centuries. With Kant's question—How is metaphysics possible?—the metaphysical enterprise and tradition fundamentally changed, however. Michel Loux (1998, 8–13) characterizes this change in terms of a split: with Kant the tradition of metaphysics was split into two strands, both of which continue to our day. The pre-Kantian, Aristotelian conception of metaphysics still continues today in efforts to provide knowledge of the ultimate nature and structure of the world itself. The ontological disputes concern the question of what "really" exists and the identification and characterization of the categories under which things fall.[8] According to the Kantian strand, on the other hand, metaphysics is a descriptive enterprise, which does not claim knowledge of the most fundamental structures of reality, but whose aim is the characterization of our conceptual schema, the delineation of the most general features of our thought and experience.[9]

This split between Kantian and Aristotelian strands of metaphysics is the starting point of Christine Battersby's project to create a feminist metaphysics. In her seminal book *The Phenomenal Woman: Feminist Metaphysics and the Patterns of Identity* (1998) she argues that the Aristotelian bias in feminist understandings of metaphysics has severely limited reflection on important metaphysical questions. Feminist theorists are right to reject and criticize any form of metaphysics of substance for upholding an immutable and potentially oppressive hierarchy of beings. This criticism should not, however, lead to the rejection of all metaphysical inquiry. If we depart from the Aristotelian tradition of metaphysics we do not have to think in terms of fixed essences, permanent substances, or unchanging being. The common feminist argument about the oppressive nature of metaphysical hierarchies is thus based on a narrow understanding of the scope of metaphysics. Battersby strongly criticizes those feminist theorists "who would demonize metaphysics" and who see no alternative to the metaphysics of substance that has been deemed a necessary feature of phallogocentric thought. She advocates instead an ontology of becoming, which does not deal with individualized substances, but with "morphological transformations and identities that emerge through repeated patternings, intersecting force-fields, and flow" (ibid., 11–13).

Battersby is just as critical of Kant's descriptive metaphysics, however, arguing that it is intimately linked to a conception of space, time, and personal identity that is incapable of dealing with the fleshy female subject that births. She wants to construct a new ontology that makes women typical: mothering, parenting, and the fact of being born need to be fully integrated into what is entailed in being a human person or self (ibid., 2). This ontology is built on five key features that she claims characterize the female subject-position in Western modernity. In addition to natality, she emphasizes the ontological dependency of the fetus on the mother as well as the fact that women are socialized as the primary caregivers for children. This means that ontologically we cannot draw a sharp division between the self and the other: the self does not emerge out of the exclusion or abjection of the other, but both the self and the other emerge "from intersecting force-fields" (ibid., 8). Last, in our culture, female identities are fleshy identities. They are integrally linked to embodiment in a way that male identities are not. Battersby's key aim is to ask "what happens if we treat the potential for pregnancy as well as the other four features of the 'fleshy' female subject-position, as central to our notion of personhood and self" (ibid., 17). She seeks to answer this question by constructing a new ontology of the self that can account for the specificity of the female subject-position.

While I am deeply appreciative of Battersby's starting point in defending the possibility of feminist metaphysics, I also see her project as symptomatic of some of the problems that the project faces. I will not attempt to challenge the actual content of her ontological claims here, but more fundamentally examine the questions that emerge from the overall nature of her project.

Battersby's project is an uneasy combination of descriptive and revisionary metaphysics. On the one hand, she seeks to describe onto-logically the female subject-position as it is at the moment, in modern Western cultures. She argues for example, that it is a monstrous and paradoxical position given the aberrant nature of the female with respect to the "normal" male modes of selfhood in Western modernity. This means that it is important to hold onto the notion of female essence, but this essence must not be thought of in Aristotelian terms. There is no essence in the sense of sameness between women, which is consti-tuted by shared experiences or life histories. The undeniable sameness between women is a question of a shared positioning vis-à-vis the found-ing metaphysical categories that inform our notions of individuality, self, and "personhood." Feminist metaphysics must study the specificity of the female subject-position in Western modernity while acknowledging that the female subject is historically changing and that modernity is not homogeneous (ibid., 39–40).

Battersby's project is also revisionary, however, in the sense that she not only exposes how we conceive selfhood and identity, she argues for how we *should* conceive them. What makes her project distinctively feminist is her emphasis on finding a new metaphysics that would allow us to take the female as the norm. The historically and normatively con-structed female subject-position becomes a model for a new ontology based on women's paradoxical mode of being. ". . . feminists need—for political ends—to exploit the difficulties of containing female identity within the schemas provided by classical science and metaphysics, and use the resources provided by contemporary science and the history of philosophy to think selves, bodies and boundaries in more revolutionary terms" (ibid., 59).

One might want to question the problematic circularity of her proj-ect: Why should we take a subject-position constructed through an op-pressive history and metaphysics as the model for a new ontology in-tended to revolutionize that history and metaphysics? Are we not in fact ontologizing the historically specific and contingent subject-position that we want to radically transform and rethink?

Aside from these questions relating to the normative underpin-nings of her project, I want to focus on the more general methodological questions that emerge from it. Whether her project is understood as de-scriptive or revisionary both possibilities imply important methodological questions. If the project is descriptive, we must ask: How can we expose the metaphysical assumptions and background beliefs that characterize our thinking about "women" in Western modernity? What is the method for doing it? If descriptive metaphysics describes the way our world is at present and the way we are as parts of it, it then describes a situation we find ourselves in. This situation moreover forms the constitutive context for our thought and practice. How can we clarify something that forms the context for the intelligibility of our being and action? Is it possible to step outside of our thought to study the assumptions and background beliefs on which it relies?

If the project is not purely descriptive, but her primary attempt is to create a new metaphysics, we still have to deal with the same questions. It is my contention that the idea of imagining a different ontology presupposes at least two contested philosophical claims. First, it presupposes descriptive metaphysics: that we can understand and elucidate the ontology underlying our present thinking. The new metaphysics can only appear new against the background of the old one which has been shown to be problematic in some way. Second, we must be able to show that our present ontology is not necessary in any absolute sense. To return to the critical question about the relevance of metaphysics, if our thinking is to have any concrete effect on social reality, there is no sense in constructing alternative ontologies that amount to nothing but fiction or wishful thinking. Feminists are right in being deeply skeptical of all forms of speculative and revisionary metaphysics that amount to nothing more than interesting thought-experiments at best. To imagine a different future, we have to start by understanding the nature of our present.

The question of the appropriate method for uncovering metaphysical presuppositions or background beliefs is tied to the question of what exactly is the status of the conceptual schema on the basis of which reality is comprehended? The philosophers following the tradition of metaphysics inaugurated by Kant do not agree on the status enjoyed by our picture of the world. While Kant held that there was a single unchanging structure that underlay human knowledge or experience, other thinkers have emphasized the dynamic and historical character of thought. They identify alternative and distinct conceptual frameworks: one conceptual schema can disappear in favor of a new and different picture of the world.[10]

Jaakko Hintikka (1997) argues that Kant's critical metaphysics led to the important development in twentieth-century philosophy that substituted language for the conceptual schema through which we comprehend reality. The linguistic turn in philosophy has been, to a large extent, the realization of the ultimate link between language and metaphysics and an effort to come to terms with it. Hintikka argues that Kant's philosophy forms the background for the influential view in twentieth-century philosophy, which he calls "the universality of language thesis." This view forms the ultimate presupposition of much twentieth-century philosophy and is held by such varied thinkers as Frege, Wittgenstein, Heidegger, and Derrida.

According to Hintikka, the ultimate presupposition of these thinkers concerns the relationship between language and the world. Language is understood as the universal medium in the sense of being inescapable. We cannot step outside of it and describe in language the world-language relationships. Language thus forms the conceptual schema, the glasses through which reality shows itself to us, and we cannot remove the glasses. We are literally prisoners of our language: its semantics cannot be defined in that language without circularity, for this semantics is assumed in all its uses, and it cannot be defined in a metalanguage because there is no such language beyond our actual working language. In short, the semantics of our one and only language is inexpressible in it.

Hence, to decide whether or how it is possible to articulate our metaphysical commitments, we must start by trying to understand what our metaphysical schema consists of. While it is obvious that some metaphysical commitments are fairly easy to elucidate and articulate, some may be impossible. If we investigate the metaphysical background beliefs operative in scientific research, for example, some of them can be fairly easily articulated and critically scrutinized by the scientific community itself. Feminist epistemologists have shown how scientific research on sex hormones, for example, is guided by the ontological background assumption of sexual dimorphism and have attempted to question its inevitability.[11] Sexual dimorphism would thus be an example of a historically and culturally specific ontological commitment which is normally invisible and taken for granted. It is undoubtedly an important feature of the conceptual schema by which we organize our perceptions of other people and by which we judge and modify our own behavior. It forms a framework for our thought and action, but it is a commitment that can be articulated and critically questioned through various philosophical methods, as I will show in chapter 6, for example.

The issue gets more complicated, however, if we accept that language itself carries metaphysical commitments, which cannot be articulated in that language itself. If we accept, for example, that sexual dimorphism is imbedded in the structure of our language, it becomes a lot harder, if not impossible, to effectively question it and to offer alternatives. Such a view characterizes much of poststructuralist feminist theory influenced by the thought of Luce Irigaray and Jacques Derrida.[12]

Language itself inhabits a phallogocentric metaphysics that excludes women. Revisionary metaphysis in any straightforward sense would not only be irrelevant or politically dangerous, but impossible. The tradition of Western metaphysics cannot be revised or reformed, it can at most be destabilized. Language traps us in a metaphysics, which is also, however, coded with its own dissolution and deconstruction. As Derrida famously formulates this idea: "There is no sense in doing without the concepts of metaphysics in order to shake metaphysics. We have no language—no syntax and no lexicon—which is foreign to this history; we can pronounce not a single destructive proposition which has not already had to slip into the form, the logic and the implicit postulation of precisely what it seeks to contest" (Derrida 1978, 280–81).

Battersby acknowledges and anticipates the possible Derridean objection to her project of a new feminist metaphysics, but casts it aside fairly easily. She argues that while the history of metaphysics has privileged the male body, metaphysics is not a monolithic tradition. She emphasizes, in connection with Nietzsche's thought, that history must be recognized as internally multiple and as containing possibilities that might have disappeared from view, but that can be reactivated. According to her, the illusions of the self, for example, that Nietzsche warned us against were not the product of universal structures of grammar, but of history. Escaping them therefore does not require abandoning grammatical and propositional language, or disturbing its systematic operations via parody or wordplay. It is possible to find other ways of thinking as well as speaking and writing "within the evolutions and revolutions (and different temporalities) of the constellations of ideas that constitute the real" (Battersby 1998, 137). Derrida's insistence that the history of metaphysics closes itself down into a single trajectory serves to render invisible an alternative "fleshy" metaphysics which is also present in our metaphysical tradition in the thought of thinkers such as Kierkegaard (ibid., 95).

However, by founding the project of feminist metaphysics on philosophers from before the linguistic turn such as Kierkegaard, Battersby's project risks appearing to be a naive return to a metaphysical tradition undisturbed by the challenge posed by language. She accepts that "all our experience is mediated through language" (ibid., 36), but she does not explain how the new metaphysics she advocates can attach "new" semantics to "old" words. She argues, for example, that for Kierkegaard, it is the notion of "woman"—and not "man"—that provides the key to his new understanding of the self that emerges together with the other through repeated movements. But how can "woman" as the model for this new subject-position come to stand in for our traditional understanding of the self? How can we attach words to things in a new way? I contend that it is vital that any attempt to construct an alternative metaphysics responds to this challenge adequately: either it has to be content to only destabilize our metaphysical tradition or it has to show that metaphysics is not seamlessly tied to the syntax and lexicon of our language. After the linguistic turn, the question of language in metaphysics cannot be bypassed.

Foucault's Historical Ontology

It is here that I find it helpful to turn to the thought of Michel Foucault. Foucault follows the Kantian tradition of philosophy in many important respects. He was interested in Kant from very early on and wrote his complementary doctoral thesis on him.[13] This interest culminated in *The Order of Things*, and Foucault did not directly refer to Kant again until the end of 1970s. In his late writings, however, he significantly returns to him and it is in connection with Kant's philosophy that Foucault introduces the idea of philosophy as an ontology of the present, or an ontology of ourselves. This historical ontology of ourselves poses the questions: What is our present? What is the contemporary field of possible experience?[14]

In contrast to Kant, Foucault argues that the critical ontology of the present should not be practiced in the search for formal structures with universal value, but rather as a series of limited, historically specific analyses of contingent practices. "The aim is not to deduce from the form of what we are what it is impossible for us to do and to know, but to separate out, from the contingency that has made us what we are, the possibility of no longer being, doing, or thinking what we are, do or think" (Foucault 1991d, 46). While science and much of ontology aim to decipher from the confusion of events and experiences that which is necessary and can therefore be articulated as universal law, Foucault's thought moves in exactly the opposite direction: he attempted to find among necessities that which upon closer philosophical scrutiny turned out to be contingent, fleeting, and singular. Hence, although I read Foucault as following the tradition of metaphysics inaugurated by Kant, for him the conceptual schemas through which reality becomes accessible are not constituted by universal structures of human reason, but in a field of historically changing practices.[15]

Hence, what poststructuralism, and particularly Foucault's thought, contributed to the linguistic turn was the strong emphasis on the historical, social, and political aspects of the constitution of reality. Language is not only an abstract grid of intelligibility, it is also a social and historical practice incorporating power relations. Foucault insisted that we had to consider the facts of discourse not only in their linguistic dimension, but also "as games, strategic games of action and reaction, question and answer, domination and evasion, as well as struggle" (Foucault 2000b, 2). Language is a game: it is a web of intersecting practices that do not form a monolithic system.[16] In his famous exchange with Derrida, Foucault accused Derrida of reducing discursive practices to textual traces and therefore seeing in his own historically determined pedagogy the closure of metaphysics (Foucault 1998a, 416).[17]

Foucault's methodological focus on practices is sometimes read as a denial of metaphysics: instead of natural objects or things, there are only practices that are constitutive of discursive objects. The focus on practices should be read as an ontological commitment, however, not as a denial of ontology. The focus on generative practices rather than supposedly natural objects amounts to a critique of forms of natural realism. Paul Veyne (1997, 168), for example, has argued that it is precisely the step of disqualifying the natural object that gives Foucault's work its philosophical, as opposed to purely historical, stature. Foucault's central and most original thesis was the primacy of practices, but Veyne cautions against any simplistic metaphysical interpretation of them: Foucault did not discover a previously unknown new agency, called practice. Practices do constitute subjects and objects, but practice is not a prime mover or a hidden engine that creates reality; it is what people do (ibid., 168).[18]

To avoid discursive idealism—the idea that language somehow exhaustively brings things into existence—and to be able to argue at the same time that there are no natural objects, but that objects come into being only as correlates of practices, Veyne makes a distinction between preconceptual materiality and the objectifications engendered by practices. To say that madness or sexuality does not exist, means that this preconceptual materiality can be objectified in different ways in different historical practices. At one time it was objectified as madness, at another as mental illness and these objects are then further reified as "natural objects." Reality does not consist of given, natural objects because the preconceptual referent can only appear as the material of cultural construction retrospectively (ibid., 160–61, 169–71).

Discourse does not construct bodies, for example, in the sense of bringing them into existence, but we can only identify them and refer to them if they have been made conceptually intelligible and thus have already been linguistically formed in the process. Discursive practices set the boundaries of our reference and by excluding some features, experiences, and possible articulations ultimately congeal versions of reality.[19]

Hence, when Foucault's commentators label him a nominalist they generally refer to some form of social constructivism.[20] Social practices, not pure language, bring into being, or institute, a world of significations, and reality, as we know it, is the result of such an institution. All knowledge, both scientific and the taken-for-granted commonsense knowledge of everyday reality, is derived from and maintained by social practices, but comes to be understood as the description of a given, objective reality. Foucault's historical ontology does not denote the study of some metaphysical principles or essences under or above concrete practices. It denotes a specific philosophical perspective to practices, however: it attempts to expose their conceptual underpinnings, the hidden grammar that regulates them.

Foucault's thought thus formed an important strand in the effort to theorize the social construction of reality that became prominent in the 1960s and 1970s.[21] It is my contention that his most original and important contribution to this project was his conception of productive power. As his arguably most famous single sentence states: "Power produces; it produces reality; it produces domains of objects and rituals of truth" (Foucault 1991a, 194).

The idea that power produces reality can be understood in different ways, however. The ordering of reality could be interpreted as an act of power in the simple sense that it is instituted by those in power and therefore reflects their perspective on the world. To use some hackneyed examples, the heterosexual/homosexual binary is the result of homophobic power relations, just as man/woman is a conceptualization of a sexist society. In both cases the first term of the binary refers to what is the norm, privileged and unproblematized, while the second refers to the aberration, to that which differs from the norm. Sexual and gendered identities have become—partly thanks to Foucault—textbook examples of categories that are constructed not as politically neutral and natural differences, but as mutually exclusive and highly normative terms reflecting and giving expression to the power relations in society.

More importantly, however, the ordering of reality has power effects irrespective of the intentions of those in power. Knowledge necessarily produces effects of power simply by virtue of what is scientifically validated, rational, or generally accepted. Elements of everyday as well as scientific knowledge have to conform to a set of constraints that is characteristic of a given type of society in a given period. What distinguishes Foucault's analyses of social practices from those of a number of other thinkers is not only the idea that practices always incorporate power relations that directly and causally manipulate the subjects in them, but that the rules of discursive practices are intimately tied to social norms.

This means that these practices become unavoidably invested with power effects: social norms are not just technical, power-neutral rules, like traffic rules or grammar, they reflect existing social hierarchies and power relations. The intertwinement of power and knowledge must thus be understood as the mutual intertwinement of practices, disciplines, and institutions of power with practices for the production of knowledge. Social reality is the result of historically specific struggles over truth and objectivity, because the production of knowledge is internally tied to social practices and the power relations manifested in them.[22]

In sum, Foucault's politicization of ontology consists of two critical moves. First, he affirms the metaphysical view that there is a discontinuity between reality and all ontological schemas that order it, and the subsequent indeterminacy of reason in establishing ultimate truths or foundations. After this initial step whereby ontology is denaturalized—made arbitrary or at least historically contingent—the way is open for explanations that treat the alternative and competing ontological frameworks as resulting from historical, linguistic, and social practices of power. The important philosophical idea behind Foucault's hybrid notion of *power/ knowledge* is that social practices always incorporate power relations, which become constitutive of forms of the subject as well as domains and objects of knowledge. They are not subjects and objects existing in the world as pregiven constants, but are rather constituted through practices of power. This is a radical, ontological claim about the nature of reality: reality as we know it is the result of social practices, but also of concrete struggles over truth in social space.

A Feminist Ontology of the Present

Foucault clearly denies the possibility of conducting metaphysical inquiry that seeks to identify universal structures of reality. Despite his firm denial of a certain understanding of metaphysics, however, his historical studies—his archaeologies and genealogies—should not be read as simply empirical studies of particular cultural practices. They are not studies in historical sociology. Rather, they should be read as forms of historical ontology. As Ian Hacking (2002, 70) characterizes them, the aim is to understand how fundamental ordering codes, scientific objects, and conceptual divisions developed in historical practices: how our conceptions were made and how the conditions for their formation constrain our present ways of thinking.

For Foucault, history functions as the method of ontological inquiry. On the one hand, it makes it possible to reveal the ontological commitments of past epochs. The task of Foucault's archaeology was to retrospectively analyze the network of scientific discourses to reveal the depth structures that were unconscious to the scientific practitioners. On the other hand, history also makes it possible to reveal our own unconscious commitments, at least to a certain extent, by revealing their historical development and also by contrasting them to past forms of thinking.[23] Here Foucault's method comes close to Heidegger and the hermeneutical insight that it is only against the background of what is different in history that the background beliefs of our present show up.[24]

Foucault also emphasizes the possibility of *problematization* as a philosophical task. In the introduction to *The Use of Pleasure*, as well as in his interviews in the 1980s, Foucault introduced the concept of problematization, a notion he claimed was common to all his work since *Histoire de la folie*.[25] It refers to the way that certain forms of behavior, practices, and actions can emerge as possible objects of politicization, redescription, and, ultimately change. He explains that for a practice, a domain of action, or behavior to enter the field of political problematization it is necessary for a certain number of factors to have first made it uncertain, to have made it lose its familiarity, or to have provoked a number of difficulties around it. This is the result of social, economic, and political processes, but their role is only that of instigation. Effective problematization is accomplished by thought. When thought intervenes it does not assume a unique form that is the direct result or the necessary expression of the social, economic, or political difficulties. It is an original or specific response, often taking many forms, sometimes contradictory in their aspects (Foucault 1991b, 388–89).

The notion of problematization can thus be understood as the possibility of contesting and transforming ontology understood as the sedimented and normally taken-for-granted background. The politicization of ontology is not just a process of unmasking, but also one of redescription. Thought is capable of problematizing itself, of taking a step back from the practices in which it is embedded and exposing the hidden grammar, the rationality, that regulates them. It allows one to take distance from forms of behavior, and to reflect on them as a problem. The politicization of ontology thus does not mean its replacement or denial, but its problematization: "Thought is freedom in relation to what one does, the motion by which one detaches oneself from it, establishes it as an object, and reflects on it as a problem" (ibid., 388).

Hence, from the point of view of feminist theory, Foucault's thought has the benefit of describing metaphysical schemas as radically historical and as subject to political change. Such an understanding of metaphysics is indispensable for the radical feminist strategy of challenging the objectivity of oppressive categories. It is implicit in the key claim of feminism that the subordinate status of women is a fundamental feature of our culture, history, and religion and yet it is not essential or necessary.[26] To put the point bluntly, the contingency and historicity of metaphysics has made feminism in its modern forms possible.

The idea that ontology is embedded in practices also provides an answer to the feminist question about the relationship between oppressive social practices and metaphysical presuppositions. It is a mistake to understand their relationship in terms of causality: a faulty metaphysics does not cause political oppression, and political oppression does not provide a cause for faulty metaphysics. Rather, metaphysical schemas and social practices are inseparable: if we think of social practices according to the model of a game, metaphysics constitutes the intelligibility of the game and its rules, not its cause.

Both Foucault and Battersby thus insist that metaphysical schemas and traditions are not eternal or immobile and that there have always been a variety of competing ontological understandings of the world. Accepting that the "world itself" is the outcome of a struggle between competing ontologies means acknowledging that there is not just one metaphysical schema associated with political patterns of discrimination. While Western modernity offers many alternative ways to conceive of the world and ourselves, it is nevertheless evident that some of these ontologies have become dominant to the extent of being taken for granted while others have almost disappeared or are now conceived as historical curiosities.

There are also important differences, however, in Foucault's and Battersby's approaches to ontology. They both turn to history, but with a very different emphasis: whereas Foucault's historical ontology is motivated by the objective of elucidating and destabilizing our present—rendering it contingent and strange—Battersby turns to history in order to raid it "for models of mobile identities that work without underlying permanent 'objects,' 'substances' or unchanging and universal 'forms'" (Battersby 1998, 7). In her project the metaphysical tradition is mined in order for her to be able to project a new picture of ourselves on to the future: a new, more relational ontology that takes the woman as norm in definitions of self, personhood, and identity.

I have argued that Foucault's politicization of ontology challenges this project of creating a new ontology: it implies that ontology—understood as a diverse set of competing background beliefs about reality—can never be the exclusive achievement of philosophers because it is formed in a web of scientific and everyday practices. It is thus not through the supreme mental effort of the philosopher—such as the *epoche* or some ingenious moment of vision—that the ultimate truth about reality can be revealed. Nor can philosophers create new ontologies by simply pairing up words and reality in new and politically more correct ways. Philosophy can nevertheless make an important contribution to descriptive metaphysics by problematization: by exposing historically specific metaphysical schemas and by the creation of new concepts, theoretical tools, and ways of conceiving of the world. But no one person can create a new ontology. The idea that practices engender reality does not eliminate the role of the individual, but it does limit it. The web of practices in which we are embedded necessarily shapes our thought and understanding. Nothing I do can change the totality of it, but equally nothing I do is politically insignificant either. Because metaphysical schemas are embedded in practices they can be changed by human effort: feminist political practice and activism is ultimately inseparable from feminist metaphysics. Even if this effort to create a new metaphysics has to be collective and anonymous, local and partial, slow and patient, it is nevertheless the task Foucault sets for us.

In sum, I have suggested that Foucault's critical project can be read as an important attempt to problematize the relationship between ontology and politics. Rather than translating the right ontology into the right politics, he reverses the argument. The radicality of his method lies in showing how the ontological order of things is itself the outcome of a political struggle. He makes visible the historical struggles over truth and objectivity: how our understanding of reality is constituted in a piecemeal fashion in historical practices that always incorporate power relations—and often exclusion, marginalization, and violence. Metaphysics is not superfluous or irrelevant for feminist political projects because it is inseparable from them. The refusal to engage in it is itself a political act—one that I hope to have shown is seriously misguided.

2

In Defense of Experience

Joan Scott's important essay "The Evidence of Experience," first published in *Critical Inquiry* in 1991, has arguably been one of the most influential contributions to the dismissal of first-person accounts of experience in feminist theory and politics in the recent decades. Even though her critique of the evidence of experience was made in the context of historiography, the philosophical presuppositions as well as the political and methodological consequences of her argument have been widely adopted in feminist theory. Appealing to one's experience as evidence for one's theoretical or political claims has become theoretically unsophisticated at best, if not completely illegitimate in feminist debates.

My aim in this chapter is not to deny the significance of Scott's essay—it produced a timely shift in feminist theory away from a narrow focus on the issues of identity and victimization to a broader study of their constitutive conditions. However, in our current predicament, characterized by many as postfeminist, I contend that it has become necessary to reassess the philosophical coherence of Scott's argument and, crucially, its broader implications for the methodology of feminist theory and for the future of feminist politics.

The philosophical issues motivating my critique of Scott's essay thus go beyond the meaning of her work and concern feminist theory and politics more generally. I ask what it means for feminist theory and politics to redefine experience as a linguistic event the way Scott suggests. I want to demonstrate that the consequences she draws from such a theoretical move are both philosophically and politically problematic. A critical study of the evidence of experience—when experience is understood in its traditional philosophical meaning as a subjective apprehension of reality—does not have to imply metaphysical or epistemological foundationalism as Scott claims, but is indispensable for challenging them. We must hold on to the evidence of experience as an important resource for contesting sexist discourses and oppressive conceptual schemas.

My argument proceeds in four stages. In the first section, I will present a critical explication of Scott's position. In the second section, I will turn to John McDowell's account of experience in an attempt to understand what Scott means when she insists on the discursive nature of experience. In the third section, I will consider the political consequences of my epistemological and ontological defense of experience. Finally, in the fourth section, I will conclude by briefly reflecting on the methodology of feminist theory.

Words and Things

The acute political problem with the idea of a collective female experience was its exclusivity: white, middle-class feminists considered their experience to be the prototypical female experience that defines feminism and its central goals.[1] For a movement that fought precisely against exclusion—women's exclusion—such a shortcoming was fatal. The idea of a common female experience was soon attacked for other philosophical and theoretical reasons too, as modes of thought associated with postmodernism and poststructuralism gained dominance in academic feminist theory in the 1980s. The contention was that female experience, no matter how inclusive or broadly defined, was a theoretically flawed starting point for feminism, because it was constructed through the very same oppressive power relations that feminists wanted to challenge and resist. Feminist theorists, inspired by poststructuralist insights into the constitutive role of discourse, advocated the need to reorient feminist theory toward an analysis of discourses and their political effects and away from all fixed and naturalized identities.[2]

Joan Scott's essay was not only an argument for the importance of analyzing discourses in order to understand how they position subjects and produce their experiences, however. She also advocated an eradication of women's subjective or personal accounts of their experiences from feminist analyses. She notes that if experience was not so deeply imbricated in our narratives, we should abandon the notion altogether (Scott 1992, 37).[3] She accuses feminist projects intended to make the common experiences of women visible of being exceedingly naive: they preclude analysis of the workings of the patriarchal representational system and its historicity and reproduce instead its oppressive terms. They also preclude inquiry into processes of subject construction: appealing to experience as uncontestable evidence and as an originary point of explanation means taking as self-evident the identities of those whose experience is being documented. Female experience thus becomes the ontological foundation of feminist identity, politics, and history while questions about the discursively constructed nature of experience are ignored (ibid., 25). According to Scott, "it is not individuals who have experience, but subjects who are constituted through experience" (ibid., 25–26). Hence, the feminist challenge is to redefine experience completely: it must be understood as a discursive effect or a linguistic event. A prediscursive conception of experience is distorted because "it operates within an ideological construction that not only makes individuals the starting point of knowledge, but that also naturalizes categories such as man, woman, black, white, heterosexual, or homosexual by treating them as given characteristics of individuals" (ibid., 27).

Scott's argument relies on three distinct philosophical claims concerning experience. The first one is ontological: she denies "a separation between experience and language" and insists on the discursive nature of experience (ibid., 34, 37). Experience is primarily a discursive process of subject construction and only secondarily and erroneously something the subject claims to have. Second, she claims that the discourses constitutive of experience are always ideological: they reflect oppressive power relations and therefore naturalize normative categories such as man, woman, white, black, heterosexual, homosexual. These two ontological claims about the relationship between experience and language imply an epistemological claim. Experience cannot function either as evidence or as a starting point for feminist analysis because of its derivative and ideological status: the singular character of experience and its first-person perspective must be eradicated in feminist methodology. Scott thus denies the usefulness of documenting women's subjective experiences as evidence for feminist theoretical claims and urges us to turn instead to the history of concepts as providing "the evidence by which experience can be grasped" (ibid., 37).

Scott's ontological position could be labeled nominalist, although it is unclear what kind of nominalist she in fact is. The first source of confusion is that Scott does not seem to differentiate clearly between identity and experience. She notes that "identity is tied to notions of experience" (ibid., 33) and then proceeds, in my view, to conflate them. While it is fairly uncontroversial to claim that identity categories such as woman or homosexual are discursively constructed (I think this is a truism), it is a significantly different philosophical claim to hold that experience is so constructed. Scott is thus not only claiming that social identities and categories are discursively constructed, but also that the experiences of the individuals belonging to those categories are too.

She argues that we cannot assume a direct correspondence between words and things and calls such an erroneous belief the referential conception of language. We must move away from modes of thinking that "naturalise 'experience' through a belief in the unmediated relationship between words and things" (ibid., 36). The problem with such a claim is that we cannot completely sever the relationship between words and things either; otherwise, the philosophical problem of discursive idealism emerges—we become trapped inside a purely discursive realm with no traction on reality. After the linguistic turn in philosophy, it has become fairly uncontroversial to argue that certain discourses and concepts make certain kinds of experiences possible. We were not able to understand the concept of a universal political right or encounter its manifestations or violations in our everyday reality until the early Modern Age, for example. However, even if we accept such a constitutive view of language, there seems to be a number of entities in our experiential reality that are not constituted by language: stars, trees, and grass seem to be out there in the world irrespective of how we name them.[4] Hence, even though we can only identify something as something by using linguistically mediated conceptual determinations, our linguistic practices do not create the world, but must be capable of interacting with the things that we speak about. It must be possible to experience something new, something that we simply cannot name, or to experience something in a new way. Such unanticipated events force us to change our linguistic practices, which would otherwise remain completely static. To attempt to explain their dynamic character by simply stating that discourses are "contextual, contested and contingent" is no explanation at all, but only a reformulation of the initial problem.

For feminist theory, a dynamic understanding of the relationship between experience and language seems particularly important because feminism is essentially concerned with societal and conceptual change. As I argued in the previous chapter, we must be able to account philosophically for the fact that the discourses and the conceptual schemas that we use to make sense of the world can be modified through political action. The feminist criticism of Scott's position has therefore usually taken the form of denying her first ontological premise that experience could be understood as linguistic through and through. Feminist thinkers appropriating phenomenology, such as Sonja Kruks (2001), for example, have strongly argued that Scott's attempt to account for experience in terms of discursivity alone poses serious problems for feminist theory.

Kruks wants to ground female experience in the female body, and she urges us to acknowledge the significance that nonlinguistic, embodied experiences such as pain must have in feminist theory. She draws on her own experience of working as a volunteer at a battered women's shelter and argues that embodied experience forms an affective basis for solidarity among women: there is a *direct* experience of affinity among women that is possible because I can recognize as mine the embodied experiences of another woman, even while knowing that she and I are in other ways very different (ibid., 152, 166–67). Certain generalities of feminine embodiment thus enable us to feel connections with the suffering of other women, and such connections can potentially become the bases for forms of respectful solidarity among otherwise different women.

While I am sympathetic to the attempts to appropriate phenomenology for the retrieval of experience in feminist theory, I agree with Scott in that we cannot go back to treating female experience as an irreducible given the way Kruks does. It is my contention that feminist theory must "retrieve experience," but this cannot mean returning to a prediscursive female experience grounded in the commonalities of women's embodiment. I will therefore adopt here a philosophical strategy that differs from that of most of Scott's feminist critics. I will begin by assuming that Scott's ontological claim about the discursive character of experience is valid. I will then demonstrate that following this idea through does not warrant the epistemological or political dismissal of women's first-person experience that Scott advocates, but that such an epistemological argument becomes internally incoherent.

In order to proceed, we have to begin by trying to understand what it actually means to hold that experience is discursive through and through. As I noted at the outset, Scott's focus in her essay is on historiography, and her objective is not to provide answers for metaphysical problems properly belonging to the philosophy of mind and language. Her philosophical claims about experience are thus brief and vague. However, it is my contention that in order to draw the epistemological, methodological, and political consequences for feminist theory that she draws, it is imperative to understand what we are in fact claiming when we say that experiences are discursive. I will therefore provide a brief philosophical explication of such a position by turning to John McDowell. His account of experience in *Mind and World* (1994) is arguably the most cogent contemporary argument to demonstrate that experiences are conceptual down to their most basic level. My aim is not to engage in a philosophical assessment of McDowell's position, however.[5] My objective is merely to appropriate his position and to draw out its epistemological implications in order to provide a philosophically coherent explication of Scott's understanding of experience which does not reduce it to discursive idealism. In other words, I want to show that even given the philosophically best possible reading of her position, her dismissal of the epistemic value of first-person experiential accounts is unwarranted.

Rational Animals, Cognitive Dissonance, and Political Change

For McDowell, the idea that experience is linguistic through and through means denying that there could be some basic level of nonconceptual consciousness, a primary, sensory experience that simply captures the world as it is given to us. Rather, all sensory experience already has conceptual content because concepts or conceptual schemas necessarily mediate the relation between us and the world. Conceptual capacities are already at work in the perceptual experiences themselves and not only in the second-order conceptual judgments justified by some bare perceptual impressions. It is only by virtue of our conceptual schemas that the world and the self can become objects of experience at all.

When I identify colors, for example, such identification can only take place against a conceptual background that ensures that I understand colors as potential properties of things. The same holds true for forms of inner experience—experiences that have no identifiable object in the external world, such as the experience of pain. As Kruks, for example, emphasizes, pain is often understood as a paradigmatic example of an experience with no conceptual content or structure. McDowell would insist, however, that for a subject to have an experience of pain, a certain kind of conceptual understanding of what it means to be in pain is required. Although pain is essentially a passive occurrence for the subject, his or her conceptual capacities are nevertheless drawn into operation. The subject must understand being in pain as a particular case of a more general state of affairs—someone's being in pain (ibid., 37–38). In other words, she or he must understand that the pain is not exclusively tied to a first-person and present-tense mode, but that being in pain is something that can happen to someone else or to oneself at a different time.

McDowell's primary interest is not in understanding the nature of experience, however. Rather, his interest is epistemological: how empirical knowledge is possible. How can experience rationally constrain and justify our beliefs and thoughts? In answering this question, he attempts to refute two diametrically opposing positions which he labels "the myth of the given" and "coherentism." He borrows Wilfried Sellars's famous notion "the myth of the given"[6] to denote the view that there is a primary level of experience, which is nonconceptual, and he acknowledges the epistemological appeal of such a view: if we assume that there are nonconceptual impacts or bits of experiential intake impinging on us from outside the realm of thought, then this allows us to acknowledge an external constraint on our conceptual game, one that moreover seems to provide the grounding for our empirical beliefs and judgments. However, McDowell argues that unfortunately, the myth of the given is precisely that—a myth; it can provide no constraints or grounding for anything.

Empirical knowledge only becomes possible if perceptions and judgments can be rationally connected: a bare presence cannot be the ground of anything. If we conceive experience in terms of impacts on sensibility that occur outside the sphere of concepts, then we cannot appeal to this nonconceptual experience to justify conceptual judgments or beliefs. "The space of reasons does not extend further than the space of concepts, to take in a bare reception of the Given" (ibid., 14). In other words, if our conceptual, empirical judgments are based on the content of our experience and these reason-constituting relations are genuinely recognizable as reason-constituting, then we cannot confine thinking within a boundary across which the relations are supposed to hold. The relations themselves must be able to come under rational scrutiny (ibid., 53). Experiences cannot provide reasons for judgments if they are outside the reach of rational inquiry: if experiences are nonconceptual, they cannot be what thoughts are rationally based on.

McDowell also denies the coherentist upshot of this argument, however, which he attributes to Donald Davidson (ibid., 14). Davidson accepts the above argument and then simply concludes that experience can never count as a reason for holding a belief: "nothing can count as reason for holding a belief except another belief" (Davidson 1986, 310). Davidson thus denies experience any justificatory role in knowledge, because we simply have no convincing way to credit ourselves with empirical knowledge. He advocates a coherence theory of truth and knowledge, which confines knowledge to the sphere of thought. Davidson, like Scott, thus seems to believe that the myth of the given can be avoided only by denying that experience has any epistemological validity.

For McDowell, such a conclusion is intolerable. There must be some external constraint on our thought that warrants its bearing on objective reality: it cannot be reduced to "frictionless spinning in a void" (ibid., 11). While he wants to refute the myth of the given—the view that truth and knowledge must depend on rational relations to something outside the conceptual realm—he also insists that knowledge cannot degenerate into moves in a self-contained game. Experience must play a role as a legitimate source of knowledge.

McDowell's solution is to insist that our conceptual capacities are also drawn on when we perceive the world: the experiential intake is not a bare getting of an extraconceptual given, but a kind of occurrence that already has conceptual content. When we trace the ground for an empirical judgment, the last step takes us to experience. But experiences already have conceptual content, so this last step does not take us outside the space of concepts. When one forms a judgment on the basis of experience, one does not have to accomplish an impossible leap from nonconceptual data to conceptual content. However, experience does take us to something in which our sensibility or passive receptivity is operative, so we need not worry that there is no external constraint on our conceptual games or that they have no bearing on the world at all. Experience in a crucial respect is passive: in experience we find ourselves saddled with content that is not of our choosing.

McDowell and Scott would thus both hold that experience cannot be epistemologically foundational in the sense of being an originary, nonconceptual given that language would only secondarily reflect. However, McDowell demonstrates that the conceptual character of experience does not warrant Scott's epistemological claim, namely, that the evidence of experience becomes insignificant. It is exactly because experience is conceptual, down to its very basic level, that the claim it makes is epistemologically valid: because experience is conceptual, it can provide the traction on reality that warrants empirical knowledge. Hence, from the premise that experiences are constituted through discourse, it does not follow that women's experiential accounts of the world are insignificant or necessarily false. We can obviously be mistaken at times—the evidence of experience is not epistemically infallible—but it is nevertheless capable of being veridical.

At this stage we can perhaps anticipate a critical rejoinder. Scott is not only claiming that experience is discursive, she is also claiming that the discourses that constitute it are ideological. In other words, even if experience was able to tell us something veridical about the world out there, we are still left with the problem that what it tells us only reflects the dominant ideological constructions of reality. Scott might be happy to grant that in the current patriarchal ideological framework the evidence provided by women's experiences seems veridical, but that is precisely because experience and discourse are necessarily coextensive. Experience is constructed so that it corresponds to the dominant criteria of veridiction: it reflects oppressive discourses and power relations. Hence, what we would really need to ask is how experience can provide evidence that contests the dominant conceptual schemas. We would have to ask McDowell, for example, how, exactly, can experience bear critically on our accepted schemas if it is entirely conceptual? It would seem that experience can only draw into operation ideological concepts that we already have. But how can judgments ever become modified by experience if experience is only the result of the passive operation of the same concepts that are already linked into judgments?

This problem seems to bring us back to the phenomenological position. In order to account for cognitive dissonance and political change we must argue, similar to the feminist phenomenologists critical of Scott's position, that experience and discourse are not coextensive and that experience therefore provides a legitimate source of challenging sexist discourses and oppressive conceptual schemas.[7] In order to account for revisions in our stock of inherited judgments, it seems that we have to acknowledge at least a minimal nonconceptual aspect of experience, even if we accept that experience can never be completely independent of language.

For McDowell, it makes no sense to try to argue that the content of experience is *partly* nonconceptual, however, as this is just another version of the myth of the given. He argues against the attempts to do so by considering the example of recognizing colors. The proponents of the partial view would argue that the level of detail that the contents of experience have can never be captured by the concepts at the subject's disposal. In other words, our repertoire of color concepts, for example, is coarser in grain than our abilities to discriminate shades, and therefore unable to capture the fine detail of color experience. Words and phrases such as "red," "green," or "burnt sienna" express concepts of bands on the spectrum, whereas color experience can present properties that correspond to something more like lines on the spectrum with no discernible width. A purely conceptual account of experience, such as McDowell's, thus, does not seem to allow for the fact that I could recognize a completely new shade that would contest the existing schemas of color, or that such experience could lead me to recognize the ways that the current discourses/schemas distort and impoverish my experience.

McDowell responds by insisting that a person's ability to embrace colors within her conceptual thinking should not be restricted to predetermined concepts expressible by words like "red," "green," or "burnt sienna." It can also include demonstrative concepts such as "that shade" or "that shade that I saw yesterday," for example. These concepts are importantly recognitional, meaning that they can be rationally integrated into our thoughts and judgments, but not in a predetermined way. McDowell notes that thoughts are not always capable of receiving an overt expression that fully determines their content, but that does not mean that they are nonconceptual (McDowell 1994, 56–58). As we saw in the previous section, he insists that perceptual content has to be conceptual in order to function as evidence for our judgments in any way—whether to confirm them or to contest them. If the perceptual content was not conceptually organized in any way—if I did not recognize the perceptual content as a *shade* of color that was in some way different from the shades that I am currently able to name with my repertoire of words—it could not challenge or contest the existing schema of color.

The basic conceptual level of experience is thus so rudimentary and indeterminate that it can be rationally linked with a variety of judgments and articulations. There is always going to remain a distinction between having an experience and describing it, even when we acknowledge that experiences are conceptually structured. Our language games are also potentially infinitely varied, allowing for the constant contestation, modification, and transformation of our judgments, beliefs, and worldviews. The same conceptual capacities that are in operation in perceptions are exercised in judgments, and that requires them being rationally linked into a whole system of concepts and conceptions—an encompassing conceptual schema or a worldview. The linguistic and cultural tradition into which human beings are first initiated serves as a primary source of this conceptual schema, "a store of historically accumulated wisdom about what is a reason for what" (ibid., 126). However, this tradition must be subject to reflective modification by each generation that inherits it. McDowell goes so far as to state that "a standing obligation to engage in critical reflection is itself part of the inheritance" (ibid.).[8] We are continually engaged in a process of having to negotiate our conceptual schemas in light of our experiences. Whether we realize it or not, we are persistently adjusting our thinking to our experience and vice versa.

Because Scott denies the epistemological and political significance of the evidence of experience, she has problems acknowledging women's role in the renewal and transformation of the cultural and linguistic tradition in which they find themselves. She fails to recognize the continual negotiation and adjustment of thought to experience and experience to thought that must characterize the dynamism of cultural traditions. Even though women's sexual experiences, for example, are constructed through patriarchal discourses, these experiences are never wholly derivative of or reducible to them. It is possible, for example, that women have, if not a fully articulated feminist critique of their situation, at least a sense of disorientation and dissatisfaction with the dominant cultural and linguistic representations of their experience. It is exactly this dissatisfaction, this gap between their personal experiences and the dominant cultural representations and linguistic descriptions that are available to them that can generate critique as well as create new discourses capable of contesting and contradicting the old ones.

Feminist Theory and Practice

Scott's aim is not to engage in debates in the philosophy of mind, but neither is it to solve epistemological questions about the legitimacy of empirical knowledge. If her essay has broader implications for feminist theory beyond feminist historiography, these implications must concern feminist politics. Whether or not it was her intention, her essay has been read, not only as a refutation of identity politics, but as a denial of the importance of any experiential accounts in feminist politics.

I want to make clear at the outset that in defending the political importance of experience here, I am not advocating a return to forms of identity politics based on a shared experience of a naturalized identity. Scott and numerous other poststructuralist feminists have been right to challenge such a project. My aim is not to retrieve the political importance of experience in order to group people together on such a basis. My first point is more fundamental: the political importance of the evidence of experience lies in its power to motivate us to demand social change irrespective of whether our own experience confirms or coincides with it. In other words, my worry is that the politically troubling consequence of denying experience as a basis for identity politics is its unwarranted extension to all forms of feminist politics: the wholesale refusal to acknowledge that women's personal accounts of experience have any political relevance. First-person accounts of experience are indispensable, not only for a politics of interest based on a shared identity, but for a politics of solidarity based on recognition and sympathy. The evidence of experience crucially makes collective political action possible by allowing us not only to identify with other people, but to *disidentify* from the singularity of our own position.

Consider the key feminist issue of rape, for example. I am not suggesting that the evidence of experience would warrant the attempt to find commonalities in women's embodied experiences in order to identify some essential core of female identity: women are essentially beings that can be raped, for example. The experiential evidence of rape should nevertheless raise some critical realization or awareness in me. It should prompt me to question the prevailing gender relations and attitudes toward sex, and it should motivate me to act politically by supporting date rape awareness campaigns or rape crisis centers, for example. Even if many of the accounts that women gave of their experiences were epistemologically suspect, ideologically produced, and made us cringe, they are still the only rationale on the basis of which we can make radical feminist political demands and contest sexist political arrangements and social practices. A history of concepts alone will not provide any motivation for radical politics that would attempt to instigate profound social transformation. It is only when we understand how these concepts function politically in the lives of real people—how they restrict, oppress, and impoverish the experiences of the individuals to whom they are attached, for example—that we have a powerful rationale for politically contesting, problematizing, and transforming them. In other words, accounts of personal experience motivate and legitimize us to demand change irrespective of our own identity and experience—irrespective of whether we ourselves are women, men, or transgendered.

Ann J. Cahill (2002, 197) argues that the second-wave feminists' success in placing rape on the political agenda was possible only because women were finally prepared to speak the unspeakable. Women were explicitly encouraged to be more open and less self-blaming about the violence that had been done to them. Cahill acknowledges that women's first-person descriptions of rape cannot be taken as authoritative in any unproblematic sense; nevertheless, she argues that such descriptions are indispensable in the effort to raise awareness of the pervasiveness of rape. The first-person accounts of rape have been able to foreground the complexity and specificity of rape vis-à-vis other experiences of violence. Because sexual violence is committed disproportionately against women, and because women's representations of that violence are met with social disbelief and suspicion, it is crucial that women speak out about their personal experiences (ibid., 128).[9]

Second, even if we accept that experiences are culturally and linguistically constructed, through and through, this does not mean that they can have no legitimate political role to play in creating communal political action. On the contrary, recognizing that the particular cultural, economic, and political conditions of a person's development are necessarily shared implies the existence of communal experiences. As long as we recognize that such communal experiences are culturally contingent and politically constituted, and not a manifestation of an essential and naturalized identity, they can function as an important source of critical reflection and societal transformation. The realization that our experiences are normalized, impoverished, painful, degrading, or disempowering in contemporary culture may not only lead to political action and societal transformation, however. Such realization itself often requires a collective, political project. These experiences need to be articulated, shared, and critically reflected upon.

Sandra Bartky (2002, 14) has voiced the concern that an insurmountable gap lies between feminist theory and practice: we have produced sophisticated theories without any corresponding political practice. To be sure, if our theories have no traction on reality, if they are just "frictionless spinning in a void," it is easy to see how a motivational deficit could arise. Feminist theory becomes an intellectual game with no connection to real lives or experiences. I am suggesting that the episte-mological and metaphysical retrieval of experience that I am advocating here could remedy that motivational deficit by legitimizing a correspond-ing practice—consciousness-raising.

Consciousness-raising was a feminist practice that for some time already has been considered outdated, if not outright ridiculous. How-ever, if we accept the ideological nature of the discourses constitutive of experience then a defense of the political importance of the evidence of experience must imply a qualified defense of consciousness-raising. I want to suggest that we think of the consciousness-raising practices conducive to critical self-transformation and collective political action along the model of the practices of the self that Foucault advocated in his late thought. These practices could be understood as a form of consciousness-raising in the sense that their goal is a qualitative trans-formation of one's experience.

While the initial feminist reaction to Foucault's late work was largely negative, criticizing it for being individualistic, masculinist, and even nar-cissistic, more recently it has been appropriated for imaginative attempts to sketch a feminist art of life and to develop concrete ways to resist patri-archal power and gender normalization.[10] Feminist theorists have argued that consciousness-raising can be viewed from a Foucauldian perspective as a practice of freedom. Margaret McLaren (2004, 230) points out how feminist consciousness-raising exemplifies the type of self-transformation that Foucault refers to in his discussion of practices of the self because it draws upon the rules, methods, and customs of one's culture, but with the explicit aim of transforming cultural convention about gender. Mari-ana Valverde (2004, 82) also contends that a Foucauldian perspective on these practices is particularly illuminating because it refuses to view them as forms of confession (see also Taylor 2009, 229–30). Viewed as tech-nologies of the self, the aim of the feminist practices of consciousness-raising is not the exposure of deep inner self or an original and authentic womanhood, but rather the problematization of the normalized self.[11] In other words, consciousness-raising practices can be understood as prac-tices of freedom in the sense that their goal is not a naturalization of identity, but its critical deconstruction.

In *Self-Transformations: Foucault, Ethics, and Normalized Bodies* (2007) Cressida Heyes acknowledges that there is a particular difficulty in such feminist projects of self-fashioning. It is going to be problematic to assess the co-optation of feminist practices of the self by the very disciplinary technologies that structure gender normalization. She argues that Foucault's late thought can nonetheless provide important tools for rethinking our relationship to ourselves as normalized individuals and suggests that we have to reject all teleological accounts of self-development and instead adopt "new practices that remain open to forms of becoming not yet imagined" (Heyes 2007, 11). Despite the pervasiveness of the techniques of gender normalization, it is thus possible to engage in creative and critical feminist practices of the self that refuse the habituated trajectories. Heyes describes feminist practices of self-transformation as being "a kind of therapy." These practices are both ethical and spiritual and they require techniques that are "somatic, meditative, artistic as well as communal" (ibid., 108). If I read Heyes correctly, these remodeled practices of consciousness-raising would not imply simply sharing our personal stories in order to find empowering communalities between women. Rather, the aim would be a problematization of who we are and who we aspire to be—a critical reflection on the social and political conditions constitutive of our normalized experiences. Neither would the aim of these practices be to simply correct false beliefs about embodiment, but, rather, the aim would be to actually change our embodied selves by "creating new and more expansive forms of embodied self-expression" (ibid., 92).

Practices of the self are often criticized as apolitical and as compatible with the current neoliberal ethos of turning away from the shared realm of politics to the realm of private self-fashioning. However, these practices should be understood as essentially collective practices that can only gain their meaning in a shared cultural context. While it is undoubtedly true that they do not by themselves necessarily imply any radical political movements, I want to insist that the reverse is nevertheless true: radical political movements necessarily imply practices of the self. Hence, the political importance of experience is connected to the broader question of what feminist politics is and what its goals are. It is my contention that feminism as a radical political project must aim at profound social transformation, not merely at some quantitative gain such as increase in women's power, political rights, or social benefits. It has to aim to change who we are—both as men and as women. In other words, it has to assume that our experience of the world could be qualitatively transformed if our society operated along different kinds of cultural and political practices and was governed by different norms. Such transformation requires politics that is able to question and transform the cultural representations and values that shape and structure our experiences, but it also requires self-transformation—political practices that aim to change our singular experiences.

To sum up this section, my endeavor to foreground the epistemological and political importance of experience here is almost diametrically opposed to the feminist project of attempting to find essential commonalities in women's embodied experiences in order to identify some essential core of female experience. In effect, I am suggesting that we attempt the reverse: we must engage in a critical study of our experiences in order to identify the fractures—those aspects of experience that break with normative femininity, naturalized identity, and the culturally scripted accounts of female experience. An important strategy of radical feminist theory and politics has been the attempt to produce cultural representations—scientific and literary texts, films and art—that would represent women's experiences in new, alternative, and more liberating ways. For this quest to make any sense, politically or philosophically, we have to assume that women are not completely "one-dimensional"—that they recognize and are able to voice, in some way, the fact that their experiences are impoverished, painful, distorted, degrading, or disempowering in contemporary culture.[12] It also assumes that they are able to transform, at least to some extent, the norms and cultural discourses that shape experience. It does not require assuming that women's experiences are prediscursive or authentic in some sense of being outside of language and culture. As I argued in the previous section, experiences can contest discourses even if, or precisely because, they are conceptual through and through.

The Possibility of Problematization

I have argued so far that feminist politics attempting to change society in some significant way requires critical analysis of first-personal experience. Such critical analysis of experience can contest identities, norms, and conceptual schemas; it can motivate us to produce enriched cultural expressions, as well as to create solidarity with others whom we accept as different. Such analysis should not be limited to other women's experiences of oppression and suffering, but must also essentially include radical self-reflection—a reflexive interrogation of one's own experience. In this section I want to conclude my argument by showing that such reflexive analysis of experience is indispensable, not just for feminist politics, but also for the methodology of feminist theory.

Radical reflection on one's own experience must be an essential element of feminist theory: the person studying sexist society must be able to take critical distance, not only from the familiar and taken-for-granted meanings of various forms of experience, but also, and most fundamentally, from her own experience. She must try to critically analyze her own experiences, beliefs, and theories as being formed in a community with its attendant practices, beliefs, and language. It is my contention that such critical reflection on one's own experience will not provide a secure foundation for theoretical activity, but, on the contrary, provides the only possibility to problematize the existence of any such foundation.

How this radical questioning of the constitutive conditions of one's own experience can be accomplished remains a difficult question. Judith Butler (2004, 107–8) writes that "the questioning of taken-for-granted conditions becomes possible on occasion; but we cannot get there through a thought experiment, an *epoche* or an act of will. One gets there, as it were, through suffering the breakup of the ground itself." While I agree with Butler about the impossibility of a complete *epoche*, I believe that it is nevertheless possible to try to deliberately cultivate the practice of problematization: the attempt to take critical distance from dominant norms and to question at least some of the constitutive conditions of one's own experience. Even though we have to discard the possibility of a complete *epoche* which aims at freeing us from all presuppositions including those carried by language, the importance of phenomenology as a philosophical method nevertheless lies in its realization that only a first-person perspective makes possible a radical philosophical critique of naturalism.[13]

From the point of view of phenomenology, the difficulty with Scott's account is not the claim that experience is constituted through culture, history, and language. The intersubjective readings of phenomenology claim exactly that.[14] Rather, the philosophical problem is historicism: how can we study the constitution of experience through empirical accounts of factual history? Experience must be historicized, it must be studied as the effect and the end product of a historical process, but it is we ourselves who write this history. We cannot transcend our own historical point of view to find some view from nowhere capable of revealing an objective account of the constitution of our experience. Historicism would entail this mistake of adopting a view from nowhere. Neither factual history nor any empirical study in isolation can explain the constitution of our experience without falling into circularity: it presupposes that which it attempts to explain. A key phenomenological insight consists of the acknowledgment that an empirical account of the constitution of our own experience is as impossible as lifting ourselves in the air by our hair.

Scott's attack on foundationalism therefore spawns an unacknowledged foundationalism of its own. If we deny the methodological significance of first-person experiential perspective, a critical reflection on those background beliefs and ontological commitments that our own experience carries and that are constitutive of the historically objective accounts of experience becomes impossible. Without a critical scrutiny of our own experience we are left with no means to even attempt to question them.

The critical analysis of our own experience is interlocked with the study of the experiential accounts of others. It is my contention that for the critical questioning of our own experience to have any hope of succeeding, even partially, it requires that we pay critical attention to the experiential evidence of others. We must listen especially to those whose experiences have been marginalized and whose voices have been silenced, not because they are in possession of some authentic truth about reality revealed only through suffering or oppression, but simply because their perspective is different from ours. It might therefore reveal some contradictions and alternative presuppositions that are not available to us and that might therefore shake the invisible privileges built into our own perspective. A precondition for feminist theory and politics is the ability to speak and to act, but also, importantly, to listen. When we stop listening, we are bound to lose our way.

3

Foucault and Experience

Linda Alcoff has presented one of the most devastating feminist critiques of Foucault's account of sexuality (Alcoff 2000).[1] The philosophical core of her argument is that Foucault accords to discourse the unique ability to attach meanings and values to our feelings and sensations and that this has disastrous effects on how we understand sexual violence such as rape. Her discussion focuses on the case of a simpleminded farmhand that Foucault introduces in *The History of Sexuality*, volume 1:

> One day in 1867, a farm hand from the village of Lapcourt, who was somewhat simple-minded, employed here then there, depending on the season, living hand-to-mouth from a little charity or in exchange for the worst sort of labor, sleeping in barns or stables, was turned to authorities. At the border of the field, he had obtained a few caresses from a little girl, just as he had done before and seen done by the village urchins round him; for, at the edge of the wood . . . they would play the familiar game called "curdled milk." So he was pointed out by the girl's parents to the mayor of the village, reported by the major to the gendarmes, led by gendarmes to the judge, who indicted him and turned him over first to a doctor, then to two experts who not only wrote their report but also had it published. (Foucault 1978, 31)

Foucault explains the significance of the case by emphasizing the way a previously ordinary sexual incident became the object not only of collective intolerance, but of a juridical action and a medical intervention. The familiar occurrence in the sexual life of the village became an instance of a careful clinical examination and a theoretical elaboration. For him, the case illustrates the historical turning point at which expert discourses on sexuality gained dominance, and sex was brought under their jurisdiction.

Alcoff accuses Foucault of being too quick to judge the incident as too insignificant to merit the medical and legal responses, however. She points out that he clearly lacked sufficient evidence about the meaning of the encounter from the little girl's point of view. By appropriating writings by adult survivors of sexual abuse, as well as her own experiences, she reconstructs a powerful description of what such a sexual encounter would have felt like from a child's point of view.

> In encounters similar to the one Foucault described, the child exhibits a need to be held or hugged, to have affection or attention, or perhaps to obtain some basic good like money for food or shelter. The adult complies but on the condition of genital stimulation. This misresponse produces in the child pain and fear mixed with compulsion and intimidation, a duress created by uncertainty and the disparity between soothing words and painful, uncomfortable invasions, by the command to be silent and the assurance that all that is happening is ordinary and based on affection. One is told by a trusted adult to take the thing in one's mouth, to allow groping explorations, to perform distressing enactments that feel humiliating and foreign. While the child gags and whimpers (or even screams and cries), the adult sighs and moans, holding tightly so the child cannot get away. (Alcoff 2000, 54)

Alcoff is undoubtedly right in pointing out that Foucault's quickness to assume the girl's willing participation manifests a male and adult pattern of epistemic arrogance. What I want to question in this chapter, however, is her interpretation of the relationship between discourse and sexual experience that the example is supposed to imply. Alcoff ultimately accuses Foucault of ignoring the girl's experience because of his underlying, philosophically flawed view concerning experience and its relationship to discourse.

She claims that because Foucault accords to discourse the unique ability to attach meanings and values to experience he is unable to dissociate dominant discourses and bodily sensations.[2] This results in his simply ignoring the relevance of any subjective description of experience. Foucault's account of sexuality is detrimental for feminist analyses because experiences such as rape can never be reduced to dominant discourses, nor is their meaning ever as ambiguous as any statement in a language. To sum up her argument schematically, she insists that to adequately theorize sexual violence such as rape, feminist theory must accept two philosophical tenets that Foucault rejects. The first is ontological: we must make an ontological distinction between experience and language. Experience and discourse are imperfectly aligned because experience sometimes exceeds language, and it is at times inarticulate. The second is methodological: we have to have recourse to descriptions of women's personal, embodied experiences, not merely to the various discursive representations of those experiences. She suggests that feminists turn to phenomenology instead of to Foucault because it can meet both of these requirements. In these respects Alcoff's position is thus almost diametrically opposed to Scott's position discussed in the previous chapter.

Although I strongly agree with Alcoff that a philosophically sophisticated understanding of experience must be central in feminist theory, my claim is that her critique of Foucault is based on a mistaken view of his philosophical position as well as on a problematic understanding of phenomenology. I contend that Foucault does not hold experience and discourse to be ontologically coextensive, nor does he ignore the epistemic importance of subjective experience. My motive for defending him here is not to commend pedophilia or to advocate a more liberal or pluralistic sexual ethics. My aim is merely to show that his understanding of experience remains a theoretically fruitful resource for feminist thought despite his sexist treatment of this incident.

My argument proceeds in three stages. In the first section, I show that Foucault holds experience to be inherently heterogeneous because it emerges from the interplay of three elements: domains of knowledge, practices of power, and reflexive relations to oneself. Moreover, he insists that experiences can be described and rendered intelligible in multiple and competing discursive practices and conceptual frameworks. In the second section, I discuss the epistemic importance of subjective experience in his thought by returning to the case of the farmhand, Charles Jouy, as well as consider his treatment of Herculine Barbin and Pierre Rivière. In the concluding section, I juxtapose Foucault's account of experience and phenomenology.

Foucault's Conception of Experience

Foucault is not generally regarded as a philosopher of experience. On the contrary, his philosophy, and poststructuralist thought as a whole, is usually read as a critical reaction to those philosophical traditions such as existentialism and phenomenology that take lived experience as their starting point. At the same time all of Foucault's studies can be described as historical inquiries into particular modes of experience—from *History of Madness* and the experience of madness in the eighteenth century to the last volumes of *The History of Sexuality* and the experience of sexuality in ancient Greece and the Roman Empire.[3] Foucault explicitly stated in several instances that experience was a central topic of his analyses. To point out only some of them, in the preface to his early book *The Order of Things* he notes that in every culture "there is the pure experience of order" and that "the present study is an attempt to analyze that experience" (Foucault 1989, xxi). Nearly twenty years later, in the introduction to *The Use of Pleasure* he again characterizes his work as a study of experience. The goal is to understand how the modern individual could experience himself as a subject of sexuality. In order to do this, one had to undertake a genealogical study of "the experience of sexuality" (Foucault 1992, 4).[4]

Commentators who acknowledge this contrast between his criticism of philosophies of experience, on the one hand, and his focus on experience as a central object of his own study, on the other, often explain away the apparent contradiction by arguing that his understanding of experience is distinctive. The way its distinctiveness is understood, however, varies.[5]

In his late writings Foucault sought to explain and define his conception of experience. In the introduction to *The Use of Pleasure* he defines experience "as the correlation, in a culture, between fields of knowledge, types of normativity, and forms of subjectivity" (Foucault 1992, 4–5). This objective definition of experience neatly ties together the three axes of his work—regimes of truth (knowledge), relations of power (governmentality), and subjectivization (forms of relations to oneself). Thomas Flynn suggests that this definition enables us to think of Foucault's conception of experience spatially: the three axes constitute a prism and the space enclosed by these prismatic planes is "experience" (Flynn 2005, 211). According to Flynn, experience is thus desubjectivized: it leaves us with a plurality of correlations that are irreducible and nonsubsumable into a larger whole. Any analysis of experience must proceed along disparate axes that are mutually dependent on, but irreducible to, one another.

Experience is thus inherently heterogeneous because it emerges from the interplay of distinct elements: domains of knowledge (objectivization), practices of power (coercion), and reflexive relations to oneself (subjectivization). As Foucault explains in a late interview, what bothered him about his early work was that he had considered the first two domains without taking into account the third—the domain of the self. The three domains of experience "can only be understood one in relation to the others, not independently" (Foucault 1988, 243). Only after undertaking his late studies on subjectivization had he achieved a sufficiently complex understanding of experience to be able to adequately map and analyze the historically specific connections between forms of experience and domains of knowledge, practices of power, and forms of the self.

Beatrice Han-Pile argues that the problem with Foucault's late, axial definition of experience is that there are in fact two different notions of experience embedded in it (Han-Pile 2002, 152–58). On the one hand, Foucault claims that experience is an objective, anonymous, and general structure connecting fields of knowledge, types of normativity, and forms of subjectivity. On the other hand, his late understanding of the subject also presupposes a more traditional understanding of experience as a subjective self-relation. According to Han-Pile, these two notions are contradictory: experience cannot be a correlation uniting both objective (knowledge and power) and subjective elements (forms of self-consciousness). She claims that the third axis introduced in Foucault's late work is distinctly different from the other two and refers to a radically different understanding of experience.

I contend that self-reflexivity is not incommensurable with an objective analysis of experience, however.[6] The tension between the objective and subjective dimensions of experience is only a contradiction in Foucault's thought to the extent that experience itself is paradoxical: it is irreducible to either its objective or subjective dimensions. It is constituted by practices of knowledge and power—as we know from Foucault's influential studies of madness, delinquency, and sexuality—but it also importantly contains a self-reflexive and meaning-constitutive dimension, the modes of self-awareness. Instead of a clearly defined prism, we might think of it as a series of foldings: the subject must fold back on itself to create a private interiority while being in constant contact with its constitutive outside. The external determinants or historical background structures of experience and the internal, private sensations fold into and continuously keep modifying each other.

The "Foucault" entry of *Dictionnaire des philosophes*—a text that is generally acknowledged to have been written pseudonymously by Foucault himself—elaborates on the idea that experience is both constituted as well as constitutive. In marked contrast to phenomenology, he begins the presentation of his thought by singling out nominalism and the appeal to practices as his main philosophical principles: "Michel Foucault's approach is quite different. He first studies practices—ways of doing things—that are more or less regulated, more or less conscious, more or less goal-oriented, through which one can grasp the lineaments both of what was constituted as real for those who were attempting to conceptualize and govern it, and of the way in which those same people constituted themselves as subjects capable of knowing, analyzing, and ultimately modifying the real" (Foucault 1994, 318).

Practices constitute the real in the sense that both subjects and objects become intelligible only through them as certain kinds of objects and subjects. In other words, the intelligibility of our experience of the world is constituted in historically and culturally specific practices, and the philosophical analysis of ourselves must be a critical study of them.

However, practices must consist ontologically of acting and thinking subjects and the material that they act upon, even if the meanings given to these bodies, actions, and objects are constituted by the rules of the practices. Foucault insists that the methodological primacy of practices does not amount to behaving as if "the subject did not exist or setting it aside in favor of a pure objectivity" (Foucault 1994, 317). Rather, one has to analyze *a field of experience* in which subjects and objects form and transform. The analyses of practices must have as their correlate an analysis of the corresponding field of experience opened up and made possible by these practices.

The discourses of mental illness, delinquency, or sexuality say what the subject is only within a very particular truth game; but these games do not impose themselves on the subject from the outside in accord with necessary causal or structural determinations. Instead they open up a field of experience in which subject and object alike are constituted only under certain simultaneous conditions, but in which they go on changing in relation to one another, and thus go on modifying this field of experience itself (317–18).

Methodologically the analysis does not start with the already given subject in order to define "the formal conditions of a relation to object" (315). This would be the phenomenological approach. Foucault explicitly challenged the idea that the subject had ontological primacy in the constitution of experience. But neither does his analysis collapse into naturalism and attempt to determine "the empirical conditions that at a given moment might have permitted the subject in general to become conscious of an object already given in reality" (315). Instead the analysis takes the form of a critical history of thought, "an analysis of the conditions under which certain relations between subject and object are formed and modified" (315). This study of "the historical *a priori* of a possible experience" is Foucault's attempt to historicize the transcendental conditions of experience and to inquire into its constitution.[7] The same process through which such objects as madness or sexuality emerge in history also involves a corresponding process of emergence of a subject capable of knowing and experiencing such objects.

Foucault thus holds that experience is always constituted through specific cultural and historical conditions that shape even its purely personal meaning. It can be rendered intelligible and analyzed formally only as already discursively structured by acts of thought. This does not mean that it is ontologically coextensive with dominant discourse, however.

We must make an ontological distinction between subjective experience understood as a self-reflexive apprehension of reality and all linguistic descriptions of it, whether by the person herself or by other people, even when we acknowledge that experience is conceptual through and through. Subjective experiences are constituted by games of truth and power, but they in turn can affect and modify these practices. Moreover, discourse must be understood as a heterogeneous and contestable practice of competing language-games. Hence, the meaning of our experience is never reducible to one dominant discourse.

Abnormal Experiences

Foucault's axial definition of experience does not reduce experience to discourse ontologically, but neither does he ignore its epistemic importance. On the contrary, I argue in this section that his important allusions to "experiential truths" are ultimately the reason why his genealogical analyses succeed in functioning as a form of social critique rather than being purely historical descriptions.[8]

Many commentators have argued that the self-reflexive subject central in Foucault's late work signals a dramatic break in his thought. Beatrice Han-Pile, for example, has contended that as well as being internally contradictory, Foucault's late understanding of experience also introduces an abrupt change into his project (Han-Pile 2002, 153). In *The History of Sexuality*, volume 1 he had no need for self-reflexive experience in order to account for sexuality. She claims that sexuality was understood purely as the correlate of a discursive practice that constituted *scientia sexualis* as well as of the norms established by disciplines.

In contrast to such views, I contend that a self-reflexive subject is indispensable for the critical project of *The History of Sexuality*, volume 1. I return to the case of the farmhand, Charles Jouy. Whereas the feminist problem is Foucault's omission of the importance of the little girl's experience, the critical impact of the case nevertheless relies on the epistemic importance of lived experience, namely that of the farmhand. Foucault's objective is not merely to show that the authorities responded to an insignificant event in a way that was odd and exaggerated, as Alcoff claims. Rather, he attempts to show us the discrepancy between the farmhand's personal experience of the incident as "ordinary pleasure" and the medical and juridical representations of it as "a degenerate and perverse act." Although Foucault fails to display moral outrage or concern for the little girl, we are clearly asked to be at least somewhat distressed about the experience of the simpleminded and poor farmhand. Foucault tells us that he was subjected to detailed, invasive questioning about his "thoughts, inclinations, habits, sensations and opinions" (Foucault 1978, 31). The experts measured his brain span and studied his facial bone structure for possible signs of degeneracy. In the end, he was acquitted of any crime, but he was nevertheless shut away in a hospital until the end of his life.

For us to be able to read Foucault's project in *The History of Sexuality*, volume 1, as a form of social critique targeting the medicalization of sexuality, we must be made to see that the expert discourses on sexuality were problematic representations of the lived experiences of pleasure and embodiment. The experiences of the people involved—the hysterics, perverts, and homosexuals—did not seamlessly conform to the dominant discursive representations of their experiences, and this was an important source of their suffering. Foucault's focus on the case of the farmhand is not just a politically neutral, philosophical analysis of discourses and their historical changes; it is meant to demonstrate the need for a philosophical and political rethinking of our conception of sexuality. His analysis succeeds in functioning as a form of social critique only because it assumes that our experiences are dependent on but not reducible to dominant scientific discourses and social norms, and that they could be qualitatively transformed if they were governed by different kinds of discourses and types of normativity. In this instance, the implicit assumption is that the farmhand's as well as our own subjective experience of sexuality would be in some way freer, better, or richer if it were not constructed and hemmed in by medical discourses and practices. The call is for a broader range of possible experiences of sexuality— experiences currently unavailable or even unimaginable—constructed through a new or different set of cultural norms and discursive practices.

I will not go into the question of the normative grounding of Foucault's analyses here—in other words, into the question of what would constitute the criteria for a better or richer experience.[9] My point here is simply to argue that while the personal, lived, or subjective experience is not ontologically or epistemically foundational or self-sufficient in Foucault's analyses, it is nevertheless indispensable. If Foucault held that subjective experiences were simply coextensive with dominant expert discourses, as Alcoff claims, there would be no need, or possibility, for him to undertake a critique of them.

In an extended discussion of the farmhand's case in the *Abnormal* lectures (2004), Foucault emphasizes the reason he is focusing on it at such length: it signals the appearance of the abnormal individual and of the domain of abnormalities as the privileged object of psychiatry. The case allows us to mark roughly the crucial period as well as the distinct way in which the abnormal individual was psychiatrized. For Foucault, the fact that the farmhand was not charged judicially—he was acquitted of legal responsibility—but that legal psychiatry took responsibility for his case represented a completely new way in which psychiatry functioned. He claims that around 1850 to 1870 a new psychiatry was born: this psychiatry dispensed with illness, which previously had functioned as the essential justification of mental medicine, and focused instead on behavior with deviations and abnormalities. According to the new psychiatric experts, the farmhand was not suffering from any illness understood as a definite chronological process. The reason they measured his cranium and the proportion between his trunk and limbs was that they needed to identify a permanent physical constellation, a permanent stigma that would brand him structurally. "In the case of Charles Jouy and in this new kind of psychiatry, the offense is instead integrated within a schema of permanent and stable stigmata" (Foucault 2004, 298). In other words, the psychiatrists were not interested in finding symptoms of an illness, but in identifying a general condition of abnormality.

Foucault's aim is thus to analyze the distinct way in which Jouy's actions and behavior were pathologized in the new psychiatric regime. He is not claiming that before the emergence of this new kind of psychiatry either the farmhand's or the little girl's experiences were simply natural in any sense. They were discursively and normatively constituted also in the earlier period, but through a significantly different, *moral* discourse: either a religious discourse operating with the notions of sin and salvation, or a legal discourse relying on legal culpability or the absence of it. Whereas the adult experience of pedophilia was effectively medicalized as a structural abnormality in the latter half of nineteenth century, the fact that the little girl, Sophie Adams, was confined to a house of correction for indecent behavior until she came of age suggests that a corresponding psychiatrization of the child's experience was not yet conceivable.

Foucault's discussion is clearly biased in favor of the farmhand's experience—his interest focuses exclusively on the way it was psychiatrized and pathologized in the new discourses of abnormality. As Jana Sawicki aptly observes in her review of the lectures (Sawicki 2005), Jouy is the only victim in Foucault's story. Alcoff maintains that Foucault does not feel compelled to address Sophie's fate at all, and this failure to address her case coupled with the suspicion that she was in some sense willing or complicit in the act manifests male arrogance and sexism. However, I want to insist that Alcoff is mistaken in arguing that the reason Foucault overlooks Sophie's experience is because he has a theoretically flawed or impoverished understanding of experience. Foucault might be wrong in assuming that Sophie's experience of the incident is coextensive with dominant norms and therefore redundant, but this is not because he assumes that *all* experiences *necessarily* are. In exactly the same way that Foucault's critique of psychiatry relies on the recognition that dominant discourses and the subjective experiences they constitute are not seamlessly aligned, the Foucauldian feminist critique of patriarchal discourses and attitudes toward rape must recognize the correlations, but also the discrepancies, between dominant discourse and subjective experience. A Foucauldian feminist analysis would have to approach Sophie's experience in a parallel manner by focusing on the correlation as well as the discrepancy between the patriarchal and religious discourses of the time that implied that Sophie was complicit, culpable, and amoral, and what was probably, or possibly, her own lived difficulty in recognizing her complicity.

Foucault was clearly aware of the epistemic indispensability of first-person experience, and this is why he emphasized the importance of *subjugated knowledges*. Subjugated knowledges refer to forms of discourse that have been disqualified for being below the required level of erudition or scientificity: they are nonconceptual, naive, and hierarchically inferior. They are typically the knowledge of the patient, the pervert, or the delinquent, and they make possible the local critique of dominant discourses (Foucault 2003, 6–8). He was also aware, however, that descriptions of lived experience cannot be treated as epistemically foundational or self-sufficient. He does not give us an actual, first-person description of the farmhand's experience; we are left to imagine it. The farmhand's suffering remains unspoken while the experts speak and write instead. But even if we did have access to his personal account of the events, it is questionable how articulate such an account would have been. The ontological distinction between having an experience and articulating it in a specific discourse affirmed earlier means also that epistemologically a gap opens—and must remain—between lived experiences and their linguistic descriptions. Even if the accept McDowell's argument discussed in the previous chapter that experiences are conceptual through and through, linguistic description will nevertheless inevitably struggle to capture the richness and ambiguity of lived experience. Even when we acknowledge that this difficulty itself does not prove that experience is nonconceptual, the difficulty persists.

A further problem concerns the authenticity of self-description. Although she advocates phenomenology and emphasizes the need for feminist theory to include personal descriptions of embodied experience—such as first-person accounts of sexual violence—Alcoff nevertheless acknowledges the problematic status of women's experiences as products of patriarchal society. She notes that women's accounts of our own lives and their meaning cannot be accepted uncritically without relinquishing our ability to challenge gender ideology. The emphasis on personal descriptions of embodied experiences does not mean holding that a rape experience, for example, is insusceptible to discursive constructions. A rape can be experienced as deserved or undeserved, as shameful for oneself or the perpetrator, as an inevitable feature of the woman's lot, or as an eradicable evil (Alcoff 2000, 43). She thus accepts the poststructuralist critique of self-sufficient and epistemically foundational experience and insists on the phenomenological descriptions for strategic reasons: first-person accounts cannot reveal the absolute truth about sexuality, rape, or gender, but they can correct some bias. When the analyses of discourses of rape are supplemented with phenomenological accounts, we can gain a more comprehensive understanding of rape and are much less likely to suppose that it is only a discursive effect or interpretation (ibid., 52). Her claim is thus not that feminist theory should rely solely or even primarily on first-person descriptions of sexual and gendered experiences, but that our analysis of rape should be *supplemented* with "phenomenologies of rape experiences from the perspectives of survivors" (ibid.).

Interestingly, Alcoff's suggestion comes close to the strategy that Foucault adopts when trying to understand the experience of hermaphrodite embodiment. In his criticism of the modern deployment of sexuality he does not give us the first-person description of the farmhand's experience, but he does give us the personal story of another victim of the modern regime of sex: Alexina Barbin. Alexina Barbin was a hermaphrodite who lived at the end of the nineteenth century, when scientific theories about sex and sexuality were gaining prominence. She was designated as female at birth, but grew up with an ambiguous awareness of her bodily specificity. At the age of twenty-one she decided to confess her anatomical particularity to a priest and a doctor, and as a consequence was scientifically reclassified as a man by medical experts. She / he attempted to adapt her-/ himself to the new identity and live as a man, but ended up committing suicide at the age of thirty. She / he left behind memoirs recounting her/ his tragic story, which Foucault discovered in the archives of the Department of Public Hygiene.

The way the book *Herculine Barbin: Being the Recently Discovered Memoirs of a Nineteenth-Century French Hermaphrodite* is compiled is significant (Foucault 1980). Foucault effectively juxtaposes her/ his memoirs and thus the first-person, lived account of the hermaphrodite body with the third-person, medical accounts of it. The memoirs are followed by a dossier that contains the facts related to the story: names, dates, and places;

her/his birth certificate; the two reports written by doctors—one by the doctor reassigning her/his sex and another report based on the dissection of her/his corpse—as well as the articles that appeared in the press at the time.

Alexina's memoirs give us the lived, first person account of her/his ambiguous embodiment. She/he describes in guarded terms the painful and humiliating medical examination that ultimately reveals her/his "true" sex and questions the ability of scientific discourse to ever fully understand her/his ambiguous embodiment: "[A] few doctors will make a little stir around my corpse; they will shatter all the extinct mechanisms of its impulses, will draw new information from it, will analyze all the mysterious sufferings that were heaped up on a single human being. O princes of science, enlightened chemists, whose names resound throughout the world, analyze then, if that is possible, all the sorrows that have burned, devoured this heart down to its last fibers; all the scalding tears that have drowned it, squeezed it dry in their savage grasp" (Foucault 1980, 103). While challenging the narrow truth of scientific discourse, Alexina's memoirs can clearly not be simply understood as the "real" or "authentic" account either. They are fundamentally shaped by the narrative conventions as well the cultural conceptions of gender characterizing her time. As Foucault notes, they are written in "that elegant, affected, and allusive style that is somewhat turgid and outdated" and which for women's boarding schools "was not only a way of writing but a manner of living" (xii). He qualifies the conclusions he draws from the memoirs by talking about "impressions" one has "if one gives credence to Alexina's story" (xiii).

On the other hand, it is equally clear that the third-person scientific accounts and medical diagnosis of her "true" identity cannot be accepted as the definitive description of her embodiment either. Foucault notes that although Alexina wrote her memoirs once her new identity had been discovered and established, it is obvious that she did not write it from the point of view of a sex that had at last been brought to light. "It is not a man who is speaking, trying to recall his sensations and his life as they were at the time when he was not yet himself" (Foucault 1980, xiii). The tragedy of Alexina's experience is precisely the result of the fissures and disjunctions, on the one hand, and the overlapping and necessary correlation on the other, between the subject's personal understanding of his or her body and the scientific and legal discourses on its true sex.

The form of the book, not just its content, is thus highly significant for Foucault's attempts to show that while our experiential embodiment is never independent of dominant discourses and practices of power, it is not reducible to them either. Bodies assume meaning through a complex process in which competing discourses, conceptualizations, and cultural practices intertwine with private sensations, pleasures, and pains. The same method is also used in Foucault's discussion of another object of expert discourses, Pierre Rivière, in his book, *I, Pierre Rivière, Having Slaughtered My Mother, Sister, and Brother.* Pierre Rivière's memoirs of his life are juxtaposed with the documents of psychiatry and criminal justice. Foucault explains that the different discourses compiled in the form of a single book outline a combat and a series of confrontations. "The doctors were engaged in a combat, among themselves, with the judges and the prosecution, and with Rivière himself . . . the crown lawyers had their own separate combats as regards the testimony of medical experts, and the comparatively novel use of extenuating circumstances . . . the villagers of Aunay had their own combat to defuse the terror of a crime committed in their midst . . ." (Foucault 1975, x–xi).

Publishing all the documents together meant that Foucault was able to draw a map of these combats in order to "rediscover the interaction of those discourses as weapons of attack and defense in relations of power and knowledge" (Foucault 1975, xi). Rivière's own account, however, assumes the central position in this composition as the mechanism that holds the whole together. It provides "the zero benchmark to gauge the distance between the other discourses and the relations among them" (xiii).

Foucault's genealogical critique of expert discourses and their power over "abnormal subjects" requires as its raison d'être the assumption that the experiences of the subjects themselves do not seamlessly match the scientific theories (fields of knowledge) and the dominant social norms (types of normativity). All experiences are irrevocably constituted by the axis of power and knowledge, but they also contain a subjective dimension, the modes of relation to oneself. Foucault's genealogies not only assume this dimension, they explicitly problematize its correlation with, as well as its distinctiveness from, the other two axes. In order to function as a form of social critique his analyses contrast the subjective with the objective and reveal a problematic and irreducible gap: the normative and dominant discourses are juxtaposed with the subjugated knowledges in order to reveal the former as pathologizing, criminalizing, and moralizing discourses of sexuality, for example.

Foucault was fascinated throughout his life with transformative limit-experiences—experiences that were capable of tearing us away from ourselves and of radically changing the way we think and act.[10] Timothy O'Leary (2009), for example, discusses Foucault's understanding of experience and distinguishes two distinct forms of experience in his thought. He calls the first "everyday" or "background" experience;

it characterizes the general, dominant form in which being is given to a historical period as something that can be thought. The second is "transformative" experience; it is a form of experience that is rare and unusual: it is something that is capable of tearing us away from ourselves and changing the way we think and act. O'Leary emphasizes the importance of such transformative limit-experiences for Foucault because the question of resistance hinges on the question of how it is possible to gain a critical distance from the modes of everyday experience.

I have attempted to argue here, however, that Foucault's understanding of ordinary, everyday experience already contains the potential for transformation and resistance. Our only option of resistance against the normalizing effects of power/knowledge does not lie in waiting for a life-changing event capable of shattering the normalized self, nor do we have to attempt to cross its conventional limits. Our everyday experience already contains fractures and lines of fragility: it has aspects and elements that are inconsistent with its normative determinants. The potential for change emerges out of these fractures, from the space of critical self-reflection and problematization. The constituted experience and its critical transformation must not be assumed to be two categorically different things. Rather, they are both aspects of the historically heterogeneous and self-reflexive nature of experience.

Foucault versus Phenomenology

The contrast between two different dimensions of experience—constituted and constitutive—is not resolved by assuming that Foucault studies one and phenomenology the other.[11] Rather, they both try to relate these two different poles of experience, but they do it in different ways.

Phenomenology holds that experience has a constitutive as well as a constituted dimension, but it is "a philosophy of the subject" in the sense that it subsumes the objective under the subjective. The intersubjective conditions of experience, for example, must and can be disclosed through a description of the subject's structures of experience. The phenomenological method only begins with first-person descriptions of experience, however. It then crucially attempts to move beyond them, from the empirical to the transcendental level of inquiry. Phenomenological descriptions of embodiment are thus not the same as the personal narratives of rape victims, for example. Nor are they sociological generalizations highlighting the common features of varied and extensive data collected from interviews. The crucial move from the empirical to the transcendental level of description that characterizes phenomenology becomes possible because of a bracketing or an *epoche*.

There exists extensive literature on how this bracketing or *epoche* should be understood. In Husserl's original formulations it enables the investigator to bracket the validity and manner of being of the world in order to be able to describe and analyze the essence of the constituting consciousness. Some of his followers, such as Eugen Fink and Maurice Merleau-Ponty, doubted the possibility of a complete reduction to transcendental consciousness and described the *epoche* as only slackening the intentional threads that attach us to the world and thus bringing them to our notice.[12] In the minimal but crucial sense, it is the move that enables the philosopher to take critical distance from his or her experience in order to study its constitutive conditions. Although Alcoff advocates phenomenology for feminist theory, she dismisses the idea of a phenomenological reduction as "too wedded to the goal of establishing certainty" (Alcoff 2000, 48). When she contrasts "phenomenologies of rape experiences" from the perspectives of survivors to "discourses of rape" (52), it is therefore not clear what phenomenological description means to her, and how we should distinguish it from personal narrative. Without some philosophical reflection on the role of phenomenological bracketing, the distinction she makes between "phenomenologies of rape" and "discourses of rape" risks collapsing into a meaningless opposition.

In contrast to phenomenology, Foucault resists all foundational recourse to experience. But he does not contest the ontological or even epistemic indispensability of subjective experience. The problem with phenomenology, according to him, is not the attempt to theorize lived experiences. The problem is that experience is treated as foundational and epistemically self-sufficient. He insists that embodied experiences such as Herculine Barbin's, for example, can only be understood in the crosslighting of two irreducible perspectives: the subjective memory of the patient and the objective knowledge of the experts.

To conclude, I have attempted to show that experience is irreducible for Foucault's critical project in at least two senses. First, without the ontological assumption of constitutive experience we cannot understand how subjects and objects are formed in social practices. Second, the self-reflexivity of experience importantly opens up the critical perspective on our present that is the driving political motivation of Foucault's thought. I contend that his conception of experience can therefore provide a valuable philosophical tool for feminist theory in its attempt to understand and validate experiences.

Part 2

Feminist Phenomenology

4

The Problem of Language

The question of what feminist phenomenology is cannot be given an easy answer. Perhaps we must accept that this is inevitable: defining feminist phenomenology might be not only extremely difficult, but also counterproductive. One of the central aims of feminist philosophy has been to question fixed definitions, boundaries, and categories. At the same time I believe that it is important for feminist phenomenologists to engage in a critical process of self-definition, if for no other reason than to thwart the fairly often heard comment that what is called feminist phenomenology turns out on closer scrutiny not to be phenomenology at all.[1] Asking ourselves this question also means following the phenomenological imperative of ultimate self-responsibility: phenomenology must be a self-critical and self-responsible practice, a movement of thought that turns back, again and again, to investigate its own conditions and origins.[2]

Although Husserl himself took up "the problem of the sexes" as a question for phenomenological investigation, I am not interested here in what he, as the founder of the method, wrote about it—and not only because what he wrote is not very much and not very interesting.[3] Rather, my reason for leaving aside his explicit comments is based on the idea that when we evaluate the relevance of phenomenology from the perspective of contemporary concerns, it must be the method that is the driving force of phenomenology and not the individual statements of any given phenomenologist. If phenomenology is to prove itself as a valuable philosophical method in today's world, then we must be able to extract it from the cultural context of the men who invented it, and to use it for our benefit today.[4] This is also the idea that I will ultimately put into question in the chapters comprising this part, however. It is my contention that our historically changing ontological schemas are irrevocably tied up with our methods of reflection and therefore, as our world changes, perhaps it is inevitable that our methods must change too.

Feminist phenomenology is often characterized as being opposed to forms of feminist theorizing that focus on discourses and conceptual analysis. It is understood as capable of accounting for the prediscursive, personal, or lived meaning of experience and therefore offering an "embodied understanding" of various feminist issues such as gender identity, anorexia, sexual violence, and feminist ethics. Sonia Kruks (2001), for example, has argued persuasively for the importance of phenomenology and its concomitant account of lived experience for feminist theory. According to Kruks, feminist theory has allowed itself to be colonized by postmodern modes of thinking that focus on discourses and, in so doing, has unwisely cut itself off from the heritage of phenomenological and existential thought. Feminist theory would now benefit from returning to phenomenology and through it, could retrieve the central importance of lived experience.

While I agree with Kruks on the starting point of her argument—the importance of phenomenological insights and particularly of the first-person perspective for feminist theory—my aim in this chapter is to question her understanding of feminist phenomenology as being able to provide us with access to prediscursive experience. Instead, I want to put forward an alternative understanding of feminist phenomenology as a sophisticated study of the constitution of linguistic meaning. I will begin with a critical discussion of Kruks's seminal book *Retrieving Experience: Subjectivity and Recognition in Feminist Politics* (2001). I will then investigate the ways in which phenomenologists have sought to elucidate the relationship between experience and language. I will take my lead from Husserl's writings, but I will also briefly study the question in the work of his most influential students, namely Eugen Fink and Martin Heidegger. I will not present a comprehensive examination of their views on language, linguistic meaning, and experience here; to do so would require a separate book. My aim is more modest: I hope to argue convincingly that phenomenology provides a rich resource for thinking about the constitution of linguistic meaning, as well as for the fundamental entwinement of language and experience. It is my contention that it is important to consider this contribution when we pose the question of what phenomenology can offer feminist inquiry and what feminist phenomenology actually is.

The Phenomenological Retrieval of Experience

Kruks's key aim in *Retrieving Experience* is to argue for the primacy of women's lived experiences over their discursive descriptions or determinations. This leads her to the problematic position of considering "female experience" as an irreducible given grounded in a female body. Her position is not only problematic politically in that it effectively undermines those feminist strategies that attempt to fight forms of bodily essentialism, but it is also supported by suspect methodology.

In arguing for the significance of the lived experience Kruks provides the following personal, "face-to-face" account. At a time when she was working as a volunteer at a battered women's shelter in London, she arrived at work one day and encountered a Nigerian woman whose left eye was bruised and closed, her cheek grazed and lip gashed. Kruks reports that she immediately felt the woman's pain in her own body. This suggested to her that we are capable of immediate intersubjective apprehension of another's experience of pain. Kruks then quickly moves from this description of her own experience, possibly through a form of eidetic variation, to a strong claim about eidetic female embodiment:

> In my example, the person in pain was, like myself, a woman. That she was a Nigerian woman whose physiognomy, speech, life experiences, and social status were very different from mine did not interfere with my ability immediately to feel-with her pain. To clarify the place of gender here it is useful to ask a further question: Do I also feel-with the pain of a man whose face has been smashed? A bruised eye and a split lip certainly communicate another's pain to me irrespective of the gender of the sufferer, yet generally I do find that my affective response to a man's pain is weaker. . . . This is surely because, although I share with him those key invariants that make us both sentient human beings, my lived body is also significantly different from his. (ibid.,167)

Kruks thus draws her phenomenological conclusion about eidetic female embodiment without hesitation. Her first-person experience of feeling-with another woman's pain warrants her to argue for the fundamental role of embodied experience as an affective basis for solidarity among all women: ". . . what I am talking about is a *direct* experience of affinity among women that is possible (though never guaranteed) because I can recognize as also 'mine' the embodied experiences of another woman, even while knowing that she and I are in other ways very different" (ibid., 152). In other words, certain essential characteristics or generalities of female embodiment enable us to share the experiences of other women. Such bodily connections can then potentially become the bases for forms of respectful solidarity among different women.

Kruks does not seem to engage in any kind of bracketing or problematization regarding her own experience, however. She not only completely overlooks the possible charges of blatant subjectivism, but she also disregards the cultural and linguistic determinants of her experience. She does not stop to consider, for example, how violence is fundamentally coded as male, both in our culture in general and in the context of a battered women's shelter in particular. Our perceptions of a woman with a black eye or of a man with a black eye are thus necessarily structured according to our culturally normative background beliefs about gender. These background beliefs will affect our emotional responses irrespective of what type of lived body one is. Joan Scott's argument discussed in chapter two, namely that treating experience as the bedrock of evidence means forgetting questions about the discursively constructed nature of that experience, seems to hit the mark here.

Elsewhere Kruks herself acknowledges the significance of poststructuralist accounts of the historically and culturally constituted experience. Rather than discarding these insights, she endeavors to complement them with phenomenological, lived accounts of experience. She argues that experience can be accounted for on the basis of two dialectically related poles, either of which can take priority depending on the nature of our questions and goals: the explanatory pole explores experience from an impersonal or "third-person" stance, while the prediscursive or phenomenological pole explores it from a "first-person" stance, in terms of its lived meaning, as an experience to be grasped or felt rather than explained. Depending on which pole we choose to start from, we can render an account of the same experience either as a discursive effect or as subjectively lived. We can also switch between the poles and privilege one pole over the other as the starting point of feminist inquiry, depending on the nature of our questions and goals (Kruks 2001, 141).

Yet Kruks's idea of two complementary accounts of experience, impersonal and personal, or discursive and prediscursive, generates more philosophical problems than it solves. First, we are still left with a methodological problem: even if one must distinguish between having an experience and describing that experience, as long as we move in the realm of philosophy, language is needed to render an account of the lived or felt experience. Even if we want to give due attention to "experiences of bodily pain and fear that exceed discourse," for example, we can do so only by identifying and articulating these experiences. Second, the fundamental metaphysical question still remains open: to what extent is the lived or felt experience structured conceptually, even when it is not articulated at all? In short, Kruks's distinction between linguistically articulated experience and prediscursive, affective experience overlooks the philosophically pressing problem of the relationship between experience and language instead of solving it or even addressing it head-on.

I suggest that we therefore return to the question of the intertwinement of experience and language already discussed in part 1 of this book, but this time from the perspective of phenomenology. I begin with Husserl's complex account of meaning and linguistic expression in *Logical Investigations*. After analyzing some of the differing interpretations and problems of the phenomenological conception of language and its relationship to experience, we will be in a better position to assess Kruks's project and answer the question of what feminist phenomenology is.

Husserl on Linguistic Meaning

Husserl's breakthrough into phenomenology, *Logical Investigations* (1900–1901), presents a detailed account of linguistics and semantics. The First and Fourth Investigation in particular put forward a complex theory of expression and signification. This discussion of language preceded Husserl's introduction of the key ideas of the phenomenological method in Ideas I—transcendental reduction, for example. Thus, initially, the question of language in connection with the proper phenomenological method could not be asked. The second edition of *Logical Investigations*, which came out in 1913, was extensively rewritten by Husserl in light of his new understanding of phenomenology as expressed in Ideas I. The initially planned revision proved too demanding, and he therefore produced only a partially revised second edition. He writes in the foreword that "anyone who knows the old work will see the impossibility of lifting it entirely to the level of the Ideas" (Husserl 2001, 4). Husserl chose what he called "a middle course" and articulated three maxims that guided the revision: to let individual errors stand to represent steps in his own path of thinking; to improve what could be improved without altering the course and style of the original; and to lead the reader level by level to newer and deeper insights (ibid., 4–5). Needless to say, such a middle course makes it difficult to assess Husserl's final position on the question of linguistic meaning, and as a result there is an extensive literature on the topic with varying emphases and interpretations. My aim here is to explicate only his key ideas to the extent that I see them as relevant to contemporary feminist debates on experience and discourse.

Husserl opens the first of the *Logical Investigations*, titled "Expression and Meaning" by making a number of distinctions. He distinguishes between signs functioning as indications and as expressions; between what an expression intimates and what it means; between what it means and what object it names; between expressions which function solely to name and other more complicated forms of expression; as well as between objective expressions and subjective expressions, the meanings of which shift with the occasion. The crucial distinction from my point of view is the one he makes in section §9 ("Phenomenological distinctions between the physical appearance of the expression, and the sense-giving and sense-fulfilling act") between the physical appearance of the expression and the act, which gives it meaning. It is by way of such meaning-giving acts that "the expression is more than a merely sounded word. It *means* something, and in so far as it means something, it relates to what is objective" (ibid., 192). Hence, there are linguistic expressions—sound patterns or written inscriptions—and mental acts that "enliven" or "en-soul" the linguistic expression and literally give it a meaning. Husserl argues for the primary importance of these meaning-giving acts; without them we would not have words, but mere meaningless sounds or marks on paper: ". . . we think . . . that an understanding, a peculiar act-experience relating to the expression, is present, that it shines through the expression, that it lends it meaning and thereby a relation to objects. . . . It is in this sense-giving act-character . . . that meaning consists" (ibid., 208–9).

Another crucial distinction that Husserl makes is between these meaning-conferring acts or the meaning-intentions, on the one hand, and meaning-fulfilling acts, on the other hand. The latter are not essential to the expression as such, but they "stand to it in the logically basic relation of *fulfilling* (confirming, illustrating) it more or less adequately, and so actualizing its relation to its object" (ibid., 192). When the meaning is fulfilled, the intended sense of the expression—the book is on the table, for example—is intuitively confirmed. We see the book on the table. In this case, there is a double identification: the words are first made one with the meaning-intention, and this in its turn is made one with its corresponding meaning-fulfillment (ibid.). We grasp the spoken sounds in terms of their sense, and we grasp this sense in terms of a corresponding intuitive presence. Thus, expressions refer to their objects through their meanings or senses, and this reference is confirmed or fulfilled by intuition. Specific processes of consciousness—acts of meaning-intention and meaning-fulfillment—constitute the sense expressed in words. Through them, we experience a unity of expression and the thing expressed, of words and things, in expressive acts.

Husserl, similar to many other twentieth-century philosophers, thus attempted to answer the fundamental philosophical question of how words "stick" to things and meaning supervenes upon reality. How do we manage to give meaning to the noises we make and the signs we inscribe, and how are those meanings conveyed to others? Husserl begins with the fundamental philosophical insight that neither language nor the transcendent objects out in the world have any intrinsic meaning as such, but it is only by virtue of human consciousness that they can carry meaning. In other words, human consciousness is intentional: it structures its experiences by giving them meaning. Language is capable of conveying meaning because it is expressive of this intentional activity, and complex language games become meaningful because they too bear the intentionality of consciousness. Without human consciousness and its exceptional ability to relate to the world as meaningful, we would not have complex symbolic systems such as language, but only random sounds and meaningless scribbling. The use of language not only relates to intentionality, but more fundamentally, is founded on intentionality, which "enlivens" it as meaningful.

Husserl's central idea of intentionality thus also provides the key to his understanding of linguistic meaning. Intentionality is a unique and intrinsic property of consciousness by means of which its relations to the world are intentional relations of meaning. For something to be an intentional experience is simply another way of saying that it has a meaning: it is a coherent experience of something by someone.

Husserl's thought following *Logical Investigations* can be read as increasingly detailed analyses of the phenomenological structure of the acts by means of which we have intentional experiences—experiences that are directed toward specific objects in specific ways. In *Ideas I*, Husserl distinguishes a specific meaning component of the intentional act, which he calls its *noema* or *noematic Sinn*.[5] *Noema* provides the key to phenomenological accounts of meaning and is therefore central to my question of linguistic meaning here. However, there is surprisingly wide disagreement among Husserl scholars as to how we should understand this fundamental phenomenological concept. Phenomenologists such as Dagfinn Føllesdal, Ronald McIntyre, and David Woodruff Smith (whose ideas are sometimes known as the West Coast interpretation), have defended a Fregean interpretation of Husserl's theory of intentionality. According to them, *noema* should be understood as an ideal meaning entity that mediates the intentional relation between the meaning-giving act and its object. It is what prescribes or determines the object *as* it is intended and should be sharply distinguished from both the intentional act and its object. In other words, *noema* is not that toward which consciousness is directed, but that by means of which it is directed and by which we achieve a reference to the external object. It is an intermediary ideal entity, which is instrumental in our intending the objects themselves. As Smith and McIntyre write: "Husserl's theory of intentionality is not an object-theory, but a mediator theory . . . for Husserl, an act is directed toward an object via an intermediate 'intentional' entity, the act's *noema*" (1982, 87).[6]

By contract, phenomenologists such as Robert Sokolowski, John

Drummond, and Richard Cobb-Stevens (those of the East Coast inter-pretation) argue in favor of an object theory: *noema* is not to be under-stood as an ideal meaning or as an intermediary between the act and the object. It is not something that bestows intentionality on consciousness. Rather, it is the intended object itself considered in the phenomenologi-cal reflection. *Noema* is the perceived object as perceived. The object and the *noema* are the same thing only understood differently: the difference is in the way one and the same object is considered, either in straight-forward experience or in phenomenological reflective inquiry. In other words, there is nothing that mediates our experience of the world. The world is already meaningful in experience before any mediation.[7]

Each of these competing *noema* interpretations has sought to cor-roborate its reading by referring to specific textual passages in Husserl's oeuvre, and I will not attempt to answer the question here of which one is the correct reading. Instead I want to show how Husserl's thought gives rise to at least two fundamentally different understandings of linguistic meaning and its relationship to experience in phenomenology, depend-ing on how *noema* is understood. This makes it far from obvious what the phenomenological understanding of the relationship between experi-ence and discourse in fact entails.

Noematic Sinn and Linguistic Meaning

In the first of his *Logical Investigations* Husserl specifically discusses lin-guistic meaning, for which he used the German word *Bedeutung*. While a key premise of his theory is that the meaningfulness of linguistic expres-sion is integrally related to intentional experiences, meanings cannot be purely subjective events of consciousness. The use of sounds or signs to express meaning is dependent on conscious intentional activity, but meaning itself must be essentially intersubjective and shareable. Nor-mally we succeed in communicating with each other, which means that we can convey to our interlocutors a meaning whereby they can come to intend the same object.

The decisive feature of the Fregean approach or the West Coast interpretation is that it equates *noematic Sinn* with *Bedeutung*. The inten-tionality of consciousness is conceived by analogy with the reference of linguistic expressions. David Woodruff Smith and Ronald McIntyre (1982), for example, argue for the unity of linguistic expression and in-tentional meaning by contending that we only have one class of meaning entities—*noematic Sinne*—that play the same role both in language and in acts of consciousness generally. They claim that Husserl identifies *noematic Sinn* with the meaning of linguistic expressions: *Bedeutung* is simply the *noematic Sinn* expressed. In other words, the meanings that we express in language are the very same meaning entities that give structure and significance to our experience. When expressed in language, they mediate the relation of words to referents in the same way that, as contents of consciousness, they mediate the relation of intentional acts to their objects (ibid., 154).

The West Coast interpretation of *noema* thus makes the phenomenological account of experience strikingly compatible with the poststructuralist insight that experience is fundamentally structured by language and linguistic meaning. The meanings that we give to our perceptions and experiences are understood as shared linguistic meanings, not as private intentional contents. The coincidence of *noematic Sinn* and linguistic meaning entails that the contents of our subjective thoughts and experiences can be shared because they can be expressed in language. We never hope or perceive aloud, for example, but the meaning of these acts is, in principle, expressible in language. This account also implies that language cannot be understood only as a medium of communication, but as constitutive of shared reality. Growing up in a given culture with its particular linguistic tradition would imply that the meanings, the *noematic Sinne*, that we lend to our private experiences are the shared linguistic meanings that we have learned in the process of making sense of the world. Even experiences such as pain and fear that Kruks, for example, foregrounds are, in principle, communicable to others, and their general meaning is constituted intersubjectively.

Yet identifying *noematic Sinn* with *Bedeutung* seems to turns phenomenology into linguistic analysis: there appears to be no meaning apart from language. Phenomenology seems to lose any possibility of accounting for situations in which our experiences cannot find an adequate linguistic expression, for example. At times, however, Smith and McIntyre argue for a weaker formulation of their thesis. They write that "there is a close correlation, at the very least, between Husserl's conception of linguistic meaning and his conception of *noematic Sinn*" (ibid., 176). Every *Sinn* corresponds *potentially* to a linguistic meaning, because in principle every *Sinn* is expressible in language. There is or in principle there could be developed some linguistic expression whose meaning would be that *Sinn*. However, *noematic Sinn* may also currently lack the appropriate expression. Smith and McIntyre acknowledge that Husserl does not claim that every *Sinn* has actually been expressed in language, nor does he claim that actually existing natural languages—or even humanly possible languages—are rich enough to express every *Sinn*. In other words, for Husserl, intentional acts and their meanings are not *intrinsically* linguistic (ibid., 183). Hence, while holding that meaningful experiences, in a strict sense, are only possible because of language, Smith and McIntyre nevertheless seem to acknowledge the irreducibility and superabundance of sensory intuition.

Language and the Reduction

Equating *noematic Sinn* with *Bedeutung* also seems to imply a further problem, namely what happens to language in the transcendental reduction. Reduction is an essential methodological device for phenomenology, because it is what enables the phenomenologist to reveal and analyze the *noemata* of various acts. Regardless of which of the two *noema* interpretations we follow, both schools hold that the *noemata* can only be identified and analyzed after the reduction. We only become explicitly aware of them on phenomenological reflection, whereas in our usual engagements with the world we are simply aware of the actual objects out there. If the reduction is carried out radically, however, all worldly habitualities, such as conceptuality and language, should also fall subject to bracketing. Language embodies through its lexical as well as its syntactical features sedimented interpretations of the community, and, in as much as philosophers use it, they can never be certain that the ideal structures they identify are purified of naturalistic presuppositions. But how is it possible to bracket language if *noematic Sinne* are in fact identical with linguistic meanings? What kinds of meanings are we supposed to encounter after we have bracketed language?

Furthermore, even if we insist that *noematic Sinn* and *Bedeutung* can be separated from each other and that it is possible to bracket language, there still remains the problem of explicating the results of the phenomenological inquiry after the reduction. Phenomenologists are forced to bring language back to be able to explicate and communicate the findings of their phenomenological inquiries. All notions such as "intentionality" and "transcendental subjectivity" revealed by the transcendental reduction are worldly concepts already tied to shared linguistic meanings. Or should we insist that transcendental reduction results in a phenomenological metalanguage, a properly transcendental language?

Some philosophers have suggested that Husserl's aim with the reduction is remarkably similar to the strands of analytic philosophy, which seek to clarify the semantic relations between words and their referents from the perspective of a universal metalanguage, a logical calculus. Martin Kusch (1997) argues that in Husserl's thought the transcendental reduction clears away the contaminated meanings that ordinary language carries with it, and a metalanguage can communicate the findings of the transcendental level of reflection, namely the ideal meanings, *noemas.* Hence, while remaining on the level of the mundane ego, we are trapped inside our language and the naive ontological commitments it carries. Only from a different metaperspective is it possible to escape the limits of our language and gain a more accurate perception of the things themselves. Natural attitude is thus tied to natural language with all its ontological commitments to psychic and physical objects. Adopting the transcendental attitude and the phenomenological metalanguage means to become free of them and gain access to the things themselves. Reduction should thus be understood as a systematic production of a metalevel that enables us to study the semantic relations of the lower, objective level. It enables consciousness to study systematically those structures of meaning, which connect it to the world.

However, Husserl's own view on the role of language in the transcendental reduction is less clear-cut. In the introduction to the second volume of *Logical Investigations* Husserl formulates the problem of language in phenomenology. He discusses the difficulties of an analysis that aims at a description of the phenomenological structure of experience and writes: "In addition to the difficulty of reaching firm results . . . we have the further difficulty of *stating such results,* of *communicating them to others.* Completely self-evident truths of essence, established by most exact analysis, must be expounded by way of expressions whose rich variety does not compensate for the fact that they only fit familiar natural objects, while the experiences in which such objects become constituted for consciousness, can be directly referred to only by way of a few highly ambiguous words . . ." (Husserl 2001, 171).

Husserl solves the problem there by referring to a necessary transformation of sense: the description has undergone a change of sense, as a result of which it now belongs to the sphere of phenomenology (ibid.)[8] He does not, however, explain in any detail how this transformation takes place or what exactly it means, but leaves the task for his followers. He concludes his discussion of the difficulties in the way of a pure phenomenology by noting that, serious as they are, "they are by no means such as to make the whole attempt to overcome them appear hopeless. Resolute cooperation among a generation of research-workers, conscious of their goal and dedicated to their main issue, would, I think, suffice to decide the most important questions in the field" (ibid., 171–72).

One of the phenomenologists continuing this "resolute cooperation among a generation of research-workers" was Husserl's assistant, Eugen Fink. Fink took up the problem of language in connection with the reduction and set out to solve it in *The Sixth Cartesian Meditation*. He claimed at the outset that the problem would disappear if there could be a proper transcendental language, but that phenomenological inquiry does not lead to the construction of a new metalanguage, nor could it ever do so (Fink 1995, 84). "Language is indeed retained as a habituality right through the *epoche* . . . the phenomenological onlooker must make use of it, if he at all wants to give predicative expression to his cognitions" (ibid., 86).

As Husserl suggested, Fink saw a solution emerging from the necessary transformation of sense. He argues that, in taking over language, the phenomenologizing onlooker transforms its natural sense. "If this kind of transformation did not occur, then the phenomenologist would slip out of the transcendental attitude every time he spoke" (ibid., 86). Fink describes the transformation of sense as an uneasy tension, a rebellion inside the words of the natural attitude (ibid., 88–89). He emphasizes that it has important implications for the phenomenological method: although phenomenology becomes communicable through its necessary articulation in language, it must retain a radically personal character. "There is thus no phenomenological understanding that comes simply by reading reports of phenomenological research; these can only be 'read' at all by performing the investigations themselves. Whoever fails to do that just does not read phenomenological sentences; he reads queer sentences in natural language. The phenomenologizing I must always be kept in mind as transformation of ontic-naive meanings into 'analogically' indicated, transcendental-ontic meanings. It signifies a lapse into 'dogmatism' (that of the natural attitude) if explicit knowledge of this necessary transformation dies away, and the phenomenologist thereby in his explications falsifies the object of his theoretical experiences" (ibid., 92–93).

The personal or existential significance of phenomenological investigation is also the starting point for the young Martin Heidegger. His early solution to the problem of language, namely the idea of formal indication, requires a personal transformation. Reduction cannot be understood as a systematic production of a metalevel, but as a personal transformation or an existential imperative. The resulting transformation of sense does not provide us with an abstract universal language of logically connected idealities, but with a language of life, which can only be filled with meaning by personal enactment. Instead of trying to solve the problem of phenomenological language within the Husserlian understanding of phenomenology as a rigorous descriptive science, Heidegger claims that the problem of language forces us to radically rethink the phenomenological project. Phenomenology cannot be a purely descriptive science: its ultimate task cannot be just description, but more fundamentally, enactment. In other words, the problem of language points to a task that consists of not just explicating and analyzing the general structure of *Dasein*, for example, but of enacting this structure itself.

Hence, the starting point for phenomenology is not the facts of knowledge and science, but the primal phenomena of experience. The move is from the theoretical to the pretheoretical as a more original sphere. If Husserl's maxim was to go back to the things themselves, young Heidegger's call is "Let us immerse ourselves again in the lived experience" (quoted in English in Kisiel 1995, 42).[9] According to Heidegger, this immersion into life experience reveals that this experience itself is already meaningful before any effort is made to reflect on it or to describe it. "The meaningful is the primary, for it gives itself immediately, without any detour of thought across the apprehension of a thing" (Kisiel 1995, 45–46).

I contend that we can find in Fink and young Heidegger's work a sophisticated explication of another interpretative strand of phenomenology that differs radically from the Fregean strand: meanings are understood as immediate and fundamentally prediscursive. In emphasizing the immediacy of lived experience—the experience to be felt or grasped rather than explained—feminist phenomenologists such as Kruks could be understood as following this strand. This means, however, that they must counter the same philosophical objections as young Heidegger did. The return to lived experience means an attempt to retain the original richness of experiential meaning without objectifying it and transforming it through theoretical reflection. The methodological challenge thus takes the form: How can the streaming experience of life become an object of reflection without being reified? How can we describe this experience in a way that does not inevitably distort, violate, and objectify it? As I pointed out in the first section of this chapter, "The Phenomenological Retrieval of Experience," in my critical discussion of Kruks, the very same problem troubles her project. Giving due attention to "experiences of bodily pain and fear that exceed discourse," for example, can only be done by identifying and articulating these experiences. Yet how can we do this without turning them into descriptive accounts already belonging to the discursive pole and not to the lived pole of her analysis?

The Language of Life

Heidegger tackled the methodological challenge outlined above in a lecture course in 1919 (*Die Idee der Philosophie und das Weltanschauungsproblem*) by responding to Paul Natorp's objections to Husserl's phenomenology.[10] Theodore Kisiel (1995, 47–48) argues that in this course Heidegger's response to Natorp's pair of simple but ingenious objections gave birth to the solution of a formally indicating language and hermeneutics. Kisiel summarizes Natorp's objections succinctly. The first objection raises the question of whether immediate life experience is accessible to reflection. Reflection exercises an analytically dissective and dissolving effect upon the life stream, acting as a theoretical intrusion that interrupts the stream and cuts it off. In other words, reflection is already a theoretical attitude, which necessarily objectifies that which is its object, thereby making immediate experience, by definition, inaccessible to reflection.

Heidegger's response to this first objection is to point to hermeneutical intuition or understanding. This means a certain nonreflective understanding, a familiarity which life already has of itself and which phenomenology needs only to repeat. We are familiar with our experiences in an implicit, prereflective manner: there is a spontaneous access that life has to itself (Kisiel 1995, 48). As Dan Zahavi formulates Heidegger's solution, he resolutely rejects the idea that life should be a mute, chaotic, and incomprehensible principle and insists that life experience is imbued with meaning. It is intentionally structured with an inner articulation and rationality, as well as with a spontaneous and immediate self-understanding. Phenomenology must simply disclose this nonobjectifying and nontheoretical self-understanding of life experience in all its modifications (Zahavi 2003, 161).

For my question of language taken up here, however, Natorp's second objection is more important. Natorp posed the same objection to Heidegger that I posed to Kruks: phenomenology claims to be pure description of immediate experience, but there is no such thing as immediate description, since all expression, any attempt to put something into words, objectifies. Description always involves the use of generalizing concepts. We can never articulate the dynamic and elusive stream of life with words that refer to things because we will end up creating a conceptual entity, namely life experience. Or, as Kisiel formulates the objection, "How can experience conceptualize itself so that this description is part of it?" (Kisiel 1995, 48). Hence, the problem that Heidegger had to deal with is that normal or natural language distorts the more original, phenomenological meanings. Language alters these meanings by reifying them, transforming them into naturalized objects. Instead of the experiential, original meanings of life, we have linguistic meanings—words—that refer to conceptual entities—things.

Heidegger took this objection very seriously and acknowledged that with the idea of a pretheoretical science ultimately the problem of language emerges. Language necessarily presents an obstacle: it fails us. Heidegger's response to this second objection is tied to his response to the first. The spontaneous access that life experience has to itself also makes it possible to find less violent concepts, because immediate experience is already meaningful. It is not mute, but already structured like a language. There is a reflective, but also an expressive dimension built into life itself. Philosophy can overcome the dualism of rational concepts and irrational lived experiences, because life not only has a spontaneous self-understanding, but also spontaneous self-expression, which philosophy simply must read off life experience. The key task of phenomenology becomes to replace the deformed and objectifying everyday understanding with the more primary articulations of life itself. A true phenomenological description thus does not constitute a violation of life experience because it is not an attempt to impose a foreign systematicity on life. Rather it is something that is rooted in and motivated by factic life experience itself (Zahavi 2003, 161–62).

The problems of immediate access to life and to its spontaneous expression are thus solved by the ideas of nonreflective understanding and nonobjectifying conceptualization that life itself provides. Hence, Heidegger could be read as having accepted the possibility of a metalanguage, but this metalanguage would not be an abstract calculus capable of translating meanings that are originally sensory. The phenomenological level of meanings now consists of the lived language of life itself.

However, even if we accept the primal unity of words and things in life experience, a problem remains: How can the appropriate expressions be "read off" directly from experience in order to enable intuitive access to it? How can we identify the appropriate philosophical expressions, the right words to describe the pretheoretical experiences? In short, what are the criteria for a concept to be true to life and not just another violent word? Why should human existence be called *Dasein* and not Donald Duck, for example?

Heidegger's early answer is the idea of formal indication. Formal indications or formally indicative concepts are formal in the sense that they are empty. They do not have content because they only indicate a meaning. Phenomenology, because of its fundamentally conceptual character, can only approximate the immediate experience it wishes to articulate. Its expressions are only formal indications, which indicate the way toward fulfilling their sense in enactment. The concept points in the direction of experience, which has to be enacted. As Heidegger put it: "The content of such concepts does not directly intend and say what it relates to, it gives only an indication, a pointer, so that those who understand this conceptual connection are called upon to bring about a transformation of themselves into the Dasein" (Heidegger quoted in Kisiel 1995, 59). Formal indications can thus only be filled in by the philosophizing individual through his or her philosophical activity. The enactment of formal indications means relating them to what the concepts refer to in one's own lived existence.

Heidegger's idea of formal indication clearly builds upon the intentional semantics Husserl developed in *Logical Investigations*. Linguistic expressions gain meaning through the individual subject's meaning-giving acts. Heidegger avoids Husserl's problem of what happens to language in the reduction, however. He too brackets natural language to be able to reach the phenomenological level of meanings, but he does not have to bring it back transformed to be able to communicate the results. Rather than seeking to transform the sense of the existing and objectifying linguistic expressions, Heidegger puts forward new ones, the formal indications. These expressions are empty to begin with, so we do not have to succeed in bracketing and transforming their meaning. They only indicate a meaning, which must be fulfilled in personal experience.

Yet Heidegger's solution creates a host of new problems, the most obvious being that formal indications risk becoming the exclusive language of Heideggerians. The meanings of formal indications are, by definition, subjective, in the sense that they can never be conveyed through any formal set of semantic rules, but only enacted in lived, personal experience. What is supposed to stop them from being purely subjective is the ontological view of a primal unity of understanding and expression in experience, and *Dasein* as the unique possibility of this unity. However, as Zahavi points out, while *Dasein* has a spontaneous access to the language of life, it also has a tendency to fall, to lose these original meanings in the distorted meanings of everyday language. In *Being and Time, Dasein* is described not only as the possibility of authentic self-understanding, but also essentially as having a tendency to cover things up, a tendency toward self-forgetfulness and falling. This means that the articulation of the fundamental structures of life will no longer be able to rely on merely going along with life's own tendency, but rather it might be more correct to describe philosophy as a counterruinant movement (Zahavi 2003, 166–67). This means that there seems to be no guarantee that life will speak to me or, more accurately, that I will understand its language. It will only speak to me if I am able to transform myself into *Dasein* and read off the original meanings of life in an authentic experience. If I am not capable of doing this, then the language of formal indication will be empty and meaningless.

If feminist phenomenologists choose to follow the interpretative strand, which insists that meaning is essentially immediate and prediscursive, then they have to provide some answer to the methodological question of how this meaning can be theoretically analyzed and communicated to others. Otherwise it is difficult to see how feminist phenomenology could be a shared field of philosophical inquiry. While Heidegger's theory of formal indication seems to provide one possible solution, I strongly believe that it is not the solution that feminist phenomenologists seek. If feminist phenomenology developed its own specialized vocabulary of formal indications and then held that it was comprehensible only to those who are the beneficiaries of certain embodied experiences or faculties denied to others, it would be in danger of abandoning philosophy in favor of an exclusive cult. Feminist phenomenology must be an ongoing, participatory project, open to different views and responses, and therefore it cannot leave behind the realm of shared, everyday linguistic meanings, even if they are general, violent, fallen, and objectifying.

To conclude, I hope to have shown that the phenomenological emphasis on lived experience does not yet imply that this experience is prediscursive or immediate. There are different views within phenomenology itself on linguistic meaning as well as on the relationship between experience and language. It is possible to argue, with the help of Husserl's ideas, that the meaning of the "felt or lived experience" is always, in principle, expressible in language and that it is therefore, phenomenologically, equally an experience to be explained. I am in full agreement with feminist phenomenologists such as Kruks and Alcoff that feminist phenomenology can provide important theoretical and methodological tools with which to challenge the narrow focus on discourse analysis and conceptual history in feminist philosophy. However, to do this, feminist phenomenology should not identify itself too narrowly as a form of theorizing that examines experiences in terms of their prediscursive, grasped, or felt meaning. Rather, it should face up to the philosophical challenge posed by language and mine the rich heritage of phenomenological thought on language and linguistic meaning for its own objectives.

5

A Phenomenology of Birth

In addition to understanding feminist phenomenology as a form of theorizing that examines women's experiences in terms of their lived meaning, another common idea is that it makes an important contribution to phenomenological study by complementing and deepening phenomenological accounts of lived embodiment with accounts of female embodiment. Linda Fisher (2000a, 33), for example, argues that feminist critiques of omissions or lacunae in phenomenological accounts and corresponding elaborations and analyses of gendered experience serve to expand, deepen, and correct phenomenological accounts.

My concern with this kind of understanding of feminist phenomenology is that it leads to a view of feminist phenomenology as a faithful assistant to the phenomenological project rather than as a truly critical current in it. Feminist phenomenology would only be concerned with regional subthemes in phenomenology. Feminist accounts of breasted experience or pregnancy, for example, could add some missing descriptions of embodiment to the phenomenological project, but they would not essentially change the core of it in any way.[1]

The questions that I suggest we must therefore ask are: If we include in the phenomenological investigation experiences which are traditionally understood as feminist issues and relegated to the margins of phenomenology, such as being pregnant and giving birth, do these studies not change the phenomenological project in any fundamental way? Do they simply deepen or complement it while leaving intact that which has previously been discovered? If we accept the understanding of phenomenology as being concerned with properly transcendental, universal conditions or structures rather than mundane, empirical, or ontic phenomena can sexual difference really be excluded from it?

In this chapter my aim is to show that an analysis of birth does not simply point to the need to complement phenomenology with vivid descriptions of labor pains, for example, but suggests a need to radically rethink such fundamental phenomenological questions as the possibility of a purely eidetic phenomenology and the limits of egological sense-constitution. I argue that a careful study of such feminist issues as pregnancy and birth can reveal a different understanding of feminist phenomenology. A study of this kind is not only concerned with marginal or regional subthemes in phenomenology, nor does it only complement them by adding gender-specific analyses of experience. Rather, feminist phenomenology should be understood as a critical current going through the whole body of phenomenological thinking reaching all the way down to its most fundamental tenets.

The Generativity of Birth

There is a curious and exceptional fragment in which Husserl discusses sexuality phenomenologically. Even if his taciturnity and his heterosexual prejudices concerning it hardly make him a very original thinker on the topic of sexuality,[2] in terms of the question of the phenomenological importance of sexual difference this fragment is interesting. Starting from himself as a man, Husserl has serious problems accounting for procreation and ultimately for the birth of a child.

> I start from myself as a man and from my human monad which contains implicitly my immediate surrounding human world. The question arises concerning the intentionality of copulation. In the fulfillment of the drive, immediately viewed, there is nothing concerning the child which is created, nothing concerning what will have the well known consequences in the other subject: the fact that the mother will give birth to the child. (Husserl 1981, 337)

Here Husserl seems clearly to acknowledge the problems arising from an egological account of generative matters such as the birth of a new human being as well as the limits of self-temporalization in connection with it. He notes that the intersubjective act of reproduction motivates new processes in the life of the other—processes which are different from self-temporalization (ibid., 337). He ends the fragment, however, with confidence that a phenomenological investigation into the structure of his own experience would nevertheless clarify the phenomenon of pregnancy, which is reflected in it. ". . . in the explication from the side of my being in the world as a man, I experience what in the world reveals itself through further inductions, I experience what concerns the physiology of pregnancy. Teleology encompasses all of the monads. What occurs in the motherly domain is not limited to it, but is reflected throughout. But I arrive at this only as an ego that recognizes itself as a scientific man in mundane life and questions my and our monadic being and from there goes systematically further" (ibid., 337). It is my contention that the concern here with the problem of accounting for birth points not only to the need to include women's experiences to the sphere of phenomenological investigation, but more fundamentally, to the limits of egological sense-constitution. It lead to the ideas, in part implicit and in part developed in Husserl's late writings, which are usually referred to as generative phenomenology.

Generative phenomenology is a style of phenomenology Husserl instigated in the 1930s, which is concerned with the geo-historical, social, normatively significant becoming or generation of meaning (Steinbock 1995, 281). This development or modification of static and genetic phenomenology stemmed precisely from the acknowledgment of the problems of egological accounts of sense-constitution, as well as of the importance of generative matters such as the constitutive role of birth, death, and historicity.[3] It questions whether sense-constitution begins with an individual subject rather than extending beyond him or her and stemming from tradition, culture, language, and history. Generative phenomena are never given to the individual subject in experience, nor can they ever concern only one person, yet they are constitutive features in world constitution.

Anthony Steinbock (1995, 189) discusses the constitutive mutations that the questions of birth and death undergo in generative phenomenology. During the period that Husserl had only distinguished between a static and genetic phenomenology, he asserted that transcendental ego has never been born and will never die. Genetic phenomenology examines the continual process of becoming in time, but the constitution of sense and self-temporalization are studied only within the life of an individual consciousness. This means that life and death form the necessary limits of this analysis and cannot become questions for it because genetic analysis remains within the strictures of internal time-consciousness, internal to the becoming of the individual. He writes that whereas sleep is a constitutional discordance that can be integrated into individual sense-constitution, birth and death present a profound hiatus in genetic phenomenology that egological constitution cannot overcome. They are precisely the limits of subjective sense-constitution.

From the perspective of genetic phenomenology, it is thus impossible to clarify how birth and death belong essentially to world constitution. Birth and death as constitutive problems necessarily escape the parameters of a genetic transcendental phenomenology. Steinbock argues, however, that by addressing a generative framework, Husserl was obliged to adopt a transcendental perspective to birth and death. Generative world constitution extends before and after the individual subject in a community of generations. As a constituting subjectivity, I am co-constituting and co-constituted as being born into and dying out of a historical normatively significant world (ibid., 181). Within generative dimension birth and death are understood as transcendental and not merely mundane events that are involved in the constitution of sense understood as stemming from an intergenerational home world. The processes of being born and dying are involved in the generative transmission of sense through traditions, stories, and rituals, for example. Birth and death must thus be understood as essential occurrences for the constitution of the world (Steinbock 1995, 282).[4]

Christine Schües argues that birth is also the fundamental condition of possibility of intentionality. It is only by way of being born into the world, that is, through an original differentiating from prenatal existence, that humans can act and constitute sense (Schües 1997, 243). She is concerned with human birth not in the sense of biological development, but in the sense of a fundamental leap from one mode of being to another, the essential trait of which is intentionality. Birth, understood as this leap from the undifferentiated into the differentiated world of objects, gives human beings the possibility of being confronted with the differentiated world of objects for the first time, and of directing their senses toward it (ibid., 245–246). According to Schües, birth is thus not the beginning of life, but rather the fundamental leap of coming into the world in a new mode of existence, through which the already living organism is given a new being (ibid., 247).

If we accept that the principle of natality is a fundamental generative phenomenon to the extent that being born is a condition of possibility for sense-constitution, this not only makes the foundational status of the transcendental ego problematic, but it also opens up the question of the phenomenological importance of sexual difference from a new angle. Christine Schües points out that when we reflect upon the fact of being born, we are, at the same time, obliged to come to terms with the fact that being born always means being-born-from-somebody, namely the mother (Schües 2000, 112). The birth of man thus always means birth from a woman, where woman cannot be replaced by the generic term "human being" the way man supposedly always can be.

Schües argues with reference to the delivering mother, that birth should be taken to mean generative birth. Birth, in the sense of the physiological process, already presumes an abstraction. "With reference to the primal occurrence of the existence of the existent we undermine a philosophical tradition that speaks of the human in general. Birth is the first primal appearance of an essence, a singular, unrepeatable, gendered, and bodily reality for and with other human beings. This occurrence is the manifestation of a fundamental difference and relation between human beings" (ibid., 112). The perspective of natality thus opens up a series of fundamental differences: a difference between prenatal existence and being-in-the-world, a difference between an unreplaceable and a contingent relation to another existent, but also sexual difference. In connection with the phenomenon of birth as world constitutive, sexual difference is not an empirical, biological difference, but a fundamental, transcendental difference: a necessary condition of possibility for a phenomenological account of birth as well as intergenerational sense-constitution.

This opens up a new perspective to feminist phenomenology: by studying sexual difference transcendentally, it is concerned not only with marginal or regional subthemes in phenomenology, but with transcendental conditions of experience. Birth is the transcendental event which makes intergenerational sense-constitution possible, and which presupposes sexual difference.

This does not, however, imply a reductionist view, according to which the meaning of sexual difference can phenomenologically be reduced to reproduction. On the empirical level of lifeworld experiences its meanings are clearly broader, inexhaustible even. We can also consistently argue that on this level sexual difference is not in any way fundamental or even necessary difference but rather a contingent, culturally constructed and upheld difference. Its necessity and naturalness is questioned every day in various experiences and practices of gender blending, for example: in sexual communities where the dichotomy of gender is constantly blurred.[5] Neither does this contingency characterize only gender. Many feminist theoreticians have demonstrated that in natural sciences such as biology the rigid duality of sex cannot be upheld either. On the level of sex organs, chromosomes, and hormones there is no unproblematic or clear-cut difference between two mutually exclusive sexes but rather a troubling ambiguity or continuum which through various forms of "corrective surgery" is made to correspond to a cultural and conceptual dichotomy.[6] It is precisely this failure to accept the fluidity and ambiguity of sex that makes the lives of many intersexed individuals intolerable.

Nevertheless, even if we accept the contingency and fluidity of sexual difference on the level of natural sciences as well as lifeworld experiences, it is precisely when we move to a transcendental analysis of experience that sexual difference gains a more fundamental status. A generative analysis of birth, intentional experience, and intergenerational constitution of meaning will reveal a fundamental difference between two kinds of beings. This does not imply a universal, dualist ontology dividing the whole of humanity into two mutually exclusive categories. It nevertheless implies a fundamental difference which is a condition of possibility for the birth of new human beings and thus also for intergenerational constitution of meaning. To be able to acknowledge the importance of birth for world constitution, phenomenology should thus also acknowledge sexual difference as a transcendental, constitutive difference.

My argument concerning the importance of sexual difference for phenomenological investigation is thus almost diametrically opposed to the standard view according to which feminist phenomenology operates on the empirical level of lived experiences but not on the properly transcendental level of analysis. I argue that on the level of an analysis of lived experiences we must seriously question our conceptions concerning what is feminine experience or female embodiment, but on the transcendental level of analysis we cannot escape posing questions of genesis and thus therefore also of sexual difference.

The Event of Birth

If Husserl has problems accounting for the experiences of pregnancy and the birth of the child, his account of the sexual encounter does not fare much better. F. A. Elliston (1981, 333) summarizes Husserl's topology of human sexuality into three theses: Sex is a social act. Sex seeks copulation. Sex is heterosexual. He notes ironically that to disengage oneself from cultural presuppositions in order to examine them critically is indeed an infinite task.

Even if Husserl's view on sexuality would prove to be more nuanced than Elliston claims, it seems safe to say that his phenomenological analysis of it does not seem to be in any way challenging the findings of his previous phenomenological studies. Yet, as I suggested earlier, the fragment about sexuality is interesting in terms of its tensions and underlying problems: the questions of intersubjectivity and intentionality, but also the phenomenological understanding of subjectivity as reflecting consciousness.[7]

Husserl depicts consciousness in this fragment as a system of drives seeking fulfillment, one of the most fundamental ones being sexuality. Dan Zahavi (2002b, 76) argues that in Husserl's thought the intentional activity of the subject is founded upon and conditioned by an obscure and blind passivity, by drives and associations. He notes that Husserl famously declares in *Analysen zur passiven Synthesis* that his investigation of the problem of passivity could well carry the title "a phenomenology of the unconscious." For Husserl, the reflecting consciousness can thus never be totally transparent to itself, but there are constitutive processes of an anonymous and involuntary nature taking place in the underground or depth dimension of subjectivity which can only be uncovered through an elaborate archaeological effort (ibid., 76–77).

The archaeological effort of uncovering them, however, still means for Husserl a reflective investigation of the essential structures of consciousness.[8] Furthermore, sexuality as a primordial form of intentionality becomes, intersubjectively viewed, a universal teleology—a goal-directed drive. Elliston interprets that in Husserl's thought it functions as the social bond uniting the otherwise isolated monads into a community. Sexuality is essential not just to the meaning of social life but to its very existence: the other is the *telos* of the sexual drive, and the means by which future generations are born (Elliston 1981, 333). Sexuality is thus not essentially characterized by obscure and blind passivity, but by a universal teleology always in the process of fulfilling itself (Husserl 1981, 336). So, rather than sexual experience introducing a fundamental break or contradiction into the horizon of expectations, it correlates with a universal intentionality. Despite its elusive and anonymous nature, it is also characterized by first-personal givenness, which makes it *my* experience.

A contrast to Michel Foucault's account of limit-experience is illuminating here. In an essay dedicated to Bataille, as well in some of his interviews, Foucault takes up the idea of sexual experience as a limit-experience: an event outside the subject.[9] Sexual experience is an event outside the subject when it transgresses the limits of the normal lifeworld into something, which exceeds the constitutive power of our familiar normativity and in this sense it throws us outside of ourselves. It is exactly something that is difficult to comprehend as *my* experience or even as *experience*. Foucault describes the difference between the phenomenological understanding of experience and the idea of the limit-experience that has been so important for him:

> The phenomenologist's experience is basically a certain way of bringing a reflective gaze to bear on some object of lived experience, on the everyday in its transitory form, in order to grasp its meaning. For Nietzsche, Bataille, Blanchot, on the other hand, experience is trying to reach a certain point in life that is as close as possible to the unlivable, to that which can't be lived through. What is required is the maximum of intensity and the maximum of impossibility at the same time. By contrast, phenomenological work consists in unfolding the field of possibilities related to everyday experience. Moreover, phenomenology attempts to recapture the meaning of everyday experience in order to rediscover the sense in which the subject that I am is indeed responsible,

> in its transcendental functions, for founding that experience together with its meanings. On the other hand, in Nietzsche, Bataille, Blanchot, experience has the function of wrenching the subject from itself, of seeing to it that the subject is no longer itself, or that it is brought to its annihilation or its dissolution. This is a project of desubjectivization. (Foucault 2000a, 241)

Foucault's interest in limit-experience is thus not interest in normal experiences: experience is not analyzed through a phenomenological effort to isolate essential structures of consciousness or lived embodiment. He is interested in limit-experience as the permanent possibility of a surprise, a transgression of limits into something unanticipated or even unintelligible. His understanding of limit-experience would, in my view, be more akin to a phenomenological understanding of an event than of an experience.

Françoise Dastur (2000, 182) defines "event" phenomenologically as what was not expected, what arrives unexpectedly and comes to us by surprise. The event is always upsetting because it does not integrate itself as a specific moment in the flow of time, but changes drastically the whole style of existence. It does not happen in a world—it is on the contrary, as if a new world opens up through its happening. The event constitutes the critical moment of temporality—a critical moment which nevertheless allows for the continuity of time. The event, in its internal contradiction is thus the impossible, which happens, in spite of everything, in a terrifying or marvelous manner. We can speak about the event only from the perspective of an object, not subject, and in the past tense, in the mode of "it happened to me." We never experience the great events of our life as contemporaneous or as truly ours.

If for Foucault sexual experience could occasionally serve as an example of an event which happens to us and which momentarily wrenches us outside of ourselves, Dastur brings us back to the question of birth. She notes that birth is the first great event of our lives.

> We did not ask for our birth, and this is testimony to the fact that we are not the origin of our own existence . . . There is therefore a surprise in us in relation to our birth. It is the permanent surprise of being born which is constitutive of our being. It is testimony to the uncontrollable character of this proto-event. In each new event there is a repetition of the proto-event of birth. It is as if we re-experience, in a new event, this radical novelty of what happens for the "first time," as well as the impossibility of coinciding with the event itself, which in its sudden apparition disconnects the past from the future. (Dastur 2000, 186)

For Dastur, the difficult task of phenomenology is to try to think this excess to expectation that is the event. The thinking of the event requires that phenomenology cannot be content to remain an "eidetic" phenomenology—the thinking of what remains invariable in experience. It must also be a thinking of what may be and of contingency (ibid.,183).

She argues that we should not oppose phenomenology and the thinking of the event, however, but try to connect them: openness to phenomena must be phenomenologically identified with openness to unpredictability. Phenomenology can think the event because one is not completely passive in relation to it, even if its meaning must remain obscure. She notes that Husserl and Heidegger both saw a passivity within our intentional activity which can only be assumed and not chosen. Like Zahavi, she argues that Husserl's theory of passive synthesis is an important recognition of this (ibid., 186). The capacity to undergo events implies an active opening to a field of receptivity. To lack this capacity to open oneself to what happens, to no longer welcome the unexpected, would be a mark of psychosis, not of normal experience (ibid., 187).

While relying on the analysis of Husserl and Heidegger, Dastur nevertheless emphasizes through her analysis of birth a different aspect or dimension of the phenomenological subject. The subject is not primarily a self-aware, constituting consciousness, but radically defined by its capacity to undergo events the meaning of which it is not the constitutive source, but which must remain forever obscure.[10]

To briefly conclude, I hope to have shown how a phenomenological analysis of birth can radically question some of the central tenets of phenomenology. It points to generative phenomenology—to the need to study the intersubjective conditions of possibility of the subject's experience in birth, sexual difference, community, history, and language. Dastur's analysis suggests that it also points to a phenomenology of the event which questions the privileged status of the phenomenological subject in another sense: there is an unpredictability to experience capable of shattering the subject's horizon of expectations.

Whether these modifications of phenomenology—generative phenomenology and phenomenology of the event—should be understood as adequate responses to the concerns of feminist phenomenology must remain an open question. In the next chapter I am going to argue that further modifications are necessary if we want to account phenomenologically for gender. Nevertheless, they already make evident that the greatest challenge feminist phenomenology faces lies not in consolidating, but in destabilizing phenomenological thinking. Even if this means losing the firm ground on which we stand.

6

A Phenomenology of Gender

The question that I ask and attempt to answer in this chapter is this: how can phenomenology as a philosophical method of investigation account for gender? Although many feminists have expressed reservations about the possibility that the master's tools could ever dismantle the master's house, phenomenology as a philosophical method seems to have provided exceptionally useful tools for feminist inquiry. From Simone de Beauvoir's *Second Sex* to recent studies on feminine corporeality, it has formed a significant part of the growing corpus of feminist philosophy. Yet it is in no way obvious how it could account for the question of gender. To what extent is it possible to study gender within the paradigm of a philosophy of a subject or of consciousness?

The answer will obviously depend on how we understand phenomenology. In addressing this issue I will explicate four different understandings of phenomenology and assess their respective potential in terms of understanding gender. Although my characterization of these four phenomenological positions is necessarily schematic and therefore in many respects problematic and contestable, their function here is mainly to illustrate my arguments concerning gender. I will explicate a classical reading, a corporeal reading, and an intersubjective reading, but my sympathies are with my fourth interpretation, which I call a post-phenomenological reading.

The Classical Reading

In its traditional formulations phenomenology cannot address the question of gender or sexual difference at all. This possibility has to be denied on the grounds that in the proper transcendental attitude all the self-interpretations and bodily characteristics of the transcendental ego are bracketed, and in this sense it is incorporeal and above the concrete life-world. The true transcendental is universal pure subjectivity understood as consciousness, with its reality status and the reality status of its objects both placed in brackets.

Although not taking issue directly with the question of sexual difference, J. N. Mohanty, for example, argues that corporeality is not excluded from the life of transcendental subjectivity, but finds its proper place within its total structure. He notes that, although Husserl is often regarded as the paradigmatic case of a philosopher in whose thought a close connection between objective thinking, the objectification of the body, and the thesis of a universal constituting consciousness is preeminently exemplified, he does not see transcendental subjectivity as a purely logical principle (Mohanty 1985, 132). Husserlian transcendental consciousness is not merely reflective and intellectual, but it rather comprehends within itself, as a basic stratum, prereflective perceptual consciousness including the lived body as a system of intentionalities (ibid., 163). The constituting principle is a disembodied consciousness, but the constituting life of subjectivity, even in its transcendentally purified form, contains a stratum of corporeality in which the lived body itself is constituted. Thus bodily intentionality, which participates in the constitution of the world and is well recognized by phenomenologists such as Merleau-Ponty, finds its place within the total field of transcendental subjectivity (ibid.,132–33). Mohanty points out that, while Husserl acknowledged that anonymous bodily subjectivity was, in an important sense, prior to or more fundamental than mental consciousness, from the perspective of phenomenological analysis, these levels together with their structural relationships can nevertheless only be comprehended within the total life of transcendental consciousness (ibid., 164).

From the perspective of feminist phenomenology, this means that even if we emphasize the constitutive importance of corporeality or bodily subjectivity, this will not bring the question of gender or sexual difference to the proper phenomenological level of analysis, understood in this reading as an investigation of transcendental consciousness. Recognition of the importance of bodily subjectivity only implies that there must be a dimension of corporeality within the structure of transcendental subjectivity that is constitutive of the mundane phenomenon of sexed bodies. Phenomenology as transcendental analysis must rise above or look behind these mundane phenomena by studying their condition of possibility in transcendental subjectivity. And transcendental subjectivity cannot be understood as sexed, otherwise we would have to argue that there are, in fact, two different types of transcendental subjectivities.

Feminist phenomenology would thus be an oxymoron: the question of gender or sexual difference cannot arise in the phenomenological analysis of transcendental subjectivity. If it did for some reason, then we would have to simply dismiss it by pointing out that the procedure of transcendental reduction has not been properly understood or accomplished.[1]

The Corporeal Reading

The consequences of transcendental reduction in terms of gender make it understandable why most feminist appropriations of phenomenology have opted for the Merleau-Pontian version, which builds on the premise that complete reduction to transcendental consciousness is impossible. This is generally interpreted to mean that the phenomenological investigation must focus on the lived body as opposed to transcendental consciousness.[2] Merleau-Ponty's work has been appropriated in a variety of groundbreaking feminist studies on female embodiment, such as Iris Marion Young's phenomenological analyses of feminine movement, pregnancy, and breasted experience.[3] According to this approach, the phenomenological study of gender is understood as a study of the basic modalities or structures of female embodiment that are typical of feminine existence. There is thus a distinct mode of corporeal being in the world that is female or feminine, and the aim is to describe the eidetic structures of the living body, rather than constituting consciousness that characterize this feminine way of being.

Despite the sophistication of this approach in terms of the philosophical articulation and analysis of the neglected experiences of women, such as pregnancy, it also has some serious problems. If any first-person description by a woman is understood as a phenomenological account and then generalized by turning it into a description of eidetic female embodiment, we end up with a female body that is essentialized. Feminist theory has fought hard against essentialism, particularly biological essentialism, which holds that femaleness and femininity are determined by the biological structures of the body. The corporeal readings of feminist phenomenology thus threaten to push us back into defending a form of corporeal essentialism that potentially precludes political changes in the situation of women.[4]

Apart from the fact that this method of analyzing individual experiences and then deriving from them eidetic claims about female embodiment is questionable, ultimately the most serious problem with the approach, in my view, is the fact that the focus on the body is simply too limited a framework to support a philosophical understanding of gender.

In her seminal book *Toward a Phenomenology of Sexual Difference*

(2003), Sara Heinämaa appropriates Simone de Beauvoir's thought in order to argue that phenomenologically sexual difference should be understood as a difference between two embodied styles of being. Heinämaa's claim is that the philosophical context in which Beauvoir operates is phenomenological, and that she therefore does not conceive of men and women as two kinds of historical entities or as two kinds of biological organisms, but as two different ways of relating to the world. Women and men are two different variations of the human embodiment, of the human way of relating to the world, and every singular human existent is a variation of one of them or else combines elements from both. "So, the principle difference is the experiential difference between two types of living bodies, women's bodies and men's bodies" (Heinämaa 2003, 84). Every individual woman thus both realizes the feminine way or style of relating to the world and modifies it. Accordingly, we can legitimately speak about "feminine eroticism" and "feminine literature" without assuming a fixed idea, "femininity" describable by exact concepts.

Heinämaa's influential account has effectively problematized the attempts to reduce the meaning of gender or sexual difference to either side of the stalwart binary of biology versus culture. However, it is my contention that the extent to which gender or sexual difference is a philosophical question it is not an issue that can be settled by just studying bodies, even if they are understood phenomenologically as opposed to biologically. It would thus be simplistic to conclude that, on the basis of the phenomenological analysis of embodiment, the philosophical meaning of gender could be reduced to the difference between two types of living bodies.

The idea that living bodies are constituted in perception and experience as necessarily falling into two basic categories or types can be contested on purely empirical grounds. Psychological studies on children's gender beliefs show that it is unlikely that a child is able to derive in some direct empirical fashion a tidy binary structuring of gender difference from everyday life in which gender distinctions are often confusing, contradictory, and irregular. The development of a "gender schema," the framework for classifying people into appropriate genders, is a complex cultural learning process intertwined with the acquisition of language, but also with many normative issues operative in society (Johnson 2000, 140–41). Bodies themselves are also culturally molded in more and less violent ways to conform to the normative expectations of gender. The most extreme example would be the case of intersexed babies whose genitals are surgically made to resemble what are considered "normal" male or female genitalia. The reason for this intervention is, in the majority of cases, purely cosmetic. The bodies of intersexed people are thus literally made to correspond to our dualist ontology or gender schema, rather than this schema simply reflecting our perception of living bodies. Even if we did accept that human bodies do, in general, come in two basic models, and that there is therefore some kind of corporeal counterpart for the cultural gender binary, philosophically the meaning of gender still cannot be reduced to this corporeal given. The way in which we classify bodies into types, give them value and meaning depends on historically and culturally specific practices. We can only identify something as something by using linguistically mediated conceptual determinations, and our experiences therefore always have linguistic, sociocultural, and historical conditions of possibility. A philosophical study of gender therefore cannot be limited to a description of the difference between two types of living bodies, but must also encompass a study of the culturally specific ontological schemas in which those bodies and experiences gain value and meaning.[5]

The Intersubjective Reading

The intersubjective readings of phenomenology seem to open up a broader perspective on the question of gender that can account for the importance of shared normative structures such as language and historicity. Dan Zahavi (2001), among others, has effectively argued for an intersubjective transformation of Husserl's philosophy taking place in his late writings. As we saw in the previous chapter, Husserl's late thought is characterized by a decisive rethinking of the relation between the transcendental and the mundane that ultimately forced him to consider the transcendental significance of issues such as generativity, tradition, historicity, and normality.

The decisive question for the relevance of this approach in terms of gender is obviously in how we understand intersubjectivity. Zahavi distinguishes three different kinds of it operative in Husserl's work. The most common of these refers to a concrete relation between subjects. When I experience an experiencing other, the validity categories of my experience are subjected to a decisive change. By means of others, the objects of my constitutive experiences are provided with a validity that lends them independence with respect to me. Thus the categories of transcendence, objectivity, and reality are intersubjectively constituted, meaning that they can only be constituted by a subject that has experienced other subjects (Zahavi 2001, 38).

According to Zahavi, second and more fundamental interpretation is to understand intersubjectivity as an a priori structure of subjectivity. Intersubjectivity does thus not refer only to the other people's actual presence: the being of the subject as experiencing and constituting implies a reference to other subjects already prior to its concrete experience of them. There is an apodictic universal structure of intersubjectivity predelineated in every ego (ibid., 61). This fundamental intersubjectivity of the transcendental subject forms the condition of possibility for egological sense-constitution.

These two senses of intersubjectivity do not have any obvious consequences in terms of gender, however. For the constitution of objective reality it should be irrelevant whether the constitutive community of others consists of men or women. Intersubjectivity in the sense of an apodictic structure of transcendental subjectivity cannot be understood as sexually varied either.

Zahavi distinguishes a third type, however, in addition to a priori intersubjectivity and the concrete experience of others, which is effective at the level of handed-down normality. As an incarnate subject, I am always already situated in an intersubjective, historical nexus of sense. I am a member of a historical community, learning from others what counts as "normal" and thereby, as a communalized subject, participating in an intersubjective tradition. I also always understand the world and myself by virtue of a handed-down linguistic conventionality. This third type of intersubjectivity thus refers to the constitutive importance of the cultural sphere, or the *homeworld* of which the transcendental subject is a member (ibid., 65, 163).

When gender is studied phenomenologically in the light of this third type of intersubjectivity, it becomes possible to understand how experiences and living bodies are given specific gendered meanings through intersubjectively constituted systems of normality that are always tied to conventionality. Being socialized to a culture and becoming a member of it means learning from others what counts as normal in the case of gender, too. I learned very early what the norms for maleness and femaleness were in my culture. I also learned what the sanctions for failing to live up to these norms were. Although the system of normality, the gender schema, often breaks down, as very clearly happens in cases of intersexed infants or transgendered individuals, as long as these discrepancies can be classified as abnormalities, the concordance of the homeworld and its system of normality can be maintained.

This approach leaves open the possibility, however, that the system of normality could also change. If the meaning of gender is understood as dependent on culturally handed-down forms of normality and not on eidetic structures of embodiment, it should be possible to effect changes in it. As Zahavi points out, our system of normality must undergo continual correction because the concordance of the homeworld is ruptured by conflicts and discordances. Absolute concordance—that is, the world itself—must thus be understood as an ideal that can only be approached through the infinite movement of relative achievements that are carried out intersubjectively (ibid., 101–2).

Let us return to the example of intersexed individuals. As this phenomenon is now attracting more attention and these individuals themselves are able to articulate their experiences in new terms, it is possible that our system of normality concerning gender has to change or is already changing. Alternatively, we could simply consider, from our perspective, the stupidity of what philosophers have written about women in the history of philosophy, and the relativity of any concordance concerning gender should seem incontestable.

Although the intersubjective reading thus seems to solve many of the problems connected with the first two approaches, my critical question now concerns how, in practice, we can study phenomenologically the constitutive role of the third type of intersubjectivity. It is my contention that the cornerstones of the phenomenological method—the first-person perspective as radical self-investigation and the subsequent move of the transcendental reduction—in fact wipe this constitutive dimension out of the picture.

Zahavi makes it clear that transcendental intersubjectivity is not an objective structure that could be studied from a third-person perspective. It is not an ontological or an empirical postulate. It can only be disclosed through a description of the subject's structures of experience, because it can only unfold itself in the relation between singular subjects. The point of departure for a phenomenological treatment of intersubjectivity, irrespective of which type we are dealing with, must be an investigation of a subject that is related to the world and to others. The turn to intersubjectivity thus in no way serves to refute a philosophy of the subject (ibid. 165).

The first two types of intersubjectivity were revealed by analyzing the structures of perception as well as other intentional experiences. The discovery of transcendental intersubjectivity thus was not based on simple empirical observations, on the fact that I can constantly see other people around me, nor was it a dogmatic metaphysical presupposition. Husserl argued that the analysis of perceptual intentionality led to the disclosure of the apodictic intersubjective structures of the transcendental ego.[6] In the case of the third type of intersubjectivity, the type that interests me here, the situation seems different, however. The constitutive conditions in this case are not a priori intersubjective structures, but historically and culturally changing norms. They are, in fact, exactly what distorts and clouds an investigation into a priori universal structures and must therefore be bracketed in the reduction. Despite the late emphasis on the constitutive importance of the third type of intersubjectivity, the phenomenological method relies on prior ontological commitment to the universal validity of the transcendental structures of the ego. The method starts from the analysis of the first-person experience and moves from there to a transcendental inquiry into the constitution of sense by identifying a priori structures of transcendental subjectivity. This move can only be justified on the basis of an ontological commitment to the universal similarity of the subjects.[7] The differences between them can only be understood on the basis of this more fundamental similarity, and must be studied through empirical sciences such as anthropology, sociology, or psychology.

Hence, although Husserl had to recognize the constitutive importance of the third type of intersubjectivity, it must always be understood as dependent on a more primordial type—intersubjectivity as a universal a priori structure—and it is this primordial type that the phenomenological method can accommodate. It cannot show, through the same method, both that the individual subjects of transcendental intersubjectivity are always furnished with identical a priori structures *and* that the concordance of their experiences is a relative accomplishment that has historical and cultural conditions of possibility. It thus seems that, although phenomenology must acknowledge the constitutive importance of language and cultural normality, it cannot address the transcendental, constitutive significance of these mundane phenomena without giving up the reduction to transcendental consciousness.

If we give up the phenomenological reduction, however, we encounter the problem of circularity. How can transcendental intersubjectivity—now understood as comprising language and historicity—be constituted in experience if it is what ultimately makes individual constitution possible?[8] In terms of my limited question of gender, the problem appears as follows: to start the analysis from a woman's experience when trying to understand what a woman is means already assuming that which we seek to explain. Husserl's solution to the paradox is the reduction to transcendental consciousness that keeps the empirical and the transcendental strictly separate.[9] This means, however, that we seem to have come full circle and have ground to a halt. Either the question of gender cannot be investigated under the phenomenological method at all, or our investigation is doomed to a circularity that already presupposes that which it seeks to explain. The question that we must thus face is, how does the phenomenological method need to be modified for it to be able study the third type of intersubjectivity, the constitutive importance of culture, language, and historicity?

The Postphenomenological Reading

With the term "postphenomenology" I refer to a modification of the phenomenological method, which, I argue, is better able to deal with the constitutive importance of the social and cultural world. According to my postphenomenological reading, it is impossible to understand how gender is constituted through normative ontological schemas if we believe that we can, by some supreme methodological step such as the *epoche*, to leave all our ontological commitments behind. It is my contention that we should therefore accept the hermeneutical circle—at least in connection with our analysis of gender—and try to see to it that our method continuously turns back upon itself, questioning and modifying itself in an effort to articulate what it secretly thinks. This means understanding *epoche* not as total, universal, and complete, but as an endless, circular, and always partial task.

It is not enough just to give up the phenomenological reduction to transcendental consciousness and the totalizing understanding of the *epoche*, however. We also have to give up the first-person perspective as the exclusive and indispensable starting point of our analysis. In striving to understand the constitution of gendered experience it might be more helpful to start by reading anthropological and sociological investigations, medical reports on intersexed children, or psychological studies of children's gender beliefs than by analyzing one's own normatively limited experiences. Husserl himself, while extending his analyses of intersubjectivity, eventually had to broaden the purely self-reflective study of consciousness. He had to enter fields that have traditionally been reserved for psychopathology, sociology, anthropology, and ethnology.[10] Heidegger and his poststructuralist followers, including Foucault, have particularly emphasized the study of history.

Although it might seem that we have now thrown the baby out with the bath and rejected phenomenology altogether, this would be too hasty a conclusion. The philosophical investigation of gender is still understood as an investigation of the constitution of gendered *experience*, not as a conceptual analysis of language or a biological investigation of the body. It cannot be reduced to medical or sociological study, even if it cannot afford to ignore the methods and results of these and other empirical sciences. These empirical descriptions can only reveal something about the normative ontological schemas that are constitutive of our experiences when they are submitted to critical philosophical analysis. What is more, this analysis must ultimately take the form of radical self-reflection. It is ultimately *I* who must read these investigations, and it is only in relation to my experience that they can reveal something previously hidden about its constitution, its limits, and its supposedly natural and universal character.

I will return to the example of the psychological study of children's gender beliefs. The postphenomenological question, unlike the psychological one, would not be about how children learn to classify people in the right gender categories; rather, it would focus on what their beliefs reveal about us and the normativity of our adult homeworld. Ann Johnson, for example, notes that most psychological theories regarding children's gender beliefs already operate within a progressivist and biologist framework. When a young child thus says that if a girl puts on a boy's clothes she would be a boy, he or she is "mistakenly" using cultural clues such as hair length or clothing to determine gender rather than rooting a person's gender classification in "true" biological criteria. Johnson argues that, from a phenomenological perspective, however, children's gender beliefs can provide salient reminders of how we find ourselves within a never-ending chain of meaning, and at the same time put into question what we have learned to accept as unquestioned reality. She refers to the opening pages of Foucault's *The Order of Things*, noting that attending to childhood gives us access to "the exotic charm of another system of thought," which in turn reveals "the limitations of our own, the stark impossibility of thinking *that*" (Johnson 2000, 146; Foucault 1989, xv).

The study of a different system of normality thus functions as a form of reduction in the sense that it makes us aware of the hidden aspects of our own thought—it lifts the naiveté of the ordinary experience—and allows us to reveal and question its constitutive conditions, at least to some extent. It is not a shift from natural attitude to the level of transcendental consciousness, but it is nevertheless a shift to the level of transcendental investigation. The idea of phenomenological reduction would thus not be simply discarded, but it would be understood in similar terms as how Merleau-Ponty characterized it: it is the interminable effort to break our familiar acceptance of the world and to see as strange and paradoxical what we normally take for granted.[11] Compared with the corporeal reading I discussed above, however, the function of the "abnormal" and the "alienworld" would not be to reveal the "normal" and the "homeworld" as universally primary, however. The aim is not to find eidetic structures of female experience that characterize all women whether they come from Nigeria or Norway: it is rather to expose the structures that are constitutive of the sense of "normal" in *our* homeworld. As Anthony Steinbock argues, a phenomenological analysis of the social world cannot begin with individual consciousness to reach a universal We, because intersubjectivity cannot be reduced to a universal, collective singularity without the patronizing assumption that we are the entire structure (Steinbock 1995, 269). Such an analysis can only study the constitutive structures of our homeworld from within it, given the awareness that they are themselves constituted in relation to alienworlds.

Hence, the postphenomenological method would give up a complete phenomenological reduction to transcendental subjectivity, but it would, nevertheless, attempt to accomplish a partial bracketing in order to reveal something about the ontological schemas underlying our ways of thinking, perceiving and acting. It would begin with considerations that are in some sense "foreign" and therefore distanced from the subject, such as anthropological, historiographical, and medical studies, for example. This knowledge would then be appropriated in an attempt to make visible the presumptions and implicit ontological commitments in one's homeworld. Unlike the classical readings of phenomenology, it would hold that these constitutive, ontological schemas are always tied to cultural normativity—to language, history, and culture. While they are thus necessarily and irrevocably intertwined with our forms of reflection, they are, nevertheless, ultimately contingent and therefore changeable. What is "normal" and therefore assumed as natural and necessary can, in the postphenomenological inquiry, turn out to be that only within the parameters of our homeworld.

Despite this fundamental compatibility with certain forms of cultural constructivism, I am not advocating an empirical study of the objective and causal processes of cultural construction. As I argued in my criticism of Joan Scott, this would entail adopting a view from nowhere and erasing the very background beliefs and ontological commitments that are constitutive of our objective accounts. My interpretation of phenomenology does not mean that the singular and always perspectival character of experience is eradicated. The philosophical reflection on gender, just like on anything else, can ultimately only be a personal task. I must analyze my own experiences and theories as being formed in a community with its attendant practices, beliefs, and language. Most importantly, however, I must be capable of problematizing them. I must be able to take critical distance from the commonly accepted meanings of various forms of experience, but also and most fundamentally, my own. This is not possible without a first-person perspective: the subject must engage in the attentive and radical study of his or her own constitution.

In conclusion and to revert back to gender, the answer to the question I started with is that phenomenology can account for gender by helping us to understand how gendered experiences are constituted and how their constitution is tied not only to embodiment, but also to the normative cultural practices and structures of meaning. This can be accomplished by a subject who, through radical philosophical reflection, manages to take critical distance from certain forms of experience. What my postphenomenological reading suggests, however, is that in order to achieve this critical distance it might be more useful for me to read psychological reports or ethnographical studies than to analyze my own experiences of women or embodiment.

Postphenomenology would thus start with knowledge and experiences that are foreign to us, but this does not mean that the question of gender is relegated to the domain of empirical study. The method of reduction is necessary to effectuate the reflective step that opens up the realm of transcendental investigation. We must break away from the natural attitude understood as an attitude where our ontological preunderstanding of the world is not visible to us at all, to an attitude that is capable of problematizing it. At the same time, we have to accept that ontology can never be totally suspended, because it is irrevocably tied up with our language, methods of reflection, and ways of seeing the world. This means accepting the always partial and preliminary character of any philosophical investigation concerning ourselves. An analysis of experience that aims to be radical and transcendental can only ever be fragmentary and incomplete.

Part 3

Feminist Politics

7

The Neoliberal Subject
of Feminism

Foucault's analyses of power and the subject can be read as part of the contemporary politicization of the social realm and the increasing dissolution of the distinction between public and private. Similar to the feminist emphasis on the political nature of the personal, his analyses show how political subjects are constructed through mundane everyday habits and practices as certain kinds of political beings. Individuals do not enter the public, political arena as fully formed subjects who then demand rights and represent interests. The supposedly personal or private aspects of their being are already traversed by power relations, which not only restrain them, but produce them as political subjects. In *Discipline and Punish* Foucault famously shows how the abstract political subject of liberalism was in fact materially constructed through concrete and detailed disciplinary habits. He argues that the establishment of an explicit, coded, and formally egalitarian juridical framework, made possible by the organization of a parliamentary, representative regime in the eighteenth century, was accompanied by the development and generalization of disciplinary mechanisms. They constituted the other, dark side of these processes of democratic progress (Foucault 1991a, 222).

Similarly, feminist appropriations of Foucault's thought have demonstrated how feminine subjects are constructed through patriarchal, disciplinary practices as very different kinds of subjects than the autonomous, liberal model suggests: they are constructed as subjects who are dependent on others, who must suppress their aggression, egotistical interests, and ambitions and demonstrate caring and nurturing qualities. In the first section of this chapter, "The Disciplinary Production of the Feminine Subject," I will analyze this process by discussing Sandra Bartky's influential account of how the docile feminine subject is constructed through disciplinary habits and practices of beauty.

However, the first section only forms a background for the main argument of this chapter: in the last decades new and fundamentally different mechanisms and rationalities of power have come to shape our technologies of gender. It is my contention that because the constitution of the subject is a thoroughly historical and highly precarious process it is possible to detect changes in it even in the course of such relatively short periods of time as the last thirty years. In order to analyze these changes, I turn in the second section, "Neoliberal Governmentality," to Foucault's lectures on liberalism and neoliberalism. I explicate Foucault's idea of governmentality and particularly neoliberal governmentality as an alternative framework to discipline for studying the construction of the governable subject. In the final section, "The Subject of Feminism," I argue that this framework has not replaced the disciplinary mechanisms that produce the feminine subject, but rather complemented and intensified them. It is my contention that analyzing the neoliberal paradigm dominant in our society provides us with a more comprehensive conceptual model for understanding the construction of the feminine subject in its current form. I want to make the controversial claim that liberalism's allegedly masculinist conception of the subject as an independent, self-interested, economic being has also come to characterize the feminine subject in the last decades. This is not primarily due to feminism, but to neoliberalism.

The Disciplinary Production of the Feminine Subject

Sandra Bartky's seminal and much anthologized 1988 article "Foucault, Femininity and the Modernization of Patriarchal Power" was one of the first appropriations of Foucault's idea of disciplinary power to explicitly feminist issues.[1] It gives a compelling account of the way in which a docile feminine subject is constructed through the internalization of disciplinary habits. The key claim that Bartky adopts from Foucault is that an adequate understanding of women's oppression requires an appreciation of the extent to which not only women's lives, but their very subjectivities are constructed through an ensemble of disciplinary habits.

In *Discipline and Punish* Foucault argues that discipline was a historically specific technology of power that emerged in the eighteenth century and operated through the body. In disciplinary practices, habits, and patterns of behavior are broken down and constructed in new ways that are more productive for the aims of modern industrial societies. Discipline consists of various techniques which aim at making the body both docile and useful. In the eighteenth century, claims Foucault, bodies of prisoners, soldiers, workers, and schoolchildren were subjected to a new kind of discipline in order to make them more useful for mass production and at the same time easier to control. The functions, movements, and capabilities of their bodies were broken down into narrow segments, analyzed in detail, and recomposed in a maximally effective way. Disciplinary power does not mutilate or coerce its target, but through detailed training reconstructs the body to produce new kinds of gestures, habits, and skills. Individuals literally incorporate the objectives of power, which become part of their own being. The human body becomes a machine, the functioning of which can be optimized, calculated, and improved through the internalization of specific patterns of behavior.[2]

Bartky acknowledges the strengths of Foucault's analysis, but contends that he is oblivious to those disciplines that produce a modality of subjection that is particularly feminine (Bartky 1988, 64). She analyzes habits such as dieting and fitness regimes as disciplinary practices imposed on women that aim at producing an ideal feminine body. These disciplinary practices of femininity aim at an exhaustive and perpetual regulation of the body's size and contours, its appetite, posture, gestures and comportment, as well as the appearance of each of its visible parts. Expert discourses on how to walk, talk, style one's hair, care for one's skin, and wear makeup create habits conducive to the requirements of submissive femininity: feminine movement as well as feminine faces are trained to the expression of deference. The rationality of these disciplinary practices can thus only be understood in the light of the modernization of patriarchal domination. They subjugate women by normalization, by constructing them as particular kinds of subjects, not simply by taking power away from them. Feminist analysis must recognize these individual practices of feminine beauty as aspects of a large and systematic disciplinary regime—an oppressive and inegalitarian system of sexual subordination. The rationality of this disciplinary apparatus is clear: it aims at turning women into "the docile and compliant companions of men just as surely as the army aims to turn its raw recruits into soldiers" (Bartky 1988, 75).

The question of why women agree to partake in these practices and actively acquire such oppressive and painful habits clearly troubles Bartky. She acknowledges that "no one is marched off for electrolysis at gunpoint, nor can we fail to appreciate the initiative and ingenuity displayed by countless women in an attempt to master the rituals of beauty" (Bartky 1988, 75). She explains the compelling character of these practices by emphasizing how they are tied to powerful sanctions and rewards. Refusal to take part in these practices in a world dominated by men means that women face a very severe sanction: the refusal of male patronage. This can mean the loss of badly needed intimacy or even of decent livelihood (ibid., 76). The disciplinary technologies of femininity are also taken up and practiced by women against the background of a

pervasive sense of bodily deficiency: a sense of shame is a central component of normative feminine experience and a measure of the extent
to which all women have internalized patriarchal standards of bodily ac-
ceptability (ibid., 71). A generalized male witness structures woman's consciousness of herself as a bodily being, and women become self-policing
subjects committed to a relentless self-surveillance. The rewards importantly include sexual attractiveness: to possess a feminine body is usually
essential to a woman's sense of herself as a sexually desiring and desirable
subject (ibid., 78). Pain, constriction, tedium, semistarvation, and constant self-surveillance are preferable to desexualization and the loss of a
socially recognized identity.

Instead of being explicitly coerced into adopting disciplinary practices or freely choosing them as their preferred means of self-expression,
women thus internalize them as normative habits that become an integral part of their gender identity. The explanatory power of habit as the
mundane basis of gender oppression lies exactly in the way it forms a
conceptual bridge between coercion and free volition, the two untenable extremes in the debates on the nature of gender. Feminist accounts
of gender have attempted to challenge forms of essentialism, but they
have equally rejected gender voluntarism: one is not born a woman, one
becomes one, but not through a deliberate choice. Habit forms the normative mechanism that produces a stable and enduring pattern of being
and creates an illusion of a permanent gender core or essence. It is like
a second nature, which unlike the first nature allows for historical and
cultural variation and change while also incorporating the permanence
and stability that characterize our experience of gendered identity.[3]

In her 2002 article "Suffering to Be Beautiful," Bartky reiterates
the same key arguments, but she also attempts to respond to some criticisms of her earlier paper. She still argues that disciplinary practices are
importantly involved in the process whereby a female body is turned into
a "properly" feminine one. She also maintains the position that this process is, on the whole, disempowering to women. However, she now acknowledges that two themes were underdeveloped in the earlier paper.
First, she wants to respond to the criticism that she had undertheorized
the pleasure women take in turning themselves into properly feminine
subjects, by spelling out in more detail the nature of these pleasures.
The second theme she neglected was the psychic ambivalence connected
to these disciplinary practices. We have to acknowledge that the disciplines of the body are in and of themselves complex and carry ambiguous meanings (Bartky 2002, 4).

These additions make her powerful account more nuanced by acknowledging the complexity of the mechanisms of oppression involved

in the construction of the feminine subject. However, I want to pose the question of whether her analysis also needs updating in light of the fundamental changes in the ways the feminine subject is constructed, which have taken place in the time between the two versions of her article. The two articles mark interesting moments in time, 1988 and 2002, because many feminist thinkers now see the intervening years as the time of a serious backlash against feminism. Crucially, these years also mark the period in which the neoliberal hegemony became firmly established in both the USA and Europe. If we accept Foucault's key claim about the ineliminable tie between forms of power and forms of the subject, this shift in techniques of government would have necessitated a shift in the corresponding construction of the subject.

I will show in the next section that what is distinctive about Foucault's analysis of liberalism is that he does not approach it primarily as a political theory, but as a governmental practice that is constitutive of a particular type of subject as its necessary correlate. His critical analysis shows that neoliberal governmentality must be viewed as a particular production of subjectivity: it produces an economic subject structured by different tendencies, preferences, and motivations than the political or legal citizen of a disciplinary society or a society of sovereignty. The neoliberal subject is understood as an atomic individual whose natural self-interest and tendency to compete for economic rewards must be fostered and enhanced.

Neoliberal Governmentality

Foucault's lectures "The Birth of Biopolitics," delivered at the *Collège de France* in 1979, focus on the birth of liberal and neoliberal governmentality, forms of political rationality concerned with the government of the modern state. He proposes that the new liberal governmentality challenges the ideal and the project of an exhaustive disciplinary society in which the legal network hemming in individuals was taken over and extended internally by normative mechanisms (Foucault 2008, 259). His lectures on liberalism and neoliberalism can thus be read a form of self-critique: while disciplinary power had provided Foucault with a useful tool for elucidating some of the key mechanism for the construction of the subject still operative in our society, it was proving to be inadequate for understanding many others. He was concerned about the rise of neoliberal forms of governmentality characterizing his historical milieu, and the lectures should be read as a response to these concerns (ibid., 192).

His target was the "state phobia" prevalent in the social critiques of his day. Similar to his aim in *The History of Sexuality*, volume 1, which was to show that the fervent mission to liberate our repressed sexuality was fundamentally misguided, he was again trying to show how the most popular forms of social and political critique were in fact attacking the wrong enemy. "What is presently at issue in our reality . . . is not so much the growth of the state . . . but much more its reduction" (Foucault 2008, 192). His problem was not the unlimited growth of the state, its omnipotence, or its continuous and unified expansion. The risk was not that the unlimited expansion of social security, or the administrative apparatus on which it rested, would inevitably lead to a totalitarian state like the Nazi or Stalinist state. "All those who share in the great state phobia should know that they are following the direction of the wind and that in fact, for years and years, an effective reduction of the state has been on the way" (ibid., 191).

Foucault makes it clear, however, that his aim is not to give an account of how mechanisms of governmentality replaced disciplinary mechanisms, which would have replaced juridico-legal mechanisms (Foucault 2008, 107). His move from discipline to governmentality is not a conceptual substitution, but an extension. It is, he argues, still possible to identify and analyze the intensification of disciplinary mechanisms of surveillance and normalization operative in contemporary society.[4] It is also important, however, to identify and analyze a completely different kind of logic or rationality of power that is gaining importance, but that in fact has fairly long roots in traditional liberalism. While the current neoliberal governmentality continues to be deeply intertwined with sovereign and disciplinary forms of power, it has also initiated significant transformations in our practices of governing. As Foucault notes, we face "a new problem" which consists of "the transition to a new form of rationality to which the regulation of government was pegged" (ibid., 312).

To understand and analyze this new rationality, Foucault, typically, had to trace its genealogy. He identifies its emergence in the eighteenth century: the ideal society was no longer the panoptic society of all-encompassing discipline. It was no longer one in which a mechanism of general normalization and the exclusion of those who could not be normalized was needed. What emerged instead was the idea or the theme-program of a liberal society in which governing was reconceived as a practice to be organized, rationalized, and limited according to the principles of economy: the social field was left open to fluctuating processes, and minority practices were tolerated more easily because the primary responsibility of government was to support the economy. This did not mean the end of governmental interference, however; it necessitated a fundamental change in the rationality of governmental practice. Governmental action was now brought to bear on the rules of the game rather than on the players themselves. There was "an environmental type of intervention instead of the internal subjugation of individuals" (Foucault 2008, 312). This did not mean a complete nullification of the technologies aiming to influence individual behavior, such as disciplinary techniques. But it meant that a level of behavior could be identified as economic behavior, and controlled as such. Subjects were understood to be responsive not only to corporeal punishments, social sanctions, and rewards, but also, and primarily, to economic gains and losses.

Foucault thus claims that the birth of the new liberal governmentality necessitated the birth of the economic subject as its correlate. In the liberal governmentality *homo economicus* functions as a crucial element with regard to the exercise of power. Foucault's provocation against liberalism is the claim that the liberal subject is not in fact an atom of freedom in the face of all the conditions, undertakings, legislations, and prohibitions of a possible government. Liberal subjects are not natural beings with predictable forms of conduct and calculable interests. Instead, they must be understood as a certain historically constructed type of subject that enabled an art of government to be developed according to the new principles of economics. The habits instilled in these subjects no longer aimed to turn them primarily into docile and efficient machines; they aimed to construct them as consumers and entrepreneurs.

Foucault's genealogy of the economic subject begins with the British empiricists—Locke and Hume—and their philosophical accounts of the subject. His rereading of the history of philosophy proposes that it was their theories of the subject—as opposed to the Cartesian subject, for example—which represent the most important theoretical transformation in Western philosophy since the Middle Ages (Foucault 2008, 271). What British empiricism introduces to Western philosophy for the first time "is a subject who is not so much defined by his freedom, or by the opposition of soul and body, or by the presence of a source or core of concupiscence marked to a greater or lesser degree by the Fall or sin, but who appears in the form of a subject of individual choices which are both irreducible and non-transferable" (Foucault 2008, 271–72). The key notion of "interest" denotes this principle of an irreducible and non-transferable individual choice, and its emergence is the momentous rupture in Western thought (Foucault 2008, 273).[5] In political practice, it signals the emergence of a subject of interest as the core correlate of the art of government.

Foucault proceeds to draw a sharp distinction between the liberal subject understood as a subject of rights and as a subject of interests. The subjects of liberalism in political thought are traditionally understood to be primarily characterized by the fact that they have natural rights. Foucault insists that this emphasis is misleading, however, because they are equally characterized by the fact that they have subscribed to the limitation of these rights and have accepted the principle of relinquishing them. In contrast, the liberal subjects understood as a subject of interest are never called upon to relinquish their interests. The key principle of liberal governmentality is not that all individuals may pursue their interests, but that it is absolutely paramount that they pursue them. The liberal subjects are importantly correlates of the "invisible hand": a complex economic system which makes them function as individual subjects of interest within a totality which eludes them, and which nevertheless founds the totality of their egoistic choices. For there to be certainty of collective economic benefit—that the greatest good is attained for the people—it is not only possible but *necessary* that all actors are oblivious to this totality and pursue only their own interests. The collective good must not be an objective of governmentality because paradoxically only then can it be achieved (Foucault 2008, 278).[6]

In sum, the liberal subject is essentially a nonsubstitutable and irreducible atom of interest. He or she is essentially someone who always pursues his or her own interest, and whose interest is such that it converges spontaneously with the interest of others. The consequences of this insight for current neoliberal governmentality have been momentous. Two hundred years after Adam Smith and David Hume, Gary Becker, one of the leading economists of the Chicago School, understood it as a guarantee for the economic calculability of all aspects of human behavior: *homo economicus* responds systematically, in a nonrandom way, to modifications in the variables of the environment. Becker's influential work in economics demonstrates how a whole range of behavior is rational from an economic perspective, including phenomena such as altruism and addiction that were generally understood as exceptions to purely economic interests.[7] When economic rationality is defined broadly enough, individuals always prioritize their interests as they conceive them.

Furthermore, many of their actions become economically intelligible as attempts to increase their human capital. Becker's groundbreaking idea of human capital explains behavioral choices such as education and on-the-job training as investments made in people. People enhance their capabilities as producers and consumers by investing in themselves. The many ways of doing this include activities such as schooling, training, medical care, vitamin consumption, acquiring information about the economic system, and migration.[8] These investments result not just in some incalculable increase in the individual's well-being, but also in a calculable increase in his or her income prospects. Human capital comprises both innate and acquired elements. While the innate elements are largely out of our control, the acquired elements are not. If we make investments in ourselves we are able to produce higher income.[9] Neoliberal governmentality thus scrambles and exchanges the terms of the opposition between "worker" and "capitalist" by aiming to construct a society in which everybody is a capitalist, an entrepreneur of him- or herself (Read 2009, 31).

This means that economic subjects are manageable, but through different mechanisms than the docile subjects of the disciplinary society: they will always pursue their own interests and they are—not in spite of this, but precisely because of it—eminently governable. They will respond systematically and in a predictable way to strategic modifications artificially introduced into the environment. They are the correlates of a governmentality that must act, not on the body of the individuals, but on their environments by systematically modifying its variables so that economic competition is maximized. According to this governmentality, economic incentives provided by the free market will therefore automatically bring about maximal efficiency, well-being, and wealth (Foucault 2008, 270–71).

Many commentators now see the year 1979—when Foucault delivered his lecture series—as the inauguration of the formal period of dominance of neoliberal economic policy in Europe and the United States.[10] Thirty years after its expanding application, Foucault's topic and his insights appear farsighted, almost prophetic. Many of our contemporary experiences in the last three decades reflect the new hegemony of neoliberal governmentality and the corresponding form of the economic subject as an entrepreneur of him- or herself. As Trent Hamann (2009, 40) notes, several critics of neoliberalism have documented a sustained expansion of self-help and personal power technologies that range from the old "think and grow rich" school to new techniques promising greater control in the management of everything from self to anger.

Given that neoliberal governmentality has become so dominant and pervasive in contemporary society, I will next ask what its consequences are for the construction of the feminine subject. Can this model of exercising power contribute to our understanding of the feminine subject? If a docile feminine body is the correlate of disciplinary practices, what kind of feminine subject is the correlate of neoliberal practices of governing?

It should be noted at the outset that my feminist analysis of neoliberalism here and in the following chapter is limited to Europe and North America, in other words, a limited number of Western liberal capi-

talist countries that have been through significant economic restructuring along neoliberal lines over the last three or four decades. The full
impact of the neoliberal turn has been global and it has been convincingly argued by others that its most far-reaching and detrimental effects
have in fact been borne by the women in developing countries.[11] A global
analysis of neoliberalism is unfortunately beyond the scope of this study,
however.

The Subject of Feminism

It seems incontestable that the normative practices of feminine beauty
that Bartky describes have dramatically increased in both volume and
variety since 1988. The cosmetics industry has reported huge increases
in profits and technical innovations in cosmetic surgery as well as in anti-
aging techniques such as botox have become widely available and form
part of many women's normal beauty routine. Both the very young and
the very old are also included now in the target group for cosmetics as
well as other normative techniques of shaping the feminine body such
as dieting, exercising, and hair removal. There seem to be no signs suggesting that the disciplinary techniques that Bartky describes and cata-
logs have in any way waned or even come under heightened critique in
contemporary society.

I want to suggest that there have been changes in the rationality underpinning these techniques in the last decades, which have emerged in
tandem with the rise of the new neoliberal feminine subject. The spread
and intensification of neoliberal governmentality has meant that women
too have come to be seen, and to see themselves, increasingly as neoliberal subjects—egoistical subjects of interest making free choices based
on rational economic calculation. Early feminist demands for political
rights were often repudiated on the grounds that women did not have
any political interests separate from those of their husband's and father's
and therefore they had no need for political representation. Even though
women have now had equal political rights for nearly a century, the idea
that all their actions would be driven by calculated self-interest to the
express exclusion of all other values has been absent or even structurally
impossible in the liberal political paradigm. However, it is my contention that women today not only have the rights guaranteed by political
liberalism; they have now also largely become the subjects presumed by
economic liberalism—individuals pursuing their own interests and responding primarily to economic gains and losses. It has now become

fully conceivable that a woman's interest might not coincide with her husband's and children's interests anymore: women do not only want a happy home anymore, they too want money, power, and success. They are atomic, autonomous subjects of interest competing for the economic opportunities available.

The rise of this new feminine, neoliberal subject can be described and documented in different ways—by analyzing visual culture or sociological data, for example. The sociologist Angela McRobbie (2009), for example, has combined elements of feminist sociology with cultural studies in a provocative attempt to map out the field of postfeminist popular and political culture, mainly within a UK framework. She surveys changes in film, television, popular culture, and women's magazines and demonstrates how feminist content has disappeared from them in the last decades and has been replaced by aggressive individualism, by hedonistic female phallicism in the field of sexuality, and by obsession with consumer culture. Natasha Walter's *The New Feminism* (1998) and Ariel Levy's *Female Chauvinist Pigs* (2005)—two popular books targeting mainly wide, mainstream audience—document this same shift in cultural attitudes. Walter's book articulates ideas about femininity and feminism that became dominant in the United Kingdom during the course of 1980s and 1990s, and it tells a triumphant story of women's economic success. Walter insists that a woman can be a feminist and still have a white wedding, buy pornography, wear designer clothes, or even be a prostitute or a porn star as long as that has been her own choice. In other words, it is irrelevant how women speak, dress, or express sexuality as long as they are pursuing their own interests. For her, the real issues of feminism are about personal freedom, economic independence, and professional success in all areas of employment (Walter 1998, 193). In a more critical vein Levy describes the way that the increasing *pornofication* of all aspects of everyday life is no longer understood in opposition to feminist political aims, but is instead seen as evidence that feminism has already achieved its goals. The fact that women too read *Playboy* and get Brazilian bikini waxes is increasingly understood as a sign of their liberation and empowerment.

However, my argument here concerning the rise of the neoliberal feminine subject is not empirical, but essentially philosophical. This means that although it can be illustrated with empirical facts and descriptions, it cannot, by definition, be conclusively proved or disproved with them. It is premised on Foucault's best-known contribution to feminist theory, namely his philosophical insight that any analysis of power relations must recognize how these relations are constitutive of the subjects involved in them. Power cannot be conceived of as an external relation that takes place between preconstituted subjects, but has to be understood as constituting the subjects themselves: their constitution only becomes possible in the shifting, contested, and precarious field of power relations. This insight must continue to remain central when we try to understand and evaluate the impact of neoliberalism on feminist theory and politics. If we accept that neoliberal techniques of governing have come to increasingly characterize our society, and we also accept that there is an ineliminable tie between forms of power and forms of the subject, then it must follow that the neoliberal turn concerning techniques of governing has necessitated a change in the corresponding construction of the subject.

Feminist theorists such as Bartky have significantly noted, however, that Foucault's analysis of subjectivization is insensitive to the modalities of it that are particularly feminine. The masculinity of the neoliberal economic subject is usually taken for granted. An important philosophical counterargument to my claim about a neoliberal feminine subject would thus point out the clear discrepancy between liberal governmentality and the corresponding female subject. Feminist critics have convincingly argued that the idea that all of women's actions would be driven by calculated self-interest to the express exclusion of all other values has been absent or even structurally impossible in the liberal political paradigm.[12] As Wendy Brown (1995, 157), for example, has argued, the subject of liberalism as a figure of fundamental self-interest and self-orientation is quite at odds with what women have been constituted as. The autonomous woman—the childless, unmarried, or lesbian woman—has been a sign of disorderly society or of individual failure to "adapt to femininity." Such "unnatural" figures make clearly visible how the social order presumed by liberalism is itself pervasively gendered, representing both a gendered division of labor and a gendered division of the sensibilities and activities of subjects. Women's traditional role in the family has been to surrender their self-interest so that their husbands and children can attain their autonomous subjectivity. The constitutive terms of liberal political discourse and practice—individual, autonomy, self-interest—fundamentally depend upon their implicit opposition to a subject and a set of activities marked "feminine," while effectively obscuring this dependence (Brown 1995, 152).

I contend that in neoliberal governmentality, with its reductive treatment of all social issues as economic, the situation has, at least to some extent, changed. We have witnessed a significant reconstitution of family, kinship, and intimate relationships in the recent decades: they too have been permeated by the logic of the market and have become less premised on permanent familial ties. It is not structurally impossible any longer that a significant number of women could be liberal subjects in the full sense of the term—not only individual subjects of rights, but also egotistical subjects of interest. Because neoliberal governmentality has brought about the increasing commodification and marketization of the private realm—domestic and caring work, for example—the self-interest of particular women can now be bought relatively easily with the subordination and exploitation of others.

While we have to recognize that this commoditized domestic and caring work is still mostly provided by women, from a primarily economic perspective the gender of the care providers is becoming less significant too. Global neoliberal economy relies on women's labor, but also, increasingly, on the *feminization of labor.* This widely used, but ambiguous concept denotes, on the one hand, the quantitative increase of women in the labor market globally due to the growth of the service industries and the increasing demand for care work. However, it also denotes a qualitative change in the nature of labor: the characteristics historically present in women's work—precariousness, flexibility, fragmentary nature, low-status, and low-pay—have come to increasingly characterize all work in global capitalism.[13] As Rutvica Andrijasevic (2010, 5) notes, this does not mean that the gendered dualism production/reproduction no longer exists, but rather that reading it exclusively in terms of gendered division of labor does not fully capture contemporary forms of labor arrangements.[14]

Axel Honneth and Martin Hartmann (2006, 45) have also emphasized the importance of such characteristics as emotional resources and communicative skills in the "new" or "flexible" capitalism. They argue that the most important criterion describing the neoliberal revolution is no longer the workers' ability to fulfill hierarchically determined parameters within a large enterprise; it is the readiness to self-responsibly bring one's communicative skills and emotional resources to bear in the service of individualizing projects. Workers are expected to mobilize informal, emotional, "lifeworld skills" for professional goals, which results in the blending of private and public, informal and formal, skills and resources (ibid., 50). Although Honneth and Hartman do not analyze the gendered aspects of this development, the implication is that traditionally feminine abilities and characteristics such as the emotional, relational, and communicative competences which were previously expected primarily from female workers are now increasingly expected from all workers.

Hence, the irreconcilable dualisms that traditionally constitute political liberalism—public/private, individual/family, autonomy/dependency, self-interest/selflessness—do not cut neatly between the two genders anymore. They have now come to characterize increasingly the psychic life of working women torn between conflicting demands of femininity, as well as the internal divisions between different groups of women and men. This implies that women's continued subordination as a *group* is not economically required for the kind of society that neoliberalism constructs.

Neoliberal Technologies of Gender

This fundamental shift in the constitution of the feminine subject implies that women are now governed and subjected though new mechanisms, namely through the harnessing of their economic interests. Normative femininity has become firmly attached to economic gains in a new way. It is my contention that women are increasingly rationalizing their participation in the normative habits of femininity in terms of their own economic interests, not in terms of men's interests: women no longer have long, manicured nails because their male partners find this sexually attractive and arousing, but because manicured nails have now become a sign of professional and financial success, a sign that is likely to help them move forward in their career. Similarly, in interviews with cosmetic surgery patients, for example, one of the main arguments women state for undergoing the operations is the fact that it can be a career move.[15] Feminine appearance has come to be seen as an important instrument by which women can increase their human capital. The neoliberal subject views feminine appearance as well as her own body increasingly as an investment for getting the returns she wants. This means that the practices of normative femininity are no longer upheld *only* through the subtle mechanisms of discipline described by Bartky—women adopt the habits of femininity through a system of social sanctions and rewards such as shame and sexual admiration. It is upheld now also through a rationality based on financial loss and gain.

Whereas Bartky noted that successful provision of a beautiful or sexy body gained women attention and admiration but did not result in any real social power, the situation has, at least on the surface level, changed considerably. Walter seems to be right in insisting that success in normative feminine appearance is not primarily a sign of deference anymore, but has become an important sign of economic success and social power. The link between idealized femininity and economic success has become tight and pronounced. The most successful performances of feminine appearance in our society no longer symbolize subservience—waitresses, flight attendants, or secretaries. The most successful performances of feminine appearance these days are accomplished by women who have power and money: female executives and politicians. We live in a world in which appearances are more important than ever and the modern female consumer is well aware of this.

We must not be fooled into thinking that this means that the cultural meaning of femininity and its profound tie to subservience and dependency has completely dissolved, however. Nor is it the case that the structural dependence of liberalism on its "others"—beings who belong to the realm of familial selflessness and dependency making the autonomy and selfishness of others possible—would have disappeared. As long as our life form is fundamentally centered on families and on a gendered division of the sensibilities and activities of the subjects, the neoliberal, purely self-interested feminine subject would signal the collapse of our social order, a collapse that is in no way evident. While the defenders of family values loudly proclaim such collapse, we have to acknowledge that normative, subservient femininity still continues to largely provide the necessary support for the neoliberal political and economic order.

It is nevertheless significant to see that neoliberal governmentality operates with a different logic of gender subjection. Rather than disciplining the feminine subjects through the normalizing habits connected to shame, social sanctions, and sexual rewards, it installs the habits constitutive of normative femininity increasingly through their economic rationality. The focus is on the environmental variables that determine and constrict women's behavior as consumers and entrepreneurs of themselves. We must recognize that the personal freedom and choice that neoliberal governmentality entails is an integral aspect of this technique of power. The idea of personal choice effectively masks the systemic aspects of power—domination, social hierarchies, economic exploitation—by relegating to subjects the freedom to choose between different options while denying them any real possibility for defining or shaping those options.

This excessive focus on free choice has been perhaps the most insidious aspect of neoliberal governmentality for the subject of feminism. The measure of women's liberation has become the individual choices we are able to make: to become executives or prostitutes, to have white weddings or to buy pornography. Power is increasingly understood as simply another thing that women can choose. Within this framework, the fact that many women choose to stay at home or opt out of more demanding and higher-paying employment opportunities is understood straightforwardly as their own free choice. The impediments to their social and political success are personal or psychological rather than political. Because the neoliberal subject is a free atom of self-interest fully responsible for navigating the social realm by using cost-benefit calculation, those who fail to succeed can only blame themselves.[16]

The obvious problem with this excessive focus on choice is that women cannot choose power like they can choose between different wedding dresses. Women have to make their choices in a network of highly unequal power relations that not only restrict their possibilities and options, but construct their very subjectivities. Feminist analyses have shown that women develop their work aspirations and identities, for example, only within the context of, and in response to, structural features of the work world.[17] The idea that feminine subjects have static interests and identities that precede their choices as well as the power relations they are engaged in obfuscates the systematic and constitutive aspects of male power. This means that, paradoxically, their belief in unlimited possibilities and freedom of choice makes women more, not less, vulnerable to sexism.

While Bartky's analysis of feminine embodiment acknowledged the force of habit—the way that habits are never simply a matter of free choice, but are importantly tied to social norms, sanctions, and rewards—the neoliberal framework effectively erases this insight. Women still internalize social divisions and power hierarchies through mundane techniques of gender to the extent that they become part of their subjectivities. Only now these techniques as well as the hierarchies that they mirror and uphold are portrayed even more effectively as the consequence of individual choice. This shift has resulted in the intensification of these practices. The belief that women are in complete control of their lives, that traditional femininity is their free choice, and that they can achieve anything they want, not in spite of it, but with the help of it, makes them more compliant with normative techniques of gender. If we believe the neoliberal doctrine that subjects do nothing that is not in their own interest, then normative femininity must be what we truly want.

It is therefore paramount that feminists engage in critical analyses of neoliberalism as well as political resistance against it. In the next chapter I will make suggestions regarding how feminist politics should confront neoliberalism and analyze some of the political dilemmas that arise in their intersection. However, it seems clear at this point that if we want to resist the new mechanisms of power operative in our society, we have to expose and understand their constitutive effects on the feminine subjects.

8

Feminism and Neoliberal Governmentality

Feminist scholars have analyzed extensively the changes in the situation of women that have been brought about by the global neoliberal turn over the last three or four decades, but their assessments of neoliberalism's impact on feminist theory and politics vary. Some have argued that feminism must return its focus to socialist politics and foreground economic questions of redistribution in order to combat the hegemony of neoliberalism.[1] Some have further identified poststructuralism and its dominance in feminist scholarship as responsible for the debilitating move away from socialist or Marxist paradigms. A weaker version of this critique claims that poststructuralist approaches are inadequate to the task of confronting new realities brought about by neoliberalism. The stronger version claims that poststructuralist feminism is symptomatic of, or even partially responsible for, this neoliberal configuration. Hester Eisenstein (2009, 212–13), for example, has argued that the postmodern turn in women's studies scholarship in the 1980s, with its emphasis on discourse and its distrust of grand narratives, undermined a systematic analysis of the capitalist system. The contemporaneous rise of neoliberalism globally as the leading political and economic paradigm implies that feminism now has to turn away from poststructuralist and postmodern analyses that focus on individual acts of resistance and turn back toward a structural analysis of global capitalism.

I share this diagnosis to the extent that the rapid neoliberalization characterizing the last thirty years has put women and feminist thought in a completely new political situation. However, in contrast to the feminist thinkers who put the blame for the current impasse on the rise of poststructuralist modes of thought in feminist theory and advocate a return to socialist feminism, I contend that such return represents a dangerous nostalgia that would rob feminist theory of its remaining political relevance. It is my contention that the poststructuralist turn in feminist theory in the 1980s and 1990s was an important advance, only now its theoretical and political force has to be redirected toward new issues such as neoliberalism and globalization. My argument in a nutshell is that Foucault's thought provides a more nuanced diagnostic approach to neoliberalism than traditional socialist welfare feminism because it enables us to account for neoliberalism's constitutive effects. These effects include both new forms of the subject as well as new limitations on what are understood as viable and rational political options in today's society. In addition, I will show how a Foucauldian approach to neoliberalism exposes the political constitution of the economic domain itself for critical scrutiny.

Foucault's 1979 lectures on neoliberalism offer a novel conceptual and theoretical framework for the critical analysis of neoliberalism, but they have received surprisingly little attention from feminist thinkers. The level on which Foucault operates is distinctive: his genealogical analysis of neoliberal governmentality is not an attempt to provide a causal, historical explanation for the neoliberal turn.[2] Rather, he seeks to outline the historical ontology of neoliberalism thereby showing the way that neoliberal policies are rooted in deep, historical changes in our conception of the political and the practices of governing.[3] In these lectures neoliberalism is crucially treated as a form of governmentality, a rationality of governance that produces new kinds of political subjects and a new organization of the social realm. It is not reducible to a set of economic policies such as limiting the regulation of capital, maximizing corporate profits, and dismantling the welfare state. As a form of governmentality neoliberalism extends beyond economic policy, or even the economic domain as traditionally conceived.

I will show that this framework is vital for the feminist diagnosis of our contemporary political reality. I proceed in four stages. In the first two sections, "Feminism, Social Democracy, and Neoliberalism" and "The Feminist Subject," I will discuss some recent socialist feminist responses to neoliberalism and criticize their reductive treatment of it as a set of economic policies with undesirable consequences for the welfare of women. I attempt to show that despite their critical intent they fail to address neoliberalism's underlying political rationality and thus overlook its constitutive effects. In the third section, "The Cultural/Economic Distinction," I return to Nancy Fraser and Judith's Butler's germinal debate on feminist politics in the journal *Social Text* in 1997 in order to demonstrate that a critical analysis of the economic/cultural distinction must be central when we consider feminist forms of resistance against neoliberalism. In the final section, I discuss Foucault's genealogy of neoliberalism in more detail. I contend that it can provide a critical diagnostic framework for feminist theory as well as opening up new feminist political responses to the spread and dominance of neoliberalism.

Feminism, Social Democracy, and Neoliberalism

Feminist researchers critical of neoliberalism have sought to demonstrate that its advancement has largely taken place at the expense of women. Sylvia Walby, for example, argues in her recent book *The Future of Feminism* (2011) that the rise of neoliberalism and the issues accompanying it—increased economic inequalities, de-democratization and environmental crisis—create the biggest challenge for the future of feminism. She argues that the effects of neoliberalism are gendered in two ways. First, the negative impact of neoliberal policies is borne disproportionately by women. Women's jobs are most affected by cutbacks in public expenditure as they work more often in the public sector. The lack of social services and benefits further affects women more than men, since they are poorer and more dependent on those services (Walby 2011, 118). Second, Walby argues that the rise of neoliberalism has turned the political context in which feminism has to operate more hostile to the practical achievement of its goals. The decline of trade unions has meant that there are fewer allies with whom feminists can construct coalitions, and the lack of funding for public institutions has hindered the active promotion of gender equality initiatives (ibid., 114). Neoliberalism brings about social, economic, and political changes that "increase gender inequality directly, through their disproportionate impact on women's jobs and welfare, as well as creating a less hospitable political context for women's effective engagement in the public sphere and for innovative gender policies" (ibid., 158). The political remedy to the situation that Walby recommends is the traditional defense of the welfare state—some variant of socialist politics combined with feminist awareness. Walby sees feminism and social democratic politics as necessarily overlapping: feminism has an important contribution to make to social democratic projects and vice versa since they have a shared concern for the democratic regulation of the economy (ibid., 123).

Hester Eisenstein argues similarly in *Feminism Seduced* (2009) that neoliberalism has had disastrous effects on the lives of most women. While some women with higher education have succeeded in climbing the corporate ladder, reaching near parity with men in many sectors of work, women with no access to education or child care are increasingly pushed to part-time and temporary jobs with few benefits. The willingness of women to enter the workforce in massive numbers has traditionally served the interest of capital in holding wages down. The new, neoliberal economy built on temporary low-wage jobs—the so-called

McJobs—draws even more heavily on female labor, however (Eisenstein 2009, 107–9). Eisenstein argues that these structural changes in the nature of work pose a challenge to mainstream liberal feminism, which sees economic independence as a key to women's empowerment. Instead of the values of individualism and self-determination characterizing liberal feminism we must return to the ideals of collectivism and solidarity animating socialist feminism. We need a more class-conscious approach to feminist politics (ibid., 212–13).

My aim here is not to challenge the validity of Walby's and Eisenstein's assessments of the implications of the neoliberal turn on women or to deny that the implementation of socialist policies would remedy many of its problematic effects. However, I want to insist that the political challenge that neoliberalism presents to feminism calls for political measures and theoretical interventions that go beyond traditional socialist welfare policies.

Walby opposes neoliberalism to social democracy and argues that the United States adopts a neoliberal form in both gender and class regimes, while the European Union adopts a relatively more social democratic form (Walby 2011, 159). However, neoliberal policies and economic principles have also been adopted systematically by the European Union and sometimes their application has been even more consistent than in the United States. It is my contention that the idea that gender and class regimes come in two opposing types, neoliberal and social-democratic, is an oversimplified abstraction that does not bring either theoretical clarity or political efficacy to feminist analyses. Rather than being opposites, I suggest that we follow Foucault in seeing social-democracy and neoliberalism more fundamentally as representing two variants of the same governmental rationality.

What makes Foucault's philosophical interpretation of neoliberalism particularly helpful, in my view, is his critical analysis of it, not as an ideology, economic doctrine, or political regime, but as a specific, rationally reflected and coordinated way of governing: a form of liberal governmental rationality or governmentality. Neoliberalism and the state cannot be understood as simply antithetical to each other when they are understood to combine in the form of a rationally coordinated set of governmental practices. This shift of perspective to neoliberal governmentality enables Foucault to make the provocative claim that although liberal governmentality existed, socialist governmentality did not. The socialist welfare politics dominant in Europe after World War II until the neoliberal turn in the 1970s, had to operate within the dominant framework of liberal governmentality that had been developing and spreading since the eighteenth century. According to him, socialism has had to submit to liberal governmental rationality and assume the role of merely compensating for the harmful social effects of the free market. In other words, socialism has been forced to take the form of covert or unawoved liberalism. "There is no governmental rationality of socialism. In actual fact, and history has shown this, socialism can only be implemented connected up to diverse types of governmentality. It has been connected up to liberal governmentality, and then socialism and its forms of rationality function as a counter-weight, as a corrective, and a palliative to internal dangers" (Foucault 2008, 92).

It is important to take Foucault's provocation seriously. His genealogy of neoliberalism shows that the philosophical roots of the neoliberal turn are much deeper than is commonly thought—they lie in the birth of a new liberal form of governmental reason formulated, reflected upon, and outlined in the middle of the eighteenth century and expressed in political economy. Foucault's key claim is that our modern understanding and practice of liberal governance was constituted and limited by a new regime of truth—one which established a novel relationship between political power and economic knowledge. To sum up its essential features, it became possible, for the first time in history, to make scientific truth claims about the economy. Economical thinking was no longer concerned with justice—the sovereign's right to impose restrictions on trade or the fairness of the market, for example—but with truth. The new science of economics dictated that good government should not interfere with market mechanisms, which spontaneously followed their own autonomous laws and established their own truths. Because market mechanisms— Adam Smith's invisible hand—best ensured that the pursuit of private interests spontaneously led to the common good, it was irrational to place such pursuits under political control. Economic truths could not be argued against politically without falling into irrationality. This meant that once something was defined as an economic question—such as the magnitude of the income gap between the rich and the poor, for example—it was moved out of the realm of justice to the realm of truth.

Foucault also emphasizes that all forms of modern politics have become intertwined with biopolitical concerns—the maximal welfare of the population. In modernity, the people have come to be understood as a population with quantifiable biological properties, and good governance means securing the population's maximal health and longevity. The unquestioned objective of good government has become to provide the best possible quality of life by the means of economic growth: in a capitalist economic system it is generally accepted that only economic growth, a continuous increase in productivity, can deliver higher living standards for everybody and thus ensure the best life. A stable capitalist economic order, both in its neoliberal or social democratic variants, is understood to be structurally reliant on economic growth. This equation of good government with economic growth is a distinctly modern construction: GDP growth (gross domestic product) is the single most important goal of governments across the world today.

Hence, the spread of neoliberalism has been almost impossible to stop in our current governmentality according to which economic progress, defined as GDP growth, is the unquestioned political end of good government and politically neutral economic truths are understood as the essential means for achieving it. The neoliberal economic argument has simply won in this governmental game of truth: according to neoliberals, economic growth can be best achieved via free international trade, sound budgets—meaning normally fiscal austerity, which translates into cuts in welfare spending—low inflation, privatization, and the deregulation of markets. In such economic thinking commodification and privatization, for example, are understood as particularly effective means of speeding up growth given that GDP is measured in terms of market transactions. If previously noncommercial or public services, cultural products, life forms, physical space, and social relations are redefined as commodities, it clearly follows that more market transactions will be generated. And formally, this translates into further economic growth measured in terms of GDP.[4] In other words, the rise of neoliberalism has meant that whereas the policies for achieving economic growth have dramatically changed, the biopolitical end of maximal wealth and welfare of the population has remained the same.

The socialist critics of neoliberalism are undoubtedly right in demonstrating that its rise has been contemporaneous with the dramatic increase of the wealth of the elites. Since the global neoliberal turn in the 1970s, there has been an enormous spiraling of the levels of wealth in the top income categories. This new distribution of wealth is often presented as the primary aim of the neoliberal turn by its socialist critics: the neoliberal project has been a deliberate attempt to restore the power and the wealth of the upper classes.[5] However, the models of resistance to neoliberalism become more complicated if we accept that the aim of neoliberal government is to maximize everybody's material welfare, not just the welfare of the elite: as the popular slogan states, the rising tide lifts all boats. The growing disparities of wealth are then understood as the unfortunate, but inevitable consequence of neoliberal government and not as its conspiratorial aim. Against this background, the continuing crisis of the left can be attributed to the fact that supporting welfare capitalism—the welfare of all in a capitalist society—is not its distinctive political demand. Most neoliberals support this end too, but in addition they have succeeded in presenting the winning economic argument for the best means of achieving it. Since the end of the 1970s the left has repeatedly lost in the economic debates centered on the key question of economic growth. It has been forced to either accept the so-called hard economic facts or to back up its political demands with moral arguments—arguments that have appeared as misplaced compassion for those failing to give their lives proper entrepreneurial shape (Brown 2005, 56). As William Connolly (1984, 227–31) formulates the conundrum, the welfare state needs a growing economy to support its distributive programs, but the structure of the capitalist economy is such that growth can only be achieved by policies that are inconsistent with the principles of justice that underlie those programs.

Feminist analyses such as Walby's and Eisenstein's that focus mainly on the material welfare of women—their employment and social benefits, for example—thus have a hard task of showing that the neoliberal reforms are detrimental to women as long as they too engage in this debate in economic terms. In such an essentially economic debate it is by no means obvious that feminist and socialist politics necessarily overlap or that the welfare of women is best served by socialist politics. If welfare programs and feminist initiatives—such as women's shelters and rape prevention campaigns—can only be funded by a growing economy, and economic facts indicate that the growth of the economy is only possible by the implementation of neoliberal policies, then women's welfare and neoliberalism are not so obviously opposed anymore.[6] We either have to come up with better economic arguments showing how economic growth can be achieved by other means—a task that I will have to leave to trained economists—or, as feminist philosophers, we have to target our current governmentality according to which economic truths are politically neutral and the good life of the population is essentially dependent on economic growth (defined in terms of GDP). Resistance to neoliberal governmentality then means posing difficult philosophical questions such as: What is the epistemological status of economic truths? Are they value-neutral? What are their political effects? Are our current criteria for economic progress and human welfare adequate? Is economic growth a socially and ecologically sustainable goal?

The Feminist Subject

Another key issue that points beyond traditional socialist welfare politics concerns the feminist subject. As I argued in the previous chapter, the

Foucauldian approach shows that the impact of neoliberalism is not limited to the dismantling of the welfare state: as a form of governmentality neoliberalism is constitutive of our conceptions of politics and political action, but also of ourselves as political subjects. This implies that the feminist subject too, as well as our understanding of feminist politics, are shaped and constituted by our current neoliberal governmentality. "Women," "feminism," and "feminist politics" are not natural, apolitical, entities that are simply affected by certain, empirical changes in society. They are fundamentally shaped and constituted by these changes as well as our conceptions and background beliefs about the social world. Assessing the impact of neoliberal governmentality requires rethinking how our conceptions of female subjectivity, citizenship, political action, and feminist liberation, for example, have themselves changed due to the impact of neoliberal hegemony.

From a Foucauldian perspective, both Walby's and Eisenstein's analyses are problematic in assuming that the constitution of the (socialist) feminist subject is unaffected by intensified neoliberal technologies of power. If we accept the argument I presented in the previous chapter that the spread and intensification of neoliberal governmentality has meant that women too have come to be seen, and to see themselves, increasingly as neoliberal subjects—egoistical subjects of interest making free choices based on rational economic calculation—this will inevitably affect and shape forms of feminist politics too. Against this background, it is my contention that Walby dismisses rather easily the charge that feminism has been incorporated by neoliberalism. Because of her narrow understanding of neoliberalism as an economic policy opposing and threatening the welfare state she is unable to account for its constitutive effects on feminine and feminist subjects. She acknowledges that some neoliberals have claimed that neoliberalism is good for women, but insists that feminists themselves think nothing of the sort. For her, verifying such a charge would require producing empirical evidence showing that some feminist group actually agrees on the compatibility of feminism and neoliberalism. However, no such evidence exists. Instead Walby attempts to provide extensive evidence of the actual activities of feminist groups—the major feminist bodies in the United Kingdom, European Union, United States, and the United Nations—demonstrating that their goals are not compatible in any way with the neoliberal turn (Walby 2011, 21–22).

However, if we accept that women have, at least to some extent, become neoliberal subjects competing for the rewards in the new economic game, does Walby's reduction of feminist thought and practice to a limited number of governmental bodies compatible with socialist policy really signal the strength and vibrancy of contemporary feminism? Would it not rather imply that feminism was somewhat out of touch with what is happening in the lives of young women today? It is obviously important to show empirically the concrete consequences that the cuts to the public sector have on the lives of women, but it is equally important to engage in a constitutive, philosophical analysis of its impact on the kinds of subjects that we have become. Feminist politics has to be able to somehow confront the overarching governmental framework in which the measure of women's liberation has become individual economic success and the choices women are able to make.

Feminists also have to raise new kinds of questions about solidarity. I strongly agree with Eisenstein that our response to the rise of neoliberalism requires challenging the individualism and self-determination traditionally animating liberal feminism. However, it is difficult to build such solidarity on class-consciousness when women's identity as a group is not constructed economically. We need a broader and a more radical vision of feminist politics than traditional welfare socialism is able to provide. Feminism must return to a critical analysis of capitalism, but we have to transform not only our political or economic institutions, but, more fundamentally, our way of life and even ourselves. We need a politics of ourselves that acknowledges that it is through us, through the reshaping of our subjectivity, that neoliberal governmentality is able to function. I will return to the question of feminist solidarity in more detail in the next chapter.

The Cultural/Economic Distinction

The concern that feminism was moving away from socialist political imaginary and neglecting issues of economic redistribution was acute already in the political debates of the 1990s, following the collapse of the Soviet Union and the dispersal of the Left. Feminists' fascination with poststructuralism and cultural identity politics was seen as a failure to provide a systematic understanding of capitalist exploitation and to engage in class politics. The debate crystallized in an interesting way in the important exchange between Nancy Fraser and Judith Butler on the distinction between the cultural and the economic.

In her article "Merely Cultural" (1997), Butler responds to the charge that the cultural focus of poststructuralist feminist theory in the 1980s and 1990s had meant abandoning the materialist project of Marxism and had led us to the dead end of merely cultural politics—a self-centered and trivial form of politics that reduced political activism to the mere assertion and affirmation of cultural identity (Butler 1997, 265). Although Butler refuses to name anyone who actually advocates such views, the article turns into a critique of Nancy Fraser's influential book *Justice Interruptus* (1997a) and of the key conceptual distinctions organizing it. Fraser makes an analytic or heuristic distinction between socioeconomic injustices and their remedies, on the one hand, and cultural injustices and their remedies, on the other hand. This enables her to study the ways that political demands for redistribution and for recognition, respectively, can be most effectively combined. Her aim is to overcome the culture/economy split by emphasizing the importance of both types of politics—we must advocate radical transformation of cultural categories *and* the institutions of political economy.

Gender, for example, has political-economic dimensions, because it is a basic structuring principle of the political economy. Gender justice thus requires transforming the political economy: eliminating gender-specific exploitation, marginalization, and deprivation requires abolishing the gendered division of labor—both the gendered division between paid and unpaid labor and within paid labor. However, such political-economic restructuring is not enough because gender is not only a political-economic, but a cultural-valuational differentiation too. Gender injustices also include forms of androcentrism and cultural sexism: the pervasive devaluation and disparagement of things coded feminine. This devaluation is expressed in a range of harms suffered by women including sexual assault, sexual exploitation, pervasive domestic violence as well as trivializing, objectifying, and demeaning stereotypical depictions in the media (Fraser 1997a, 20). In addition to political-economic redistribution we crucially need remedies of recognition too: changing the cultural evaluations as well as their legal and practical expressions that privilege masculinity and deny equal respect to women. Fraser thus bridges the opposition that Eisenstein, for example, erects between socialist feminism and poststructuralism: traditional socialist feminist politics must be combined with the cultural politics of poststructuralist feminism.

Butler attacks the viability of such combinatory politics, however. She argues that by reiterating the distinction between the economic and the cultural Fraser only entrenches the split by falsely reaffirming the existence of two separate spheres of politics with different objectives and instruments (Butler 1997, 270–71). She seeks to contest the stability of the distinction between cultural and economic on several grounds—she refers to currents of neo-Marxist thought as well as to the work of anthropologists such as Mauss and Lévi-Strauss (ibid., 274–76)—but the crucial move in her critique, in my view, is not the destabilization of this distinction, but its politicization. She suggests that instead of being a purely ontological, theoretical, or analytical distinction, the cultural/economic—distinction has a political function.

The way Butler explicates this political function is very brief, however. She claims that it is "tactically invoked for the purposes of marginalizing certain forms of political activism," namely queer politics (Butler 1997, 268). In other words, the distinction gives support to a social and sexual conservatism by making questions of sexuality and queer politics secondary to the "real business of politics" (ibid.). She also seeks to politicize the distinction in a second sense by briefly referring to Marx's *Precapitalist Economic Formations*, in which Marx "seeks to explain how the cultural and the economic themselves became established as separable spheres—indeed, how the institution of the economic as a separate sphere is the consequence of an operation of abstraction initiated by capital itself" (ibid., 274). In the section of the *Grundrisse* to which Butler refers, Marx analyzes the historical development that led from precapitalist economic formations to capitalism. He seeks to identify the historic prerequisites for the development of capitalism—laborers with nothing but their labor power to sell, on the one hand, and capital, on the other hand. Through various historical processes of dissolution an economic formation developed which was based on exchange-values and money, as opposed to use-values and forms of property corresponding to small-scale production. This process made possible the transformation of money into capital, and it separated the laborer from his own means of production.[7]

As is often the case with Marx, it is debatable whether this is intended as a historical argument or as an argument concerning the inevitable logic of capitalism. Butler's use of phrases such as "initiated by capital itself" gives the impression that she reads it in the latter sense. While such reading accomplishes a politicization of the economic/cultural distinction by revealing that this distinction is essential for the exploitation of laborers by capitalists, politicizing it in this way is not particularly helpful in the contemporary feminist context as it does not enable us to get a grip on the historically specific political challenges that neoliberalism presents.

In her response to Butler, Fraser emphasizes that she does not understand or utilize the cultural/economic distinction as an ontological distinction, but as a distinction that is historically specific to advanced capitalism.[8] She contends that Butler has resurrected one of the worst aspects of 1970s Marxism and Marxist-feminism by relying on an ahistorical reading of Marx and by putting forward an "overtotalized" view of capitalist society: "What gets lost is the specificity of capitalist society as a distinctive and highly peculiar form of social organization" (Fraser 1997b, 284). Fraser follows Karl Polanyi in arguing that in prestate, precapitalist societies the cultural/economic distinction was essentially unstable: neither distinctively economic relations nor distinctively cultural relations existed. A single order of social relations handled both economic and cultural integration. However, such matters are relatively uncoupled in capitalist society, which is characterized by gaps between status and class, culture and economy. Nineteenth-century industrial society, in which economic activity became isolated and imputed to a distinctive economic motive, was historically a singular departure.[9] Fraser thus defends her position against Butler's attempt to destabilize the distinction between the economic and the cultural by insisting that the distinction can be usefully applied to capitalist society in order to understand its historically specific character and the ways that it is structurally differentiated (ibid., 287).

While emphasizing the historical specificity of the distinction Fraser refuses to acknowledge that it serves a political function—either of marginalizing queer politics or of stabilizing capitalism. She denies outright that she has used it tactically to marginalize queer sexualities. Empirical evidence refutes Butler's second, Marxist claim that capitalism relies on this distinction. According to Fraser, observing contemporary capitalism makes evident that it does not attempt to push gays and lesbians outside of the economic sphere; instead it has readily seen the economic advantages of accommodating them and viewing them as potential consumers (ibid., 285). The distinction between the cultural and economic is thus not a political distinction in either of the senses advocated by Butler. It is simply an analytically useful distinction for understanding the specificity of capitalist society.

Despite their differences, both Butler and Fraser turn to analyses of capitalism in their attempts to account for the institution of the economic/cultural distinction. They do not question how the political formation of the economic domain has changed in the current neoliberal governmentality. I strongly agree with Fraser that we must not understand the economic/cultural distinction as a fixed, ontological distinction, but as historically specific to advanced capitalism. However, in my view Fraser brushes aside too quickly the possibility that this distinction might have a political function. Butler's use of phrases such as "tactically invoked" and "initiated by capital itself" is unfortunate as it suggests that these political effects are reducible to deliberate tactics and specific political interests.[10] I therefore suggest that we turn to Foucault next in order to critically investigate the political effects of the economic/cultural distinction in neoliberal governmentality.

A Genealogy of the Economic

Foucault's lectures on liberal and neoliberal governmentality provide us with a genealogy of the economic—not a history of the concept, but a genealogy of the governmentality that established the economic as a autonomous realm of reality with its own laws and regularities. For Foucault, physiocrats such as François Quesnay and their economic doctrine represent "the founding act of economic thought" in the sense that with them not only a whole new conception of the economy emerges, but, crucially, the free market starts to operate as the principle of good government (Foucault 2007, 33).[11] In *The Order of Things* (1989), Foucault had already shown how economic analysis remained on the level of an analysis of wealth in the seventeenth century and how, in the eighteenth century with the physiocrats, a new domain of knowledge, political economy, was opened up. In the lecture series *Security, Territory, Population* (2007), he is no longer interested in the emergence of political economy "in terms of an archaeology of knowledge," but he now wants to "consider it from the perspective of a genealogy of techniques of power" (Foucault 2007, 36). With the physiocrats, political economy emerges not only as a science, but also as a technique of intervention in the field of reality understood as the economy. Their study of market mechanisms was thus both a scientific analysis of what happens and a program of what should happen.

Foucault argues that it would be wrong to simply concede that physiocratic economic theory produced a shift in economic policy as its practical consequence (Foucault 2007, 34). What occurred instead was a fundamental reorganization of the theoretical field of economics as well as of the techniques of government. Physiocrats rejected any analysis of economic processes in terms of morality and approached them instead as autonomous, natural phenomena governed by scientific laws and regularities. With their doctrine of "economic government" the art of government too reached a certain threshold of "science" (ibid., 116). "The word 'economy' designated a form of government in the sixteenth century; in the eighteenth century, through a series of complex processes that are absolutely crucial for our history, it will designate a level of reality and a field of intervention for government" (Foucault 2007, 95). Hence, through the work of the physiocrats the modern conception of economy emerged as an autonomous sphere of society and as an object of scientific knowledge in political history. This was highly significant for our conception of good government and, more generally, for our understanding of the political. The establishment of an autonomous and self-regulating economic sphere was not a deliberate political act tactically invoked or initiated by anybody, but this does not mean that it had no political effects. A key aim of Foucault's genealogy is precisely an analysis of these political effects on our social reality.

In terms of contemporary politics, perhaps the most worrying political effect of the autonomy of the economic sphere has been the exclusion of many economic and political decisions from the realm of democratic governance. The identification of policy issues as economic rather than as social, cultural, or political means that they are understood as morally and politically neutral and can therefore be removed from democratic decision-making processes to the exclusive territory of economic experts and financial institutions. As neoliberal governmentality spreads, this depoliticization of the social realm becomes more pronounced because a key feature of neoliberal governmentality is the potentially unlimited expansion of the economic: it attempts to bring all aspects of life under economic rationality. Its key aim is not the creation of free market economy, but free market society.

Foucault shows in his lectures how the Chicago School economists took this idea to the extreme. They found that the generalization of the economic form of the market to the whole of society functioned effectively as a grid of intelligibility and as a principle of decipherment for social relationships and individual behavior. It was possible to reveal in traditionally noneconomic processes, relations, and behavior a number of formal and intelligible relations (Foucault 2008, 243–45). Economy was no longer one domain among others with its own particular rationality, it was increasingly understood as the rationality of the entirety of human action.[12] An essential feature of neoliberal governmentality is not just the eradication of market regulation, for example, but, more fundamentally, the eradication of the border between the social and the economic: market rationality—cost-benefit calculation—must be extended and disseminated to all institutions and social practices. Every social practice and policy—not only economic policy—must be submitted to economic profitability analyses and organized according to the principles of competition.

Foucault's lectures importantly question the common perception of neoliberalism as a lack of government. He insists that it is a specific governmental form and doctrine that aims to create a society organized according to competition. Competition is not a natural phenomenon or a pregiven foundation of society that only has to be allowed to rise to the surface and be discovered. Instead, competition is a formal mechanism that allows inequalities to function in a way that is stimulating for the economy and effective in terms of allocating resources. In other words, a competent government must undertake the task of producing an effective market by means of competition (Foucault 2008, 120–21). While the key problem in the liberalism of Adam Smith in the eighteenth century had been to cut out a free space for the market within an already given political society, the problem of neoliberalism was rather how the overall exercise of political power could be modeled on the principles of a market economy. It was a question not of freeing an empty space, but of taking the formal principles of a market economy and projecting them onto the general art of government (ibid., 131). "Neoliberalism should not therefore be identified with laissez-faire, but rather with permanent vigilance, activity, and intervention" (ibid., 132). It is an intervening liberalism: it has to intervene everywhere in order to create effective competition in free markets and to actively oppose all inferior methods of coordinating individual efforts, such as central planning. Planning is required, but it has to be planning for competition, not instead of it.[13]

Hence, even if we accept Fraser's claim that the cultural/economic distinction characterizes capitalist societies as opposed to precapitalist ones, we have to ask how the dividing line between the two spheres has shifted in contemporary society dominated by neoliberal governmentality and the rapid expansion of the economic sphere and its market rationality. Is the distinction still theoretically meaningful when everything, from the quality of the care a mother gives to her child to the production of knowledge, can be, and increasingly must be, viewed as an economic matter? What are the political effects of this expansion of the economic? Neoliberal governmentality effectively undermines the relative autonomy of all, but the economic domain. It entails the erosion of social practices, political activities, and institutions that are not organized along market rationalities, but are based instead on moral values and political ideals, for example. When all political decisions are submitted to "value-neutral" economic assessment, forms of radical politics, including feminist politics, become meaningless.

Perhaps the greatest political challenge neoliberalism presents to feminist politics therefore concerns the extension of the economic realm itself. We have to study critically the political processes and the criteria that determine the allocation of social issues in the spheres of the cultural and the economic rather than just accepting this distinction as a politically neutral tool. Feminist resistance to neoliberalism would ultimately have to mean deliberately pushing back the encroachment of the social by the economic with a broader vision of politics and of the good life. The feminist response to neoliberalism cannot therefore be limited to issues of economic redistribution: how wealth can be distributed more evenly among the sexes, for example. We must also raise more fundamental questions about the limits of the markets and of economic rationality itself. Feminist theory and politics should form a strong and vocal strand in the public, political, and moral debate on the acceptable limits of the markets—a debate our societies acutely need today.

One area in which such feminist debate must be central is sexuality. While second-wave feminism was initially almost unanimously opposed to all forms of sex work, condemning it as a form of patriarchal domination or even male violence, during 1970s and 1980s a feminist position gradually developed that was strongly pro-prostitution. Today feminists are starkly divided between so-called abolitionist and sex workers' rights perspectives. Abolitionists generally identify prostitution with the selling of the body and consequently of the self. It is a self-estranging activity destructive of woman's humanity.[14] This position is countered by sex workers' rights advocates, who insist that what is sold in prostitution is not the body, but a service, and that what a client pays for is a sex worker's time and not indiscriminate access to her body. They criticize the abolitionist position as moralizing and utopian: the best way to protect vulnerable women is not to eradicate the market for sex by legislative means, but to use political power to organize that market in a way that makes it safer and less exploitative for sex workers. Sex work must be understood essentially as a service sector job determined by the operative conditions of the labor market as well as other factors regulating the supply and demand of sexual services. As Wendy Chapkis (1997, 82), for example, argues, viewing erotic labor as a form of service work is less grand and poetic than imagining the prostitute's soul in mortal danger through the commodification of its most intimate aspects, but such formulation has the advantage of pointing critics in the direction of practical interventions such as workplace organizing and broader political campaigns to increase the status and respect accorded to those performing the labor.[15]

While the economic approach has undoubtedly made it easier to recognize and analyze the specific forms of exploitation that sex workers face, we should nevertheless be wary of how such feminist position converges with neoliberal governmentality—the expansion of market rationality to all areas of life. While in Fraser's schema pornography and prostitution are still understood, not only as economic issues, but importantly also as cultural harms that require remedies of recognition, in neoliberal governmentality they must be treated solely as economic issues concerned with adequate working conditions, toughening markets, and forms of entrepreneurial conduct. As one of the call girls interviewed in Chapkis's book states, the most serious impediments to a sex worker's success are "dysfunctional behavior and limited investments skills" (Chapkis 1997, 102). The sex workers' rights position thus operates according to the same economic logic as neoliberalism aiming to only ameliorate the destructive effects of free markets through the implementation of labor regulations. It is therefore important to consider how such a purely economic approach to sex work may contribute to the increasing difficulty of raising critical questions about the moral limits of markets—the fundamental question of what we as society believe should be for sale. If part of the appeal of the free markets lies in the fact that "markets do not wag fingers," I believe that there are new reasons to insist that feminist politics must, in many instances, continue to do so.[16]

I am thus suggesting that feminists must continue to critically question sex work, however, they should not do so from a universalist moral perspective concerned with static female subjects and their natural and fundamental human rights. As feminist research has demonstrated, sex worker's subjectivities are complex and do not easily fit into the binaries between forced/voluntary, victim/free agent, active/passive. From a Foucauldian perspective, their subjectivities too have to be examined in relation to the governmental rationalities, power relations, discursive regimes, and juridical norms that constitute them. It is also important to note how human rights discourse can cut both ways: abolitionists are opposed to prostitution because they view it as a violation of women's human rights, but the sex workers' rights advocates utilize human rights discourse too when arguing that states' attempts to criminalize sex work or penalize sex workers is a denial of the human right to self-determination to those who make an individual choice to enter prostitution.[17]

A critical feminist perspective on sex work thus does not have to fall back on universalist human rights discourse, but, in the context of neoliberal governmentality, sex work should be approached as an issue concerned with the politically constituted and contestable limits of the markets. While I acknowledge that particular forms of rights discourse might well have strategic utility in the political contestation of the power of the markets, ultimately we need more radical political tools than human rights in order to fundamentally contest our current neoliberal governmentality.[18]

In sum, while in Marxist and socialist analyses neoliberalism is often seen just as an intensification of capitalism, it is in fact a distinctive organizing principle for both economic and social life. As Wendy Brown writes, the political rationality of neoliberalism could be read as issuing from a stage of capitalism that simply underscores Marx's argument that capital penetrates and transforms every aspect of life—remaking everything in its image and reducing every activity and value to its cold rationale. However, such analysis would not bring into view the form of governmentality neoliberalism replaces and the new form it inaugurates. Neither would it expose the modalities of resistance neoliberalism renders outmoded and those that must be developed if it is to be effectively challenged (Brown 2005, 44–45).

While I have attempted to argue that Foucault's thought provides us with valuable tools for the acute diagnostic task that the rise of neoliberalism presents for critical inquiry, I acknowledge, however, that his thought alone will be inadequate for the prescriptive task that must follow—for the political project of designing and promoting alternative rationalities for the regulation of the practices through which we are governed and govern ourselves. In addition to far-reaching environmental politics, radical Marxist-feminist projects might well prove themselves invaluable for that task. Nevertheless, I hope to have shown that we cannot simply return to socialist or Marxist feminisms as if poststructuralism had never happened, nor can we simply complement them with the merely cultural politics of poststructuralism. We face new challenges that have to be met with the sharpest political and theoretical tools that we have at our disposal. Foucault's thought should remain one of those tools.

9

Feminist Politics of Inheritance

Sisterhood was a crucial concept for the political aims of the second-wave feminist movement, but today it seems evident that while some of us are still feminists, we are no longer sisters. The problems of this notion quickly became evident: sisterhood took for granted the commonality of women's experience, while hiding the differences associated with class, race, sexuality, and age. African-American feminists, for example, quickly exposed the hypocrisy and dishonesty of those white feminists who advocated solidarity among women while remaining complacent to privileges following from race and class.[1] The rise of postmodernism and poststructuralism as the dominant theoretical paradigms in feminist theory further undermined the idea of women as a collective political identity. Gender became a historically contingent and resignifiable fiction arduously maintained by an ongoing performance. It was not a fixed foundation for a shared political destiny, but only one of the normalizing axes constitutive of subjectivity. The charge was that, to the extent that feminist theory adhered to a founding and exclusive preoccupation with women and feminism, it entrenched itself as a conservative barrier to critical political theory and practice (Brown 2005, 132).[2] The "new" or "third-wave" feminists thus had to move away from an exclusive focus on women and engage with emerging interdisciplinary fields such as queer studies, animal studies, and critical race theory in order to build alliances with other excluded "others."

This development in feminist theory was generally welcomed as a sign of maturity, but the idea of simply abandoning the political ideals animating sisterhood—solidarity and shared political responsibility among women—also created a great deal of anxiety and bitter debate among feminists. In the "essentialism debates" that characterized feminist philosophy through the 1990s, a key concern was the very possibility of feminist politics once the existence of women as a collective political identity was called into question.[3] As Kate Soper succinctly expressed the problem: "Feminism, like any other politics, has always implied a banding together, a movement based on the solidarity and sisterhood of women, who are linked by perhaps very little else than their sameness and 'common cause' as women. If this sameness itself is challenged on the ground that there is no 'presence' of womanhood, nothing that the term 'woman' immediately expresses, and nothing instantiated concretely except particular women in particular situations, then the idea of a political community built around women—the central aspiration of the early feminist movement—collapses" (Soper 1990, quoted in Mouffe 1992, 381).

To forestall such a fatal collapse, feminist political theorists developed sophisticated arguments for rethinking women as a collective, political identity. The guiding idea in most of these feminist reformulations has been that we have to let go of fixed identity and the sameness of women as a normalizing and exclusionary fiction, yet maintain the category of women as a strategically necessary platform for a shared political project. Chantal Mouffe (1992, 373), for example, argued that accepting that social identities are essentially unstable discursive structures does not mean that we cannot retain notions such as "women" as a signifier referring to a collective identity. She suggests that once the existence of a common essence has been discarded, the status of such identities as "woman" or "homosexual" must be conceived in terms of what Wittgenstein designated as "family resemblances," and their unity must be seen as "the result of the partial fixation of identities through the creation of nodal points." Precarious forms of identification can be established around the category "women" that provide the necessary basis for feminist identity and feminist struggle.[4]

The rationale for building feminist political coalitions is thus strategic: effective feminist politics requires that women from very different subject-positions are able to come together, build coalitions, and construct a "we" around shared political goals without having to subscribe to a predetermined sameness or communal experience of womanhood. The most important advantage of poststructuralist feminism is "its usefulness for contemporary feminist political practice. Such practice is increasingly a matter of alliances rather than one of unity around a universally shared interest or identity" (Fraser and Nicholson 1990, 35). In other words, feminists should strike up alliances and build coalitions around specific issues, goals, and projects for the sake of political efficacy.

While I share the sense of importance that must animate feminism as an effective political project, my critical concern is that a purely strategic understanding of feminist political identity in fact closely mirrors the current, neoliberal understanding of the subject dominant in our society and discussed in the previous chapters. As several political thinkers have demonstrated, our experiences and relationships in contemporary neoliberal societies have become excessively individualistic and instrumental. For strategic reasons feminism as a political project requires building coalitions across generations, classes, and races. But could we also build coalitions irrespective of their strategic efficacy, purely out of a sense of collective responsibility and solidarity? Has such an idea—that of animating the metaphor of sisterhood—really become both politically dated and theoretically impossible? Has it become impossible to create a sense of political responsibility between women on any other grounds than individual, strategic interests that bind us together only as long as we need each other? Is it possible that such strategic understanding of feminist politics that builds on single issues and an individual sense of empowerment is actually reactionary rather than radical?

As an alternative to the feminist political projects based on single issues and strategic individual interests, I want to investigate theoretically the possibility of building feminist politics on solidarity: a sense of collective political responsibility among women. While the idea of solidarity among women has always been an integral aspect of feminist political projects, after the crisis of identity politics, it has resurfaced as a significant theoretical alternative to shared identity as a basis of feminist politics. As Naomi Scheman (1997, 152–53) writes, "the issue . . . is not who is or is not really whatever, but who can be counted on when they come for any of us: the solid ground is not identity but loyalty and solidarity." The challenge then becomes how to rethink the basis of this feminist solidarity in a way that does not rely on the naturalized identity of woman.[5]

I want to investigate here the idea of feminist solidarity that is not based on the assumed sameness of all women's experience—some idealized and predetermined notion of sisterhood—but on a shared feminist past. The notion of sisterhood implied not only the sameness of the experiences of women, but being "sisters" also suggested the idea of belonging to the same "family"—in other words, a shared inheritance and history. My aim in this chapter is to ask what a feminist politics of inheritance could mean for us today.

It is my contention that such a project requires rethinking the philosophical understanding of history that underlies our political aspirations and commitments, as well as rethinking the conception of the political that is animating feminist projects. I will attempt such a rethinking with the help of Walter Benjamin and Jacques Derrida. Before turning to appropriate their ideas, however, I will begin by considering Wendy Brown's influential argument in *States of Injury* (1995) against a politics based on a shared history of oppression.[6]

Wounded Attachments and the Solace of History

While the dominance of poststructuralism as a theoretical paradigm in gender studies has resulted in a strong emphasis on the contingency of gender and even sex, it has also underscored historicity: history must be understood as fundamentally constitutive of our subjectivity as well as of our social ontology. This means that we are not simply the products or effects of the past, but our subjectivities carry sedimentations of a collective history that bind us together whether we like it or not. Our identities as women and as feminists are the unwanted inheritance of sexism that lies beyond any notion of personal choice. In a poststructuralist theoretical framework we could thus consistently argue that a shared past constitutes at least some grounds for an attempt to construct a shared political identity that stretches beyond single issues.

However, Wendy Brown's *States of Injury: Power and Freedom in Late Modernity* (1995) presents a powerful argument against any such attempt. Her key claim is that feminist attachment to the identity of "woman" that is constituted by its history of oppression necessarily leads to political impotence and defeatism. She appropriates Nietzsche's idea of *ressentiment* to argue against turning toward a history of suffering as a source of collective identity. For Nietzsche, *ressentiment* names an attempt to displace suffering by reworking the pain into a negative form of action, an imaginary revenge. The revenge is achieved by establishing suffering as the measure of social virtue and by casting strength and good fortune as self-recriminating. Revenge thus becomes a substitute for the capacity to act, and it produces an identity that is both bound to the history that produced it and a reproach to the present. The subject constituted and structured by *ressentiment* necessarily becomes invested in its own subjection because thereby recognition is acquired. This recognition is predicated on injury, only this injury is now righteously reevaluated (ibid., 70).

Hence, while politicized identities such as "woman" and "homosexual" present themselves as pure self-affirmation, Brown's contention is that on closer analysis they reveal themselves to be structured by *ressentiment*: they are predicated on injury and require their sustained rejection by a "hostile external world" (Brown 1995, 70). As a protest against marginalization and subordination, a politicized identity becomes firmly attached to its own exclusion: an understanding of sustained and unfair suffering becomes a basis for one's sense of who one is. Identity is "premised on this exclusion for its very existence as identity, and its formation as exclusion also crucially augments the suffering entailed in subordination by finding a site of blame for it" (ibid., 73–74).

Identity politics structured by *ressentiment* can only reverse the structure of blame without genuinely subverting it. An investment and reliance on a shared history of suffering as a basis of an identity "breed a politics of recrimination and rancour, of culturally dispersed paralysis and suffering, a tendency to reproach power rather than aspire to it, to disdain freedom rather than practice it" (Brown 1995, 55). Brown's contention is that identity politics is thus necessarily characterized by a debilitating paradox: the past cannot be redeemed unless the identity of women ceases to be invested in it, and women's identity cannot cease to be invested in the past without women giving up their identity (ibid., 73). Feminist identity politics thus shows how political resistance ends up reifying the very structures and identities that it opposes.

Brown suggests that we need to transform our wounded investments and fashion a more radically democratic and emancipatory political culture. This requires paying attention to Nietzsche's counsel on the virtues of forgetting: if identity structured by *ressentiment* resubjugates itself through investment in its own pain, then memory is the house of this activity. It is therefore necessary to engage in a Nietzschean "forgetting of this history, in the pursuit of an emancipatory democratic project" (Brown 1995, 55). What such a forgetting would entail is not very clear in Brown's account, however. Immediately after suggesting it, she acknowledges that counseling feminists just to forget might seem "inappropriate if not cruel" (ibid.). She reformulates the challenge as an attempt to "configure a political culture that could remember without longing for a revenge," that would keep guard "against abetting the steady slide of political into therapeutic discourse, even as we acknowledge the elements of suffering and healing we might be negotiating" (ibid., 75).

She ends her attack against feminist identity politics based on a shared history of suffering by advocating a politics that would supplant the language of "I am"—with its defensive closure of identity and its insistence on the fixity of position—with the language of "I want this for us." Similar to Mouffe, Brown thus wants to rescue feminist politics by premising it on shared future goals, not on a shared past. In her view, this is an "I want" that "distinguishes itself from a liberal expression of self-interest by virtue of its figuring of a political or collective good as its desire" (Brown 1995, 75). She thus anticipates and defends her position against the charge of neoliberal individualism which I raised earlier by insisting that the future goals "I want for us" are not dictated by liberal self-interest. Rather, they are collective political goods.

But even if I want a collective or political good instead of a purely selfish good, it is still difficult to see how in Brown's political future anything but self-interest would bind women together to fight for these goods. Our political commitments can only be conceived of in voluntarist terms in the vocabulary of "want" since we have discarded any notion of binding identity, as well as having been cured from *ressentiment* by letting go of the memory of our shared suffering. I can join the feminist coalition when something that I value or want is on the menu, but ultimately there is nothing other than individual interest binding me together with other women.

In addition to her main argument, which focuses on feminist political strategy, Brown objects to the idea of a politics premised on a shared past on the grounds that such an idea relies on a faulty philosophy of history. She contends that we have to acknowledge that our late modern understanding of history itself has been rapidly changing: history has disintegrated as an intelligible narrative and as a coherent category. She refers to Foucault and argues that history's presumed continuity and objectivist foundation have effectively been refuted, and history has become a force with no direction, a war without end. "We know ourselves to be saturated by history, we feel the extraordinary force of its determinations; we are also steeped in a discourse of its insignificance, and above all, we know that history will no longer . . . act as our redeemer" (Brown 1995, 71).

It is my contention that Brown's brief turn to the philosophy of history is crucial and contains a solution to her problem. I suggest that we have to investigate the following questions: Instead of simply forgetting and letting go of our "wounded attachments," could feminists rethink our relationship to history in a way that was more conducive to forms of feminist solidarity? More specifically, could the dispersal of history as an intelligible narrative of progress signal a rethinking that could redeem our politics against the charges of *ressentiment*? What if our history of oppression was understood as nonlinear, multidirectional, and fragmented?

Benjamin and History as Remembrance

One of the seminal thinkers who raised our suspicion about history as a linear narrative was Walter Benjamin. Benjamin's engagement with the philosophy of history was an acute acknowledgment of how our understanding of history is inevitably interconnected with our conception of the political.[7] His radical critique of Enlightenment philosophies of time was a direct response to what he perceived as the failure of the social democratic movement prominent in Germany at the time to stand up to the rise of fascism. Theses X–XIII of his famous "Theses on the Philosophy of History" engage in a critique of social democracy, which is criticized not only for its political and economic conformism, but also and most seriously, for its commitment to the conception of history as progress. "One reason why Fascism has a chance is that in the name of progress its opponents treat it as a historical norm" (Benjamin 1992, 249). Because the social democratic politicians had simply capitulated to fascism, it was now urgent to find "a conception of history that avoids any complicity with the thinking to which these politicians continue to adhere" (ibid., 250). The political vision capable of opposing fascism had to be much more radical than social democracy; its critical edge would extend all the way down to our philosophy of time and conception of history.

For Benjamin, the problem with the idea of progress was that it presupposed the determining presence of a teleology, a pregiven goal toward which we were inevitably moving. It was thus based on a deterministic conception of history that overlooked the singularity of historical events. It also obviated the Marxist idea of the importance of conflict as the inherent condition for the movement of history, as well as masking the fact that history was always a narrative by the victors.[8] Most problematically, however, the idea of progress functioned as an unsurpassable justification for the status quo. Pernicious political conservatism could be validated through the narrative of continuous improvement: under the prevailing constellation of power relations things had improved and would continue to improve in a continuous and predictable way. Benjamin believed that the social democratic movement shared the technocratic ideology of fascism—its unwavering belief in the inevitable technological progress of mankind. This ideology had preserved the hegemony of the ruling class, as they were in control of the technological means of production. "Nothing has corrupted the German working class as much as the notion that it is moving with the current. It regarded technological developments as the fall of the stream with which it thought it was moving" (Benjamin 1992, 250).

Benjamin's attack in the "Theses" also targets two central features of traditional historiography. First, he was skeptical of the idea that history could be written as a continuous narrative such as the idea of progress presupposes. It could not amount to "telling the sequence of events like the beads of a rosary" (Benjamin 1992, 254). The historian who forces the past into a historical continuum, a coherent narrative, ignores the singularity of historical events and overlooks those minor events that do not support the status quo. History thus becomes a selective process of forgetting. For Benjamin, history must instead become an instrument of remembrance capable of rupturing and undermining the consistency of the comforting narratives that we tell ourselves: the task of the "historical materialist" is to blast open the continuum of history (ibid.). Similar to the Foucauldian genealogist, the historical materialist must construct counterhistories and "brush history against the grain" (ibid., 248).

Second, Benjamin was critical of positivist or objectivist historiography: the idea that history provides us with a neutral account of objective facts that the historian simply discovers and records. Such an endeavor is based on a completely false conception of time as homogeneous and empty. Benjamin insisted that time cannot be filled like an empty container with historical facts, processes, and events. Time does not move on, mechanically and indifferently. Julian Roberts (1982, 206) explains Benjamin's distinction between clock time and calendar time by noting that clock time continues indefinitely, forever accommodating, indifferently, the events that fall into it. The time marked by calendars, however, does not just roll on mechanically. Rather it punctuates existence with "days of remembrance," moments that gather up time into points of concentration. On the day of remembrance things remembered suddenly become topical and reenter existence in the moment of recollection. This, Benjamin argues, is the proper character of time and not the regular ticking of clocks that levels all events into an indifferent continuum. History is not a collection of empty time containers waiting to be filled with a mass of facts, nor is it the cold advance of infinite progress, but rather "the sudden pause of impassioned recollection."

While objectivist historiography attempts to give us "the eternal image of the past," Benjamin's historical materialist must supply us with "a unique experience" with the past (ibid., 254). Through remembrance, we can have an experience with the past that is momentary and unique, as opposed to an experience of the past as complete and eternally present to us. To understand the past historically thus does not "mean to recognize it 'the way it really was.'" Instead, one must "seize hold of a memory as it flashes up" (ibid). It is not enough to *know* history; we have to have an experience with history that is capable of changing the present, of changing who we are. The past must be an active partner, not the passive object of our experience.

Benjamin's monadic theory of time is thus a profound critique of the idea of time as an absolute and objective continuum. Yet its perhaps most contested and original feature is the idea of a messianic interruption: the possibility of a complete, revolutionary break with all previous history.[9] The messianic indicates a temporality of politics that defies all forms of historical determinism. History harbors unforeseeable breaks and ruptures and politics cannot become an attempt to fulfill our "true destiny" because the expectations we have concerning our future are never realized as such.

However, if the messianic signals an absolute discontinuity between the past and the present, between the conditions of our present historical existence and those that will follow after the radical interruption, it also seems to imply problematic consequences for political action, especially regarding the idea of a politics of inheritance. Does the possibility of a radical rupture between the present and the past not in fact cut us completely loose from the past? Does it not promise the end of time or a moment of redemption that will one day make history whole and complete?

While commentators often emphasize the messianic as indicating the possibility of a completely new world, Benjamin significantly introduced the idea of "a weak messianic power" in Thesis II. This weak messianic power is crucially orientated not toward an unforeseen future, but toward the past.

> The past carries with it a temporal index by which it is referred to redemption. Doesn't a breath of the air that pervades earlier days caress us as well? In the voices we hear, isn't there an echo of the silent ones? Don't the women we court have sisters they no longer recognize? If so, then there is a secret agreement between past generations and the present one. Then our coming was expected on earth. Then, like every generation that preceded us, we have been endowed with a weak messianic power, a power on which the past has a claim. That claim cannot be settled cheaply. (Benjamin 1992, 389–90)

Weak messianic power can be understood as the redemptive power of memory: memory can bear the traces of historical suffering. Similar to a strong power, such as a revolution, weak messianic power also suggests an attempt to break with the past, but by means of redeeming the past through remembrance. The past makes a claim on us insofar as it is marked by an incompleteness, which persists into the present: the past transmits injustices and unrealized possibilities into the present. The present must bear these injustices because the past has a claim on us: we are the possibility of its redemption. In this sense "we have been expected on earth": we are not able to change the past, but we have the unique ability to remember it. As Jürgen Habermas (1987, 14) writes in his illuminative essay on Benjamin, Benjamin ascribed to all past epochs a horizon of unfulfilled expectations, and to the present he assigned the task of experiencing this corresponding past through remembering in such a way that we can fulfill its expectations with our weak messianic power.

Benjamin recorded his exchange with Max Horkheimer on the issue of the completeness of history in Convolute N of *The Arcades Project*.[10] Horkheimer had argued that Benjamin's idea of the incompleteness of history was idealistic if completeness was not included in it. In other words, we have to acknowledge that past injustices really occurred and were thus completed: "The slain are really slain" (Benjamin 2002, 471). Taking Benjamin's idea seriously could only lead to theology: "If one takes the lack of closure entirely seriously, one must believe in the Last Judgement" (ibid.). Horkheimer suggested that Benjamin should make a distinction between positive and negative events in history. Horkheimer would thus be prepared to accept a modified version of Benjamin's view in which only positive events and experiences, such justice and joy, remained incomplete. The negative events, on the other hand—injustice, horror, and suffering—had to have a different relation to time: these events were irreparable and thus complete. One had to accept this because to believe anything else would be "idealistic." Ultimately, all human suffering was sealed by death.

Benjamin responded to Horkheimer's criticism by making an important distinction between history as a science and as a form of remembrance: "The correlative to this line of thinking may be found in the consideration that history is not simply a science but also and not least a form of remembrance. What science has 'determined,' remembrance can modify. Such mindfulness can make the incomplete (happiness) into something complete, and the complete (suffering) into something incomplete" (ibid). In other words, while the horrendous facts of history have really happened and cannot be erased or denied, history does not simply record them the way science would. History must also be a form of remembrance binding us to these events of the past, yet in a relationship that remains open and allows or even forces us to have a transformative experience with it. The past only exists in remembrance and only through remembrance can it be redeemed in the sense that the suffering and injustice it carries is not completed, sealed, and forgotten. Each generation bears the responsibility not only for the fate of future generations, but also for the fate suffered by past generations.

Thus, regarding politics, remembrance does not amount to a simple act of restitution—setting past injustices right. Because the past is and remains essentially incomplete, we cannot complete it by somehow making things right now, once and for all. The past cannot be fully possessed or completed by the present. Something of it always escapes the present, leaving it an incomplete task. However, politics becomes essentially a project that is not only directed to the future, but also, significantly, to the past. It becomes a project haunted by ghosts.

Derrida and the Ghosts of the Past

Derrida's book *Specters of Marx* is based on two lectures that he gave in 1993 at a conference concerned with the future of Marxism. Instead of looking forward to the future, Derrida crucially turned to look back and began by suggesting that we must learn to live with ghosts, with those who are no longer present.[11] We must learn to live with them in the name of justice because what we call justice must carry on beyond present life, life as my life or our life: "No justice . . . seems possible or thinkable without the principle of some responsibility, beyond all living present, within that which disjoins the living present, before the ghosts of those who are not yet born and who are already dead . . ." (Derrida 2006, xviii).

This learning to live with ghosts or specters indicates "a politics of memory, of inheritance, and of generations" (Derrida 2006, xviii–xix). Politics is thus not concerned solely with the present or even with the future, but also crucially the past. Not only are we responsible to those with whom we share the world now, but we are also responsible to those not yet born and those who are already dead, "be they the victims of wars, political or other kinds of violence, nationalist, racist, colonialist, sexist, or other kinds of exterminations, victims of oppressions of capitalist imperialism or any of the forms of totalitarianism" (ibid., xviii).

For Derrida, doing justice to the dead requires coping with two difficult aspects essential to any inheritance. First, he insists that a politics of inheritance can only be built on the acknowledgment that an inheritance is always radically and necessarily heterogeneous. The heterogeneity of past legacies opens them up to multiple receptions, none of which can be predicted in advance. This implies a second difficulty, namely that we are both active and passive in relation to our heritage. Inheritance is something that is violently imposed on us, and yet we must make a choice regarding our response to it. "An inheritance is never gathered together, it is never one with itself. Its presumed unity, if there is one, can consist only in the injunction to reaffirm by choosing. . . . If the readability of a legacy were given, natural, transparent, univocal, if it did not call for and at the same time defy interpretation, we would never have anything to inherit from it. We would be affected by it as by a cause—natural or genetic" (Derrida 2006, 18).

Derrida insists that one never chooses to inherit—inheritance is a relation within which one always finds oneself. However, while emphasizing this, he also denies that inheritance would be a purely passive enterprise in which whatever comes is accepted. "Inheritance is never a *given*, it is always a task" (Derrida 2006, 67). A legacy implies the injunction "to reaffirm by choosing" in one's response to it. Derrida also uses the notions of filtering, sifting, criticizing, and sorting. In other words, certain elements of a tradition will be conserved only if others are forgotten and ignored. As Samir Haddad (2013, 27) observes in his seminal study of Derrida's conception of inheritance, legacies conjoin necessity and choice in a very specific way. As finite beings, we can never place any parts of a legacy forever outside our limits, beyond any possibility of recovery. While reaffirming a legacy is thus not a choice in the sense that a legacy violently elects us and even ignoring or denying a legacy is a way of reaffirming it, Derrida nevertheless insists that there are different ways that this reaffirming can be carried out. There is an active dimension of inheritance in which the heir has a role to play in making a difference to what is transmitted. Hence, while there is much that is necessary in inheritance, at the same time choices can be made in how one receives legacies from the past.

Haddad (2013, 38–39) also emphasizes that the temporal structure of an inheritance cannot be reduced to a linear temporality, because of the curious interchangeability of the past and the future embedded in an inheritance. It originates in the past, but because it is always a task, it also remains before us. Similar to Benjamin, Derrida insists that the time of inheritance is one of disrupted linearity: inheritance can be located just as much in what is to come as in what has already been. As a task, an inheritance can never be simply set right or erased through our actions because all attempts to do so will only produce a trace as their necessary consequence, ghosts that live on.

Derrida's key problem in *Specters of Marx* is how to interpret Marx's texts in a way that does justice to the critical project at their core, and I will not attempt to investigate or take a stance on this issue. However, in a somewhat parallel manner, I want to ask now what it means to be a feminist in relation to the legacy of feminism. What is our responsibility to those women already dead because of various forms of sexism and gendered violence, for example? What is the significance of a specifically *feminist* remembrance?

Toward a Feminist Politics of Inheritance

Whereas Brown argues that the past, irreversibly marked by suffering, cannot be redeemed unless women cease to invest their identity in it, I want to insist on the possibility of redemption in such an investment. Any attempt to move the debate on the future of feminism to purely strategic ground will remain problematic because to operate effectively in the present or the future we have to think through our relationship to the past. We have to confront the task that is our feminist inheritance.

As Brown argues, history itself has become dispersed, fragmentary, and multidirectional. Its fragmentary nature means, however, that it is not a monotonous narrative of oppression, suffering, and powerlessness; rather if we "brush it against the grain," it also shows radically different pictures of courage, solidarity, and strength. These counterhistories do not constitute an identity structured by *ressentiment*, but by pride and a sense of belonging. If we accept the claim that history cannot be told as a narrative, but instead has to be experienced as an ongoing task, the legacy of feminism could be a source of strength and solidarity. The past does not determine our being, but leaves radically open both the final shape of our identity as well as our future. The goals and outcomes of feminist politics cannot be defined or predetermined by any imaginary continuum of history. We are not simply the anticipated outcome of a sealed history of suffering, but feminist politics is precisely the possibility of the radical disruption of our history.

Just as there is no single Marxist legacy, there is no single feminist legacy, but rather several. Feminist politics must acknowledge the radical heterogeneity of the tradition from which it emerges. We cannot turn to the past in order to find a definitive account of the essential nature of ourselves or of our present. Fidelity to feminism or solidarity with the victims of sexist oppression does not mean adopting a fixed legacy. It requires having to choose between differing, often incompatible, interpretations of our history while acknowledging the limits and the fallibility of that choice. The past will not provide a revelation of our being. We have to work to break its determining power, toward blasting the causal continuum of our history of oppression. And yet we must also remember.

As Horkheimer insists, the slain are really slain. In other words, no matter how far toward freedom and equality women have come today, countless women have nevertheless died and suffered needlessly: they have been battered to death in their own homes, raped, and sexually abused; they have died of illegal abortions or preventable diseases simply because they were women. Nothing we do today can alter these facts or make them right. Nevertheless, if we follow Benjamin's idea of history as remembrance, then this suffering is never complete in the sense that its meaning cannot be altered. It cannot be altered by us through some heroic act of restitution, but it can be altered *in* us. It is not important just to *know* our history; we have to have an experience *with* it, an experience that is able to transform us and disturb our present. The dead have a claim on us that cannot be settled cheaply. How we are going to redeem their suffering is obviously not an easy task, but it is nevertheless the task of a feminist politics of memory, inheritance, and generations. To use Derrida's language of ghosts, the ghosts of the past will continue to unsettle and disrupt the present. They will not lay quiet or settle into our conceptual frameworks and historical narratives, but will continue to haunt us in the sense of both connecting us to the past and of disrupting and opening the present to the future.

I want to conclude with a thought experiment. In order to imagine what a feminist politics of inheritance would mean, ask yourself this: If, one fine day, we lived in that utopian society in which the rigid markers of sex and gender had finally disappeared along with all the oppressive structures and hierarchical power relations based on them, would our debt to the dead then be settled? Could the legacy of feminism then be erased and forgotten? Would the ghosts then lie quietly? Benjamin's insistence on the incompleteness of history is crucial because it means that the past, our shared history of sexist oppression, for example, can never be simply laid to rest. The ghosts of the past generations are always with us, disrupting the complacency of our narratives of progress and disturbing any settled sense of who we are. Acknowledging this does not imply victimhood, *ressentiment*, or revenge. It implies an incompleteness of our identity that at the same time is the possibility of our belonging. The challenge is to find ways of acting politically that acknowledge the weak messianic power with which we are endowed and to struggle to utilize that power for redemption—in other words, for remembrance, the only kind of redemption possible on earth.

Notes

Introduction

1. See, for example, Foucault 1988a, 95.
2. See, for example, Foucault 1988b, 257; 1992, 14–24.
3. See, for example, Hekman 1990; Bigwood 1991; McNay 1991.
4. It is a matter of intense debate as to what extent Foucault's position changes between his archaeological and genealogical phases. While some commentators see archaeology as a form of structuralism and emphasize a radical break between archaeology and genealogy, others insist on the profound continuities of Foucault's project. See, for example, Dreyfus and Rabinow 1982; Han-Pile 2002; Oksala 2005.
5. See, for example, Merleau-Ponty 1994, 170.
6. Most feminists acknowledge not only the difficulty, but also the undesirability of defining feminist philosophy too strictly. Linda Martin Alcoff and Eva Feder Kittay (2007, 8), for example, suggest that it should be understood as an open research program or an area of inquiry within philosophy that consists of set of questions rather than a particular set of propositions or shared methodological commitments. In this way it would be analogous to other research areas within the discipline of philosophy such as epistemology, for example, which poses questions about knowledge while precluding any consensus among epistemologists over how to define knowledge. Allison M. Jaggar and Iris Marion Young (1998, 2) make a similar point. They acknowledge that although feminism certainly presupposes a substantive ethical or political commitment to opposing women's subordination, this commitment is too indeterminate to entail specific answers to most philosophical questions.
7. Feminist philosophers have revealed the deep-seated sexism in the history of philosophy and thereby forced philosophy to reexamine its self-understanding as a universal and value-neutral form of inquiry. See, for example, Lloyd 1984; Irigaray 1985a; Le Doeuff 1991.

Chapter 1

1. See, for example, the Academy of Finland, report on "The State and Quality of Scientific Research in Finland 2012."
2. Compare to Lowe 1998, 5.

3. See, for example, Fraser and Nicholson 1990; Butler 1992.

4. For some definitive accounts, see, for example, Elshtain 1981; Lloyd 1984; Irigaray 1985b; Beauvoir 1988.

5. The term "ontology" was introduced by Christian Wolff in the eighteenth century to give a name to a branch of metaphysics alongside cosmology, psychology, and theology concerned with the study of being in general. In contemporary use it is often used as a synonym for metaphysics as the systematic study of the ultimate nature of reality. The word "ontology" harbors an ambiguity, however: it refers both to the fundamental order of reality and to the study of this fundamental order. The famous metaphysical debates on modernity take issue precisely with this ambiguity in different ways, for example, while Kant's solution was to establish the separation between the noumenal and phenomenal worlds, Nietzsche's attack against metaphysics denied the possibility of any objective ontology at all.

6. The acknowledgment of the inevitable connection between ontology and politics has taken center stage in political philosophy in recent decades. The importance of ontological inquiry in political philosophy is often established through an emphasis on the distinction between "politics" and "the political": political science deals with the empirical field of "politics," whereas political philosophy is not about the facts of politics, it is about the nature of "the political." See, for example, Mouffe 2005, 8–9. For an overview of the conceptual difference between "politics" and "the political," see Marchart 2007.

7. Gilles Deleuze's thought in particular has been enthusiastically received and appropriated by many feminist thinkers. It has been understood to provide a way of radically reconceptualizing some of the fundamental concepts and categories that organize our thought. For some recent feminist appropriations of Deleuze's thought, see, for example, Olkowski 1999; Braidotti 2002; and Grosz, 2004.

8. Although the Aristotelian conception of metaphysics can be understood to continue mainly in the tradition of analytic philosophy, contemporary analytic philosophy is a diverse tradition and contains many different approaches to metaphysics. As well as debates on ontology, contemporary metaphysical debates deal with topics such as causation and laws of nature, modality, personal identity, free will, and the nature of time. On contemporary debates on metaphysics in analytic philosophy, see, for example, Sider, Hawthorne, and Zimmerman (eds.) 2008. While the Continental tradition can be claimed to mainly follow the Kantian strand in critical ways it also contains attempts to think metaphysics that build on pre-Kantian thinkers such Spinoza.

9. For Kant, this descriptive enterprise is in fact only one aspect of metaphysics, which splits into two parts: speculative metaphysics deals with unanswerable questions about *noumenal*, non-spatio-temporal reality, whereas descriptive metaphysics analyses *phenomenal* reality—existence within the parameters of the space-time world.

10. See, for example, Heidegger 1977; Foucault 1989.

11. See, for example, Longino 1990, 103–32.

12. Luce Irigaray's thought is a pioneering effort to radically rethink meta-

physics. Her criticism of the masculine metaphysics of our Western philosophical tradition and her strategies of destabilizing it from within is a thread that runs through all her works. Because of the multifaceted nature of her work and the commentators varying readings of it, it is not an easy task to pin down Irigaray's position with regards to metaphysics, however. Some commentators read her in the postmodern framework and argue that her project is mainly critical and de-structive of metaphysics. Others emphasize the phenomenological background of her thought and read her as making not metaphysical but experiential claims. Some finally argue that her principle goal is in revisionary metaphysics: to open up an alternative to a metaphysics of substance by thinking an ontology founded on being two. See, for example, Irigaray 1985a, 1985b, 2004.

13. For an excellent discussion of this early work, see Han-Pile 2002. On the parallels between Foucault's thought and Kantian criticism, see, for example, Djaballah 2008; Allen 2010.

14. See, for example, Foucault 1988a, 95.

15. Foucault confirms the centrality of social practices for his thought on numerous occasions. He singles them out as the constant object of his studies: what unites and gives coherence to his always partial and local analyses is that they have the realm of practices as their homogeneous domain of reference. See, for example, Foucault 1991d, 48; 2001, 1512.

16. On the similarities between Foucault and late Wittgenstein, see David-son 1997. Also Thomas Flynn (1994, 30) has compared Foucault's conception of practice to Wittgenstein's concept of game: a practice is shaped in a preconcep-tual, anonymous, socially sanctioned body of rules that govern one's manner of perceiving, judging, imagining, and acting.

17. Derrida's side of this exchange consisted of his critical essay on Fou-cault's *History of Madness*, "Cogito and the History of Madness." See Derrida 1978.

18. Unfortunately some of Veyne's own formulations are suggestive of a mysterious agency granted to practices or even of discursive idealism. He com-pares the process of how practices engender their corresponding objects to how apple trees produce apples, for example. See Veyne 1997, 160.

19. Compare to Butler 1993.

20. Paul Veyne (1994), Thomas Flynn (2005) and Ian Hacking (2002), for example, have all argued that Foucault's historical nominalism is a form of social constructivism. Foucault noted that when it came to thinking about power, one needed to be a nominalist. See Foucault 1978, 93.

21. Cf. Berger and Luckmann 1967; Castoriadis 1987.

22. Even though Foucault thus seems committed to a view that is often called contextualism in the philosophy of science—the social and political con-text of scientific knowledge inevitably shapes its content—it is debatable to what extent he is committed to the view that all scientific truths are equally laden with social and political values, interests, and presuppositions. He clearly held that knowledge was a social practice. All societies have practices and institutions for the production of knowledge, and the development of science is necessarily a social rather than an individual activity. This view does not, however, imply that all theories or pictures of the world are equally true or false: it does not rule out

the possibility of reaching objective truths. Rather than understanding objectivity as independence from all socially formed criteria, we can understand it as an achieved consensus of the (scientific) community. Similarly, reality or the world itself is, at best, a political consensus, never adhered to by all. See, for example, Longino 2002; Hacking 2002.

23. Whereas most practices are based on spatially local and temporally contingent ontological schemas, it is arguable that some ontological assumptions concerning space, time, and substance, for example, could be universal. If they are, they are then, by definition, impossible for us to identify as they form the glasses that we cannot remove.

24. See Oksala 2005, 74–76.

25. See, for example, Foucault 1988b, 257; 1992: 14–24.

26. See, for example, Beauvoir 1988.

Chapter 2

1. A study of female experience would therefore lead to a form of gender essentialism, which Angela Harris, for example, has described as "the notion that a unitary, essential women's experience can be isolated and described independent of race, class, sexual orientation, and other realities of experience" (Harris 1990, 585).

2. Nancy Fraser (1997a, 152–53) elegantly sums up the tripartite ways in which a philosophical conception of discourse can foster more interesting theoretical perspectives. First, it can help us understand how people's social identities are discursively constructed in historically specific social contexts. It can thus be used both to understand social identities in their full sociocultural complexity and to demystify static, single-variable, essentialist views of gender identity. Second, it can help us understand how, under conditions of inequality, social groups are formed and unformed in response to struggles over social discourse. Third, a conception of discourse can illuminate how the cultural hegemony of dominant groups in society is secured and contested. Therefore, it can shed light on the prospects for emancipatory social change and political practice.

3. I refer here to a later version of her essay published in a collection titled *Feminists Theorize the Political* in 1992.

4. Ian Hacking (2002), for example, argues that strict nominalism leaves our interaction with the world, and our description of it, a complete mystery. For him, nominalism about human artifacts presents no problem. We manufacture pencils; that is why they exist. Nominalism about grass, trees, and stars, however, is a problem.

5. For recent critiques of McDowell's position, see, for example, Dreyfus 2005; Schear (ed.) 2012.

6. See Sellars 1997.

7. Linda Alcoff (2000, 46) has appropriated phenomenology to argue that it is not only a metaphysical error to claim that experience and language are co-

extensive, but that the political consequences of such a view are disastrous. She discusses the phenomenology of rape and takes as an example the controversy over the term "date rape" and the ongoing refusal of U.S. state laws to recognize rape within marriage. In connection with these forms of sexual violence, she urges us to consider the political consequences of holding experience and language as coextensive. A position that links experience to discourse too securely might argue that, prior to the discourse of date rape, the experience itself could not occur, or at least not the sort of experience we now associate with date rape. Thus, date rape could be said to be a fiction invented by feminists, which is now having material effects in needlessly traumatizing impressionable, young women. Although it is clear that the changes in discourse have effected changes in the experiences of such traumas, it is also clear that we have more than adequate reason to believe that rapes occurred on dates and in marriages before the 1970s, when these issues first became widely discussed. See also Alcoff and Gray (1993).

8. McDowell holds that we share with animals a perceptual sensitivity to features of our environment, but that we have this capacity in a special, conceptual form. Conceptual thinking is thus not an exemption from nature; rather, it is our special way of living an animal life (ibid., 64–65). Human children are initiated into conceptual capacities through their upbringing, and these capacities become part of their second nature. Human beings are thus not set apart from animals in some "splendidly non-human realm of ideality" (ibid., 88). We are animals, but the kind of animals whose natural being is permeated with rationality (ibid., 85).

9. Sonja Kruks (2001, 139) similarly argues that, for those who suffer domestic violence, it can be an empowering process for experiences to be shared. In presenting their experiences, individuals may come to realize that their own predicament is part of a wider problem and that forms of resistance they have not previously envisaged might be possible.

10. For feminist critiques of Foucault's late work, see, for example, McNay 1992; Soper 1995.

11. See also Sawicki 1991, 44.

12. In his classic work, *One-Dimensional Man* (2002), Herbert Marcuse analyzes a situation in which consumerism, advertising, mass culture, and capitalist ideology integrate subjects effectively into the capitalist system and make them "one-dimensional": subjects have lost their ability for dissent, autonomy, and critical thought; they are content with their lot and unable to perceive any alternative dimension of possibilities that would transcend the present. The system that manufactures, superimposes, and administers their needs presents itself as the best and only possible means of satisfying them.

13. Many feminist phenomenologists discard the transcendental reduction. They usually turn to Merleau-Ponty and reiterate his view on the impossibility of a complete reduction: "The most important lesson which the reduction teaches us is the impossibility of a complete reduction" (Merleau-Ponty 1994, xiv). See, for example, Alcoff 2000; Kruks 2001.

14. See, for example, Steinbock 1995; Zahavi 2001.

Chapter 3

1. See also Alcoff 1996.

2. Alcoff also accuses Foucault of the contrary view, however: Foucault views pleasure as antithetical to power when it is disinvested of dominant discursive meanings. She reiterates the criticism originally advanced by Judith Butler according to which Foucault naively posits pleasure outside of power and discourse. See Butler 1990; Alcoff 2000, 53.

3. See, for example, O'Leary 2009.

4. See also, for example, Foucault 1991b, 116–17; 1991c, 333.

5. On discussions of Foucault's conception of experience, see, for example, Han-Pile 2002; Flynn 2005; Oksala 2005; Djaballah 2008; O'Leary 2009.

6. Kant's transcendental deduction, for example, was an attempt to show, through a purely analytic analysis of experience, the reflexivity of all cognition. All experience had to incorporate self-awareness or reflexivity, and cognition involved a special reflexive act of bringing representations to awareness—the apperception of representation.

7. It has been widely debated whether Foucault succeeds in this project or not. See, for example, Dreyfus and Rabinow 1982; Gutting 1989; Han-Pile 2002; Oksala 2005.

8. On experiential truth in Foucault's thought, see, for example, Prado 2006, 93–96.

9. This question has been extensively discussed by Foucault's critics and commentators. See, for example, Habermas 1987; Fraser 1989.

10. See, for example, Foucault 2000a, 241.

11. See, for example, Kruks 2001.

12. See, for example, Merleau-Ponty 1994, xiii.

Chapter 4

1. The possibility of addressing the question of gender or sexual difference phenomenologically can be denied on the grounds that, in the proper transcendental attitude, all self-interpretations and bodily characteristics of the transcendental ego are bracketed, and in this sense it is incorporeal and above the concrete lifeworld. The true transcendental is universal pure subjectivity understood as consciousness, with its reality status and the reality status of its objects both placed in brackets. I will discuss this objection in more detail in chapter 6. While phenomenologists have been dismissive about the possibility of feminist phenomenology, feminists have also been skeptical of the compatibility of the two projects, claiming that phenomenology is unavoidably universalizing, essentialist, masculinist, and antipolitical. See, for example, Allen 1982–83; Butler 1989.

2. See, for example, Husserl 1970, 133.

3. On Husserl's writings on "the problem of the sexes," see, for example, Husserl 1970, 188; Husserl 1981.

4. Linda Fisher (2000b, 7), for example, defends the feasibility of feminist

phenomenology by arguing that the failure of a given phenomenologist to discuss gender or sexual difference cannot be taken as indicative of the inability of phenomenology itself or of the phenomenological approach to engage such issues. Identifications between the disciple and the discourse, the practice and practitioner, can never be seen as seamless and absolute; otherwise, for example, we would never see any feminist interaction with the traditional disciplines or orientations. The real issue is not whether phenomenologists are able to engage the issue of gender, but whether phenomenology is.

5. Husserl sometimes appears to use the terms interchangeably. In *Ideas I*, however, he distinguishes three inseparable moments in the *noema*: the thetic characteristics, the noematic sense or Sinn and the determinable X. See Husserl 1982, 309–16. The noematic Sinn is the component that determines the sense or the meaning of the object as experienced.

6. It is important to note that even though *noema* is an ideal meaning entity according to the West Coast interpretation, it is not an ideal object—some kind of mental picture or ideal representation standing between our minds and the world out there. *Noemata* carry out the work of achieving intentional relations, but they do not represent external objects in the way words or pictures represent things.

7. For an illuminating account of the differences between the East Coast and West Coast interpretations, see Zahavi 2004.

8. Similarly, in his late work, *The Crisis of European Sciences*, Husserl takes up the problem of language in his analyses of the lifeworld, and again moves it aside rather quickly. There he writes that, after the transcendental reduction has been performed and the lifeworld has become a mere "component" within transcendental subjectivity, words taken from the sphere of the natural attitude become dangerous and "the necessary transformation of their sense must therefore be noticed" (Husserl 1970, 174).

9. Theodore Kisiel gives a detailed account of young Heidegger's lectures in *The Genesis of Heidegger's Being and Time*. My presentation of them here relies considerably on Kisiel's account and his translations. The lectures discussed are *Die Idee der Philosophie und das Weltanschauungsproblem* (1919) and *Grundprobleme der Phänomenologie* (1919/1920). For the German originals, see Heidegger's *Gesamtausgabe*, Heidegger 1999 and 1993.

10. Natorp set forth his critique in *Allgemeine Psychologie nach kritischer Methode* (1912).

Chapter 5

1. See, for example, Young 1990.

2. F. A Elliston (1981, 332) writes in his introduction to the English translation of this fragment that Husserl's taciturnity hardly distinguishes him from most turn-of-the century thinkers, for with the notable exception of Bertrand Russell, none of his contemporaries said anything significant of the subject of sexuality.

3. Husserl seems to have been aware of the necessity of generative investigation even when he does not explicitly develop one. His *Cartesian Meditations*, for example, puts forward an egological account of sense-constitution, but he also claims there that the investigation implies further study to deal with the problems of birth and death, which have not yet been touched on. They belong to a higher dimension and presuppose such a tremendous labor of explication pertaining to the lower spheres that it will be a long time before they can become problems to work on (Husserl 1995, 142). Anthony Steinbock (1995, 4) argues that we do not find fixed, clear-cut stages in Husserl's work, but that there are strains of thought or methodological motivations running throughout, often becoming interwoven with other strains or motivations. When developed systematically and consistently, however, these strains have distinct and irreducible implications.

4. Steinbock develops a phenomenology of the social world on the basis of Husserl's writings in his book *Home and Beyond* (1995). He argues that in Husserl's *Nachlaß* we find a novel dimension of phenomenology being explored and anticipated, a dimension he refers to with the expression "generativity" (*Generativität*). It captures matters such as birth and death, language and tradition. Generative problems entail a dimension of sense-constitution that takes place historically, geologically, and intersubjectively. Generative phenomenology does not begin with individual consciousness in arriving at the universal structures of experience, but takes as its departure the generative structure of homeworld/alienworld. The homeworld and the alienworld become constitutive conditions for the possibility of sense emergence, and these conditions are themselves formative of subjectivity.

5. Judith Butler has famously argued for this point in her book *Gender Trouble*. See Butler 1990.

6. See, for example, Kaplan and Rogers 1990.

7. This understanding of the subject is one of the nodal points of the poststructuralist critique of phenomenology. Michel Foucault, for example, argues in *The Order of Things* that, while modern thought has focused on the thinking subject as the precondition of knowledge, the modern cogito—for example, Husserl's transcendental ego—is not any more transparent to itself. It cannot reduce the whole being of things to thought in the way Descartes' cogito could without "ramifying the being of thought right down to the inert network of what does not think" (Foucault 1989, 324). The cogito cannot provide epistemic immediacy and self-certainty because there are prereflective conditions of knowledge, which obfuscate the evident truths of reflection. Modern subjectivity is permeated by an unthought which eludes reflection, but which nevertheless must determine the ways of questioning it.

8. The task is to make explicit through reflection something that, by definition, eludes reflection. Through reflective inquiry the depth dimension of subjectivity becomes thematic and loses its prereflective elusiveness. As Dan Zahavi (2002, 82) notes, reflection does not merely repeat or copy the original experience, it changes the givenness of the experience reflected upon—otherwise there would be no need for reflection. Thus, the paradox inherent in reflection

means that we are obviously confronted with a fundamental limit: when I reflect, I encounter myself as a thematized ego, whereas functioning subjectivity always eludes my thematization and remains anonymous (ibid. 84). Zahavi argues that this does not constitute a major skeptical challenge for the phenomenological enterprise, but only creates a harmless and unavoidable impasse. First, although reflection cannot apprehend the anonymous life in its very functioning, neither is it supposed to. The aim is to lift the naïveté of prereflective experience, and not to reproduce it. Second, although it must be acknowledged that there are depth dimensions in the constitutive process, which do not lie open to the view of reflection, this does not necessarily imply that they remain forever completely ineffable, beyond phenomenological investigation. They can be disclosed, not through direct thematization, but through an indirect operation of dismantling and deconstruction (ibid., 84–86.)

9. See Foucault 1998b, 69–87; Foucault 2000a, 241, 248.

10. Lisa Guenther develops an interesting feminist phenomenological account of birth in her book *The Gift of the Other: Levinas and the Politics of Reproduction* based on Levinas's thought. She argues, similarly to Dastur, that birth always "refers to a past that antecedes and interrupts the remembered or represented past in which I constitute myself as an autonomous, self-possessed subject" (Guenther 2006, 4). She shows how this idea has profound ethical consequences: our understanding of the moral subject as an entirely self-possessed individual is at odds with the understanding of oneself as born to an Other. She argues that we should consider philosophically the ethical significance of birth as a maternal gift of time and existence.

Chapter 6

1. The phenomenological investigation of sexual difference can also be denied on the basis of Heidegger's thought. Drucilla Cornell (1999, 4) writes that the Heideggerian position might run, broadly, as follows: questions of sexual difference cannot follow directly from an analytic of finitude, because the marking of *Dasein* as differentiated by sex is a secondary phenomenon. An analytic of finitude that would proceed along the lines of *Being and Time* must not include secondary characteristics in its analysis because these would involve the philosopher in engaging with ontic and not ontological questions—questions of anthropology in Heidegger's sense, rather than questions of philosophy. Jacque Derrida is perhaps the best-known critic of Heidegger's view. He has questioned whether sexual difference can be reduced to a secondary characteristic of *Dasein*. See Derrida 1983.

2. The way Merleau-Ponty's denial of the possibility of a complete reduction is interpreted varies. Sara Heinämaa (2002), for example, argues against interpretations that claim Merleau-Ponty abandons Husserl's reductions. According to her, Merleau-Ponty's critical comments are directed against intellectualist interpretations of Husserl's methodic ideas. The phenomenological reduction should be understood as involving passions and passivity.

3. See Young 1990. On other influential feminist accounts appropriating Merleau-Ponty's thought, see, for example, Weiss 1999; Heinämaa 2003. Many feminist theorists have also expressed strong reservations about Merleau-Ponty's avoidance of the question of sexual difference and of his apparent generalizations regarding subjectivity and embodiment, which tend to take men's experiences for human ones. On feminist criticisms of Merleau-Ponty accusing him of manifesting a masculinist bias, see, for example, Allen 1982–83; Butler 1989; Grosz 1994; and Irigaray 2004.

4. Linda Fisher (2000a, 29) defends feminist phenomenology against the charges of essentialism by arguing that a general account need not be equivalent to the absolutist sense of generic, but should be understood rather as the thread of invariance; not a model that fits all, but structural invariance *within* variance, that gives shape and coherence to it. Feminist phenomenology should not be understood as a form of reifying and homogenizing essentialism that suppresses any variations, but the attempt to articulate the tension of general and specific.

5. For more on poststructuralist criticism of feminist phenomenology see, for example, Butler 1989; Scott 1992.

6. Zahavi (2001, 125) shows how the intersubjective constitution of meaning is revealed in Husserl's thought through an analysis of the constitutive processes of the subject. To every experience of an object, there essentially belongs a reference to further possible experiences, since the absent aspects of the object are co-intended through, and beyond, the intuitively given appearance. Since these possible experiences are incompatible in principle with my currently actual experience, it is a matter of the experience of possible others. I can only constitute an object because my horizontal relatedness to the world contains structural references to the perceptions of possible others. My experiences of the world therefore contain an intersubjective dimension a priori.

7. Husserl also states this explicitly in *Cartesian meditations*, for example: the individual subjects of transcendental intersubjectivity are furnished with mutually corresponding and harmonious systems. See, for example, Husserl 1995, 125.

8. David Carr (2002, 121), for example, argues that transcendental intersubjectivity itself has, in the final analysis, to be submitted to phenomenological reduction to reveal how it is constituted.

9. Merleau-Ponty seems to a certain extent to accept the circularity of his position and the superimposition of the empirical and the transcendental aspects of experience. He formulates the problem himself when he writes, for example: "Now if the transcendental is intersubjectivity, how can the borders of the transcendental and the empirical help becoming indistinct? For along with the other person, all the other person sees in me—all my facticity—is reintegrated into subjectivity, or at least posited as an indispensable element of its definition. Thus the transcendental descends into history" (Merleau-Ponty 1964, 107). Foucault's criticism of Merleau-Ponty focuses precisely on this circularity. He argues that the analysis of lived experience (*expérience vécu*) superimposes the transcendental and the empirical by giving the empirical contents transcendental value. What is given in experience and what renders experience possible correspond to each other in endless oscillation. See Foucault 1989, 321–322, 336.

10. See, for example, Zahavi 2001; Steinbock 1995.
11. See, for example, Merleau-Ponty 1994, xiii–xiv.

Chapter 7

1. For other feminist appropriations of Foucault's idea of disciplinary power, see, for example, Bordo (1989) and (2001).

2. Foucault (1991b, 135) argues that in the seventeenth century a soldier, for example, still learned his profession for the most part in actual fighting in which he proved his natural strength and inherent courage. But by the eighteenth century a soldier had become a fighting machine, something that could be constructed through correct training.

3. The idea of gender as an acquired habit characterizes both poststructuralist approaches, such as Butler's performative gender theory, as well as phenomenological attempts such as Iris Marion Young's analysis of typically feminine ways of movement. See Butler (1990); Young (1990).

4. Trent Hamann (2009, 48), for example, points to the alarming explosion of the U.S. prison populations as well as the worldwide escalation of the use of surveillance technologies. According to him, the open acknowledgment of the use of torture by the U.S. government can also be recognized as one of the signal characteristics of sovereign power.

5. Foucault discusses a frequently cited passage from Hume's *Enquiries* in which he proposes that we ask a man why he uses exercise. The man would answer that he wants to keep his health. If we pushed the inquiry further and asked why he wants to keep his health, he would note that sickness is painful. However, he would not be able to answer the final question of why he hates pain. Foucault argues that for Hume, individual choice is irreducible in the sense that it becomes a regressive end point in the analysis of human behavior. It is also nontransferable, which does not mean that we could never choose to place another person's interest before our own. However, even in that case of an altruistic choice the principle of my choice is still based on my own feeling of pain and pleasure—only it is another person's satisfaction that causes me more pleasure than my own. Foucault (2008, 272) refers to Hume's famous aphorism in *A Treatise of Human Nature*, in which Hume argues that it is not "contrary to reason to prefer the destruction of the whole world to the scratching of my finger" (Hume 1975, 293).

6. Foucault notes that what is usually stressed in Smith's famous theory of the invisible hand is the "hand," in other words the existence of something like providence which would tie together all the dispersed threads. But for Foucault, the other element, "invisibility," is at least as important. The total rationality will always remain invisible, which means that no economic agent can or should attempt to pursue the collective good but should focus on pursuing solely his or her own interests; see Foucault 2008, 279–80.

7. See, for example, Becker 1995, 218–39 and 329–42.

8. The theory of human capital developed by economists of the Chicago

School such as Gary Becker and Theodore Schultz in the 1960s and early 1970s was an attempt to fill a gap in formal economic analysis by offering a unified explanation of a wide range of empirical phenomena that had either been given ad hoc interpretations or had baffled investigators. Becker, for example, refers to well-known phenomena such as the fact that earnings typically increase with age at a decreasing rate, and that unemployment rates tend to be negatively related to the level of skill. See Becker 1962 and 1964; Schultz 1962.

9. The most striking example that Foucault discusses is the mother-child relationship (2008, 229–30, 243–44). A neoliberal economic analysis would treat the time the mother spends with the child, as well as the quality of the care she gives, as an investment that constitutes human capital and on which she can expect a return. Investment in the child's human capital will produce an income when the child grows up and earns a salary. Similarly, economic analyses of marriage could be read as attempts to decipher what is traditionally considered noneconomic social behavior in economic terms. Social relationships could be considered forms of investment: there are capital costs and returns on the capital invested.

10. See, for example, Palley 2005.

11. On the global effects of neoliberalism see, for example, Jaggar 2006; Ong 2007; Eisenstein 2009; Fraser 2009.

12. Feminist critiques of liberalism have become a central strand of feminist political philosophy. As Mary Dietz writes in *Turning Operations: Feminism, Arendt and Politics* (2002, 28), over the past two decades they have become a kind of cottage industry within feminist theory. Feminists have critically examined the implications of liberalism for ethical and moral theory, as well as challenged the assumptions that underlie liberal thought and inform its politics. Many of these critiques eschew the liberal focus on rights protected by the state and criticize the abstract individualism, rational egoism, as well as the instrumental conception of social relationships that informs liberal political theory. A crucial issue underlying the different strands of feminist critique has been the philosophical repudiation of the liberal subject. It has taken two main forms. Feminists have argued that the idea of an atomistic individual that underlies liberal thought is ontologically false because subjects are importantly relational and constituted by their attachments and primary social relationships. The second strand of the feminist critique has focused on the male-bias prevalent in liberalism's understanding of the subject: the rational, highly competitive, and self-interested subject might be an accurate characterization of the male subject, but it does not correspond to female experience. In other words, to the extent that there is reality to liberalism's understanding of the subject, it is a narrow and biased account because it rests on an allegedly masculinist conception of the subject as an independent, self-interested, economic being. On feminist critiques of the liberal subject, see, for example, Pateman 1979 and 1988; Elshtain 1981; Jaggar 1983; Held 1984.

13. For different definitions of the concept *feminization of labor*, see, for example, Morini 2007, 41–44.

14. Andrijasevic refers to feminist scholars such as Arlie Hochshild (1997, 1983) and Elizabeth Bernstein (2007) who have made important contributions

to mapping out the new emerging configurations of intimate life and emotional labor. They have studied customer-oriented relational work and sex work, respectively, and shown how emotional labor has been transposed from the sphere of domesticity to that of commerce.

15. See, for example, Elliott 2008.

16. As many critics of neoliberalism have argued, exploitation and domination is rendered invisible as political phenomena when individuals' social situation is judged as the effect of his or her own choices and investments. Neoliberal rationality thus allows for the avoidance of any kind of collective structural or governmental responsibility for social and economic inequality (Hamann 2009, 44). See also, for example, Brown 2005; Harvey 2005; and Read 2009.

17. See, for example, Schultz 1998.

Chapter 8

1. See, for example, Eisenstein 2009; Walby 2011.

2. For such accounts, see, for example, Harvey 2005; Patomäki 2008. Patomäki (2008, 135–36) emphasizes the importance of the closing of the gold window by Nixon in 1970. According to him, this decision to delink the dollar and gold was one of the nodal points that generated a new set of global competitive trends that point forty years later to an immanent rupture in global history.

3. His usage of neoliberalism in these lectures is nonstandard from the current point of view because he traces its earliest form to 1930s Germany. The lectures analyze the neoliberal program in two forms. The initial German form was represented by proponents of the Freiburg school of economists such as Walter Eucken and Wilhelm Röpke, and the other, American form, was the neoliberalism of the Chicago school, which was derived from the former but was in some respects more radical.

4. Compare to Patomäki 2008, 163.

5. David Harvey (2007, 21), for example, has presented the powerful argument showing that it was the genius of neoliberal theory to provide a benevolent mask full of wonderful-sounding words such as "freedom," "liberty," "choice," and "rights" to hide the grim realities of this restoration of naked class power. For Harvey, resistance to neoliberalism requires that we rejuvenate class politics and unmask the truth: we must expose neoliberalism for what it truly is, namely a covert attempt to restore class privilege.

6. Walby's own socialist feminist analysis emphasizes the importance of such central neoliberal objectives as economic growth and the need to increase women's human capital. See, for example, Walby 2011, 152.

7. See Marx 1965, 471–514.

8. Fraser begins by rejecting what she takes to amount to a mere misunderstanding of her position before tackling the genuine disagreements. She emphasizes rightly that the way she understands misrecognition is material: it is an institutionalized social relation, not a psychological state or something merely symbolic. Butler's argument that because gays and lesbians suffer material, eco-

nomic harms their oppression is not properly categorized as misrecognition is thus simply a mischaracterization of her claim. In Fraser's conception, injustices of misrecognition are just as material as injustices of maldistribution. The material harms cited by Butler—the instances in which lesbian and gays are excluded from state-sanctioned notions of the family and the accompanying benefits, for example—thus constitute paradigmatic cases of misrecognition (Fraser 1997b, 282).

9. See Polanyi 2001, 74.

10. Lisa Duggan (2003, 83) also interprets Butler to be arguing that the economy/culture distinction is "a kind of *ruse* of capitalist liberal discourse."

11. Physiocrats were a school of economists founded in eighteenth-century France. Their key tenet was the belief that land was the source of all wealth, but they also advocated the idea that profoundly influenced Adam Smith and economic liberalism that government policy should not interfere with the operation of natural economic laws. Foucault discusses the physiocrats in several instances in the lectures *Security, Territory, Population* (2007)—the lectures that preceded *The Birth of Biopolitics*.

12. See, for example, Becker 1962, 1964.

13. See, for example, Hayek 1944, 13, 27.

14. See, for example, Barry 1995, 32.

15. Those who view prostitution as an inherently abusive practice generally support prohibition of the act and punishment of some or all parties involved. In contrast, those who view prostitution as a form of labor tend to advocate policies designed to enhance worker control through decriminalization, regulation, and worker self-organizing. While decriminalization entails only the removal of criminal penalties for sexual commerce, legalization implies state regulation of the trade (Chapkis 1997, 131, 155).

16. Compare to Sandel 2012.

17. Rutvica Andrijasevic (2010, 57–58) describes the process of negotiating the U.N. Trafficking protocol, for example, as having been contested by two main feminist NGOs: first, the Human Rights Caucus, defending the position that prostitution is a form of legitimate labor, and second, the International Human Rights Network, adamant that prostitution was a violation of women's human rights.

18. For an illuminating discussion on Foucault's position on rights discourse and the political potential of rights as a form of opposition to neoliberal governance, see McNay 2009, 70–74.

Chapter 9

1. bell hooks (1981), for example, argued that the white feminists' version of sisterhood was informed by race and class assumptions about white womanhood. This version took political solidarity for granted rather than approaching it as a goal to be achieved.

2. See also, for example, Butler 1990; Brown 1995; and Spelman 1998.

3. For an excellent analysis of these debates and of the central philosophical issues at stake in them, see Heyes 2000. Heyes (2007, 20–21) shows how
feminists have presented essentialism as a term that "can capture a range of
widely debated and controversial themes in feminist thought, including illegitimate generalizations, ahistoricism, and certain understanding of identity politics." As well as bringing clarity to the debates, she shows (77–102) how Wittgenstein's notion of family resemblances can help feminists to locate themselves
outside of the problematic stalemate of trying to incorporate the multiplicity
of differences between women while also having to make generalizations about
them. The notion offers an ontological critique of essentialism, but it also makes
it possible to use the category of women meaningfully as a basis for feminist politics. Women bear family resemblances to each other, but they do not all fit any
single definition.

4. See also Heyes 2000.

5. Cressida Heyes (2007) has taken up this question in her investigation of
feminist solidarity after queer theory. She defends the importance of solidarity
between feminists and transsexuals by appropriating the idea of family resemblances: there are important overlaps between the normalizing techniques targeting transsexual bodies and female bodies. She is "not arguing for a one-size-
fits-all theory of embodied identities," but attempts to show that "we all feel the
weight of a culture where identities and bodies are supposed to line up" (Heyes
2007, 62).

6. For other accounts that emphasize futurity in feminist theory, see also,
for example, Grosz 1999.

7. Andrew Benjamin (2005, 1), for example, contends that the key question
for Walter Benjamin was the relationship between politics and time. The latter's
concern with history essentially involved a reconfiguration of the way the political
and the temporality of history interconnect.

8. Benjamin (1992, 248) claims that the cultural monuments celebrated
by official history could not be understood outside the context of their origins,
namely oppression and exploitation: "There is no document of civilization which
is not at the same time a document of barbarism."

9. The notion of the messianic is often deemed politically problematic
because of its religious connotations. It is taken as evidence that Benjamin was,
variously, a true, crypto- or pseudo-religious thinker who fell back on a regressive form of Jewish mysticism. On the tension between the political and religious
aspects of Benjamin's thought prominent in his commentators' assessments, see
Masuzawa 1985.

10. In *The Arcades Project* Benjamin studied fragments of the past—the
"rags" and "refuse" of the early days of mass culture in the nineteenth-century
Parisian arcades—that resist incorporation into the historicist's continuous
narrative.

11. Martin Hägglund (2008, 82) explains that ghosts or specters can be
understood as haunting reminders of the victims of historical violence or those
excluded from the formation of society. According to him, the notion of spectral-
ity is not, however, exhausted by the ghosts that question the good conscience of

a state, a nation, or an ideology. Rather, Derrida's aim was to formulate a general *hauntology* in contrast to the traditional ontology that thinks of being in terms of self-identical presence. What is important about the figure of the specter, then, is that it cannot be fully present; it has no being in itself, but indicates a relation to what is no longer or not yet.

Bibliography

Alcoff, Linda. 1996. "Dangerous Pleasures: Foucault and the Politics of Pedophilia." In *Feminist Interpretations of Michel Foucault*, ed. Susan Hekman, pp. 99–135. University Park, Pa.: Pennsylvania State University Press.

———. 2000. "Phenomenology, Post-Structuralism, and Feminist Theory on the Concept of Experience." In *Feminist Phenomenology*, ed. Linda Fisher and Lester Embree. Dordrecht: Kluwer Academic Publishers.

Alcoff, Linda, and Laura Gray. 1993. "Survivor Discourse: Transgression or Recuperation?" *Signs: Journal of Women in Culture and Society* 18, no 2: 260–90.

Alcoff, Linda Martín, and Eva Feder Kittay. 2007. "Introduction: Defining Feminist Philosophy." In *The Blackwell Guide to Feminist Philosophy*, ed. Linda Martín Alcoff and Eva Feder Kittay, pp. 1–13. Oxford: Blackwell Publishing.

Allen, Amy. 2010. *The Politics of Our Selves: Power, Autonomy, and Gender in Contemporary Critical Theory*. New York: Columbia University Press.

Allen, Jeffner. 1982–83. "Through the Wild Region: An Essay in Phenomenological Feminism." *Review of Existential Psychology & Psychiatry* 18, nos. 1, 2, and 3: 241–56.

Andrijasevic, Rutvica. 2010. *Migration, Agency and Citizenship in Sex Trafficking*. New York: Palgrave Macmillan.

Barry, Kathleen. 1995. *The Prostitution of Sexuality*. New York: New York University Press.

Bartky, Sandra Lee. 1988. "Foucault, Femininity and the Modernization of Patriarchal Power." In *Feminism and Foucault: Paths of Resistance*, ed. I. Diamond and L. Quinby, pp. 61–85. Boston: Northeastern University Press.

———. 2002. *"Sympathy and Solidarity" and Other Essays*. Lanham, Md.: Rowman & Littlefield.

Battersby, Christine. 1998. *The Phenomenal Woman: Feminist Metaphysics and the Patterns of Identity*. London: Routledge.

Beauvoir, Simone de. 1988. *The Second Sex*. London: Picador.

Becker, Gary. 1962. "Investment in Human Capital: A Theoretical Analysis." *Journal of Political Economy* 70, no. 2, part 2: "Investment in Human Beings," 9–49.

———. 1964. *Human Capital: A Theoretical and Empirical Analysis with Special Reference to Education*. New York: National Bureau of Economic Research.

———.1995. *The Essence of Becker*, ed. R. Febrero and P. Schwartz. Stanford: Hoover Institution Press.

Benjamin, Andrew. 2005. "Introduction." In *Walter Benjamin and History*, ed. Andrew Benjamin, pp. 1–2. London and New York: Continuum.

Benjamin, Walter. 1992. *Illuminations*, ed. Hannah Arendt, trans. Harry Zohn. London: Fontana Press.

———. 2002. *The Arcades Project*. Cambridge, Mass. and London: The Belknap Press of Harvard University Press.

Berger, Peter, and Luckmann, Thomas. 1967. *The Social Construction of Reality: A Treatise in the Sociology of Knowledge*. New York: Random House.

Bernstein, Elizabeth. 2007. *Temporarily Yours: Intimacy, Authenticity and the Commerce of Sex*. Chicago and London: University of Chicago Press.

Bigwood, Carol. 1990. "Renaturalizing the Body." *Hypatia* 6, no. 3: 54–72.

Bordo, Susan. 1989. "The Body and the Reproduction of Femininity: A Feminist Appropriation of Foucault." In *Gender/Body/Knowledge*, ed. Allison Jaggar and Susan Bordo, pp. 13–33. New Brunswick, N.J.: Rutgers.

———. 2001. "Feminism, Foucault and the Politics of the Body." In *Up against Foucault*, ed. C. Ramazanoglu, pp. 179–203. London: Routledge, 1993.

Braidotti, Rosi. 2002. *Metamorphoses: Towards a Materialist Theory of Becoming*. Cambridge, U.K.: Polity Press.

Brown, Wendy. 1995. *States of Injury: Power and Freedom in Late Modernity*. Princeton, N.J. and Oxford: Princeton University Press.

———. 2005. *Edgework: Critical Essays on Knowledge and Politics*. Princeton, N.J. and Oxford: Princeton University Press.

Butler, Judith. 1989. "Sexual Ideology and Phenomenological Description: A Feminist Critique of Merleau-Ponty's Phenomenology of Perception." In *The Thinking Muse: Feminism and Modern French Philosophy*, ed. by Jeffner Allen and Iris Marion Young. Bloomington: Indiana University Press, 85–100.

———. 1990. *Gender Trouble: Feminism and the Subversion of Identity*. London and New York: Routledge.

———. 1992. "Contingent Foundations." In *Feminists Theorize the Political*, ed. Judith Butler and Joan W. Scott, pp. 3–21. London: Routledge.

———. 1993. *Bodies that Matter*. London and New York: Routledge.

———.1997. "Merely Cultural." *Social Text* 52/53, vol. 15, nos. 3 and 4: "Queer Transexions of Race, Nation, and Gender," 265–77.

———. 2004. *Undoing Gender*. London: Routledge.

Cahill, Ann. 2001. *Rethinking Rape*. Ithaca, N.Y.: Cornell University Press.

Carr, David. 2002. "Response to Drummond and Zahavi." *Human Studies* 25, no. 1: 117–23.

Castoriadis, Cornelius. 1987. *The Imaginary Institution of Society*. Cambridge, Mass.: MIT Press.

Chapkis, Wendy. 1997. *Live Sex Acts: Women Performing Erotic Labor*. New York: Routledge.

Connolly, William. 1984. "The Dilemma of Legitimacy." In *Legitimacy and the State*, ed. William Connolly, pp. []. Oxford: Blackwell.

Cornell, Drucilla. 1999. "Opening Remarks." In *Is Feminist Philosophy Philosophy?*, ed. Emanuela Bianchi, pp. 3–9. Evanston, Ill.: Northwestern University Press.

Dastur, Françoise. 2000. "Phenomenology of the Event: Waiting and Surprise." *Hypatia* 15, no. 4 178–89.

Davidson, Arnold I. 1997. "Structures and Strategies of Discourse: Remarks Towards a History of Foucault's Philosophy of Language." In *Foucault and His Interlocutors*, ed. Arnold I. Davidson, pp. 1–20. Chicago: University of Chicago Press.

Davidson, Donald. 1986. "A Coherence Theory of Truth and Knowledge." In *Truth and Interpretation: Perspectives on the Philosophy of Donald Davidson*, ed. Ernest LePore, pp. 307–19. Oxford: Basil Blackwell.

Derrida, Jacques. 1978. *Writing and Difference*. New York and London: Routledge.

———. 1983. "*Geschlecht*: Sexual Difference, Ontological Difference" *Research in Phenomenology* 13, no. 1: 65–83.

———. 2006. *Specters of Marx: The State of the Debt, the Work of Mourning and the New International*. Trans. Peggy Kamuf. New York and London: Routledge.

Dietz, Mary. 2002. *Turning Operations: Feminism, Arendt and Politics*. London: Routledge.

Djaballah, Mark. 2008. *Kant, Foucault, and Forms of Experience*. London and New York: Routledge.

Doeuff, Michele Le. 1991. *Hipparchia's Choice: An Essay Concerning Women, Philosophy, Etc.* Cambridge, Mass.: Blackwell.

Dreyfus, Hubert L. 2005. "Overcoming the Myth of the Mental: How Philosophers Can Profit from the Phenomenology of Everyday Expertise." *Proceedings and Addresses of the American Philosophical Association* 79, no. 2: 47–65.

Dreyfus, Hubert L., and Paul Rabinow. 1982. *Michel Foucault: Beyond Structuralism and Hermeneutics*. Hemel Hempstead, U.K.: Harvester Wheatsheaf.

Duggan, Lisa. 2003. *The Twilight of Equality? Neoliberalism, Cultural Politics and the Attack on Democracy*. Boston: Beacon Press.

Eisenstein, Hester. 2009. *Feminism Seduced: How Global Elites Use Women's Labor and Ideas to Exploit the World*. Boulder: Paradigm Publishers.

Elliott, A. 2008. *Making the Cut: How Cosmetic Surgery Is Transforming Our Lives*. London: Reaktion Books.

Elliston, F. A. 1981. "Introduction to Universal Teleology." In *Husserl, Shorter Works*, trans. M. Biemel, pp. 335–37. Notre Dame, Ind.: University of Notre Dame.

Elshtain, Jean Bethke. 1981. *Public Man, Private Woman*. Princeton, N.J.: Princeton University Press.

Fink, Eugen. 1995. *Sixth Cartesian Meditation: The Idea of a Transcendental Theory of Method*, trans. Ronald Bruzina. Bloomington: Indiana University Press.

Fisher Linda. 2000a. "Phenomenology and Feminism: Perspectives on Their Relation." In *Feminist Phenomenology*, ed. Linda Fisher and Lester Embree, pp. 17–38. Dordrecht: Kluwer.

———. 2000b. "Introduction." In *Feminist Phenomenology*, ed. Linda Fisher and Lester Embree, pp. 1–15. Dordrecht: Kluwer.

Flynn, Thomas. 1994. "Foucault's Mapping of History." In *The Cambridge Companion to Foucault*, ed. Gary Gutting, pp. 28–46. Cambridge: Cambridge University Press.

———. 2005. *Sartre, Foucault, and Historical Reason, Vol. 2. A Post-Structuralist Mapping of History*. Chicago: University of Chicago Press.

Foucault, Michel. 1978. *The History of Sexuality, Vol. 1, An Introduction*. Trans. Robert Hurley. London: Penguin.

———. 1988a. "The Art of Telling the Truth." In *Michel Foucault: Politics, Philosophy, Culture: Interviews and Other Writings, 1977–1984*, ed. Lawrence Kritzman, trans. Alan Sheridan and others, pp. 86–95. New York and London: Routledge.

———.1988b. "The Concern for Truth." In *Michel Foucault: Politics, Philosophy, Culture: Interviews and Other Writings, 1977–1984*, ed. Lawrence Kritzman, trans. Alan Sheridan and others, pp. 255–67. New York and London: Routledge.

———. 1989. *The Order of Things: An Archaeology of the Human Sciences*. London and New York: Routledge.

———. 1991a. *Discipline and Punish: The Birth of the Prison*. London: Penguin.

———. 1991b. "Polemics, Politics, and Problematizations." In *Foucault Reader*, ed. Paul Rabinow, pp. 381–90. London: Penguin.

———. 1991c. "Preface to *The History of Sexuality*, vol. 2." In *Foucault Reader*, ed. Paul Rabinow, pp. 333–39. London: Penguin.

———. 1991d. "What Is Enlightenment?" In *Foucault Reader*, ed. Paul Rabinow, pp. 32–50. London: Penguin.

———. 1992. *The Use of Pleasure. The History of Sexuality, Vol. 2*, trans. Robert Hurley. London: Penguin.

———. 1994. "Foucault, Michel, 1926–." In *Cambridge Companion to Foucault*, ed. Gary Gutting, trans. Catherine Porter, pp. 314–19. Cambridge, U.K.: Cambridge University Press.

———. 1998a. "My Body, This Paper, This Fire." In *Aesthetics, Method and Epistemology: Essential Works of Foucault, 1954–1984*, vol. 2, ed. J. Faubion, pp. 393–418. New York: New Press.

———. 1998b. "A Preface to Transgression." In *Aesthetics, Method and Epistemology: Essential Works of Foucault, 1954–1984*, vol. 2, ed. J. Faubion, pp. 69–88. New York: New Press.

———. 2000a. Interview with Michel Foucault. In *Power: Essential Works of Foucault, 1954–1984*, vol. 3, ed. J. Faubion, pp. 239–97. New York: New Press.

———. 2000b. "Truth and Juridical Forms." In *Power: Essential Works of Foucault, 1954–1984*, vol. 3, ed. J. Faubion, pp. 1–89. New York: New Press.

———. 2001. "Interview de Michel Foucault." In *Dits et écrit II, 1976–1988*, ed. D. Defert and F. Ewald, pp. 1507–15. Paris: Gallimard.

———. 2003. *Society Must Be Defended: Lectures at the Collège de France, 1975–1976*, ed. Mauro Bertani and Alessandro Fontana, English series ed. Arnold I. Davidson; trans. David Macey. Harmondsworth, U.K.: Allen Lane, Penguin.

———. 2004. *Abnormal: Lectures at the Collège de France, 1974–1975*, ed. Valerio Marchetti and Antonella Salomoni, English series ed. Arnold I. Davidson; trans. Graham Burchell. New York: Picador.

———. 2007. *Security, Territory, Population: Lectures at the Collège de France, 1977–78*, ed. Michel Senellart. Basingstoke, U.K.: Palgrave Macmillan.

———. 2008. *The Birth of Biopolitics: Lectures at the Collège de France, 1978–79*, ed. Michel Senellart. Basingstoke, U.K.: Palgrave MacMillan.

———, (ed.). 1975. *I, Pierre Rivière, Having Slaughtered My Mother, My Sister, and My Brother: A Case of Parricide in the 19th Century*. Lincoln: University of Nebraska Press.

———, (ed.). 1980. *Herculine Barbin: Being the Recently Discovered Memoirs of a Nineteenth-Century French Hermaphrodite*, trans. Richard McDougall. Brighton, U.K.: Harvester Press.

Fraser, Nancy. 1989. *Unruly Practices: Power, Discourse and Gender in Contemporary Social Theory*. Cambridge, U.K.: Polity Press.

———. 1997a. *Justice Interruptus: Critical Reflections on the "Postsocialist Condition."* London: Routledge.

———. 1997b. "Heterosexism, Misrecognition, and Capitalism: A Response to Judith Butler." *Social Text* 52/53, vol. 15, nos. 3 and 4, "Queer Transexions of Race, Nation, and Gender": 279–89.

———. 2009. "Feminism, Capitalism and the Cunning of History." *New Left Review* 56: 97–117.

Fraser, Nancy, and Linda Nicholson. 1990. "Social Criticism without Philosophy: An Encounter between Feminism and Postmodernism." In *Feminism/Postmodernism*, ed. by Linda Nicholson, pp. 19–38. London and New York: Routledge.

Grosz, Elizabeth. 1994. *Volatile Bodies, Toward a Corporeal Feminism*. Indianapolis: Indiana University Press.

———. 1999. "Thinking the New: Of Futures yet Unthought." In *Becomings: Explorations in Time, Memory, and Futures*, ed. Elizabeth Grosz, pp. 15–28. Ithaca, N.Y.: Cornell University Press.

———. 2004. *The Nick of Time: Politics, Evolution, and the Untimely*. Durham, N.C.: Duke University Press

Guenther, Lisa. 2006. *The Gift of the Other: Levinas and the Politics of Reproduction*. Albany: SUNY Press.

Gutting, Gary. 1989. *Michel Foucault's Archaeology of Scientific Reason*. Cambridge, U.K.: Cambridge University Press.

Habermas, Jürgen. 1987. *The Philosophical Discourse of Modernity*. Cambridge, U.K.: Polity Press.

Hacking, Ian. 2002. *Historical Ontology*. Cambridge, Mass.: Harvard University Press.

Haddad, Samir. 2013. *Derrida and the Inheritance of Democracy*. Indianapolis: Indiana University Press.

Hägglund, Martin. 2008. *Radical Atheism: Derrida and the Time of Life*. Stanford: Stanford University Press.

Hamann, Trent. 2009. "Neoliberalism, Governmentality, and Ethics." *Foucault Studies* 6: 37–59.

Han-Pile, Béatrice. 2002. *Foucault's Critical Project: Between the Transcendental and the Historical.* Trans. Edward Pile. Stanford: Stanford University Press.

Harris, Angela. 1990. "Race and Essentialism in Feminist Legal Theory." *Stanford Law Review* 42, no. 3: 581–616.

Hartman, Martin, and Axel Honeth. 2006. "Paradoxes of Capitalism." *Constellations* 13, no. 1: 41–58.

Harvey, David. 2005. *A Brief History of Neoliberalism.* Oxford: Oxford University Press.

Haslanger, Sally. 2000. "Feminism in Metaphysics: Negotiating the Natural." In *The Cambridge Companion to Feminism in Philosophy,* ed. Miranda Fricker and Jennifer Hornsby, pp. 107–26. Cambridge: Cambridge University Press.

Hayek, Friedrich. 1944. *A Road to Serfdom.* Chicago: University of Chicago Press.

Heidegger, Martin. 1977. *The Question Concerning Technology and Other Essays.* New York: Harper & Row.

———. 1993. *Grundprobleme der Phänomenologie.* Gesamtausgabe Band 58. Frankfurt am Main: Vittorio Klosterman.

———. 1999. *Zur Bestimmung der Phänomenologie.* Gesamtausgabe Band 56/57. Frankfurt am Main: Vittorio Klosterman.

Heinämaa, Sara. 2002. From Decisions to Passions: Merleau-Ponty's Interpretation of Husserl's Reduction. In *Merleau-Ponty's Reading of Husserl,* ed. Ted Toadvine and Lester Embree, pp. 129–48. Dordrecht: Kluwer.

———. 2003. *Toward a Phenomenology of Sexual Difference: Husserl, Merleau-Ponty, Beauvoir.* Lanham, Md.: Rowan & Littlefield.

Hekman, Susan. 1990. *Gender and Knowledge: Elements of Postmodern Feminism.* Cambridge, U.K.: Polity Press.

Held, Virginia. 1984. *Rights and Goods: Justifying Social Action.* New York: Free Press.

Heyes, Cressida. 2000. *Line Drawings: Defining Women through Feminist Practice.* Ithaca, N.Y. and London: Cornell University Press.

———. 2007. *Self-Transformations: Foucault, Ethics, and Normalized Bodies.* Oxford: Oxford University Press.

Hintikka, Jaakko. 1997. *Lingua Universalis vs. Calculus Ratiocinator: An Ultimate Presupposition of Twentieth-Century Philosophy.* Dordrecht: Kluwer.

Hochshild, Arlie. 1983. *The Managed Heart: Commercialization of Human Feeling.* San Francisco and Los Angeles: University of California Press.

hooks, bell. 1981. *Ain't I a Woman: Black Women and Feminism.* Boston, Mass.: South End Press.

Hume, David. 1975. *A Treatise of Human Nature,* ed. Selby-Biggc. Oxford: Clarendon Press.

Husserl, Edmund. 1970. *The Crisis of European Sciences and Transcendental Phenomenology: An Introduction to Phenomenological Philosophy,* trans. David Carr. Evanston, Ill.: Northwestern University Press.

———. 1981. "Universal Teleology." In *Husserl, Shorter Works,* trans. M. Biemel, pp. 335–37. Notre Dame, Ind.: University of Notre Dame Press.

———. 1982. *Ideas Pertaining to a Pure Phenomenology and to a Phenomenological Phi-*

losophy, Vol. 1: General Introduction to Pure Phenomenology, trans. F. Kersten. The Hague: Martinus Nijhoff.

———. 1995. *Cartesian Meditations*. Dordrecht: Kluwer.

———. 2001. *Logical Investigations*, 2 vols., trans. J. N. Findlay. London: Routledge.

Irigaray, Luce. 1985a. *Speculum of the Other Woman*. Ithaca, N.Y.: Cornell University Press.

———. 1985b. *This Sex which Is not One*. Ithaca, N.Y.: Cornell University Press.

———. 2004. *An Ethics of Sexual Difference*. London: Continuum.

Jaggar, Alison M. 1983. *Feminist Politics and Human Nature*. Totowa, N.J.: Rowman and Allanheld.

———. 2006. "Saving Amina: Global Justice for Women and Intercultural Dialogue." *Ethics & International Affairs* 19, no. 3: 55–75.

Jaggar, Alison M., and Iris Marion Young. 1998. "Introduction." In *A Companion to Feminist Philosophy*, ed. Alison M. Jaggar and Iris Marion Young, pp. 1–6. Oxford: Blackwell Publishing.

Johnson, Ann. 2000. "Understanding Children's Gender Beliefs." In *Feminist Phenomenology*, ed. Linda Fisher and Lester Embree, pp. 133–51. Dordrecht: Kluwer.

Kaplan, Gisela T., and Rogers, Lesley J. 1990. "The Definition of Male and Female Biological Reductionism and the Sanctions of Normality." In *Feminist Knowledge, Critique and Construct*, ed. Sneja Gunew, 205–28. London: Routledge.

Kisiel, Theodore. 1995. *The Genesis of Heidegger's Being and Time*. Berkeley: University of California Press.

Kruks, Sonia. 2001. *Retrieving Experience. Subjectivity and Recognition in Feminist Politics*. Ithaca, N.Y. and London: Cornell University Press.

Kusch, Martin. 1997. "Husserl and Heidegger on Meaning." In *Lingua Universalis vs. Calculus Ratiocinator: An Ultimate Presupposition of Twentieth-Century Philosophy*, ed. Jaakko Hintikka, pp. 240–68. Dordrecht: Kluwer.

Levy, Ariel. 2005. *Female Chauvinist Pigs Women and the Rise of Raunch Culture*. New York: Free Press.

Lloyd, Genevieve. 1984. *Man of Reason*. Minneapolis: University of Minnesota Press.

Longino, Helen. 1990. *Science as Social Knowledge: Values and Objectivity in Scientific Inquiry*. Princeton, N.J.: Princeton University Press.

Loux, Michel J. 1998. *Metaphysics: A Contemporary Introduction*. London and New York: Routledge.

Lowe, E. J. 1998. *The Possibility of Metaphysics: Substance, Identity, and Time*. Oxford: Clarendon Press.

Marchart, Oliver. 2007. *Post-Foundational Political Thought: Political Difference in Nancy, Lefort, Badiou and Laclau*. Edinburgh: Edinburgh University Press.

Marcuse, Herbert. 2002. *One-Dimensional Man*. London: Routledge.

Marx, Karl. 1965. *Grundrisse. Foundations of the Critique of Political Economy*. London: Penguin.

Masuzawa, Tomoko. 1985. "Tracing the Figure of Redemption: Walter Benjamin's Physiognomy of Modernity," *MLN* 100, no. 3, "German Issue": 514–36.

McDowell, John. 1994. *Mind and World*. Cambridge, Mass.: Harvard University Press.

McLaren, Margaret. 2004. "Foucault and Feminism: Power, Resistance, Freedom," in *Feminism and the Final Foucault*, ed. Dianna Taylor and Karen Vintges, pp. 214–34. Urbana and Chicago: University of Illinois Press.

McNay, Lois. 1991. "The Foucauldian Body and the Exclusion of Experience." *Hypatia* 6 no. 3: pp. 125–40.

———. 1992. *Foucault and Feminism*. Cambridge, U.K.: Polity Press.

———. 2010. "Self as Enterprise: Dilemmas of Control and Resistance in Foucault's *The Birth of Biopolitics.*" *Theory, Culture & Society* 26, no. 6: 55–77.

McRobbie, Angela. 2009. *The Aftermath of Feminism: Gender, Culture and Social Change*. London: Sage.

Merleau-Ponty, Maurice. 1994. *Phenomenology of Perception*, trans. Colin Smith. New York and London: Routledge.

———. 1964. *Signs*. Evanston, Ill.: Northwestern University Press.

Mohanty, J. N. 1985. *The Possibility of Transcendental Philosophy*. Dordrecht: Martinus Nijhoff.

Morini, Cristina. 2007. "The Feminization of Labour in Cognitive Capitalism." *Feminist Review* 87: 40–59.

Mouffe, Chantal. 1992. "Feminism, Citizenship, and Radical Democratic Politics." In *Feminists Theorize the Political*, ed. Judith Butler and Joan W. Scott, pp. 369–84. London and New York: Routledge.

———. 2005. *On the Political*. London and New York: Routledge.

Natorp, Paul. 1912. *Allgemeine Psychologie nach kritischer Methode*. Tubingen: J. C. B. Mohr.

O'Leary, Timothy. 2009. *Foucault and Fiction: The Experience Book*. London: Continuum.

Oksala, Johanna. 2005. *Foucault on Freedom*. Cambridge: Cambridge University Press.

———. 2006. "Female Freedom: Can the Lived Body Be Emancipated?" In *Feminist Interpretations of Maurice Merleau-Ponty*, ed. Gail Weiss and Dorothea Olkowski, pp. 209–228. University Park, Pa.: Pennsylvania State University Press.

———. 2012. *Foucault, Politics, and Violence*. Evanston, Ill.: Northwestern University Press.

Olkowski, Dorothea. 1999. *Gilles Deleuze and the Ruin of Representation*. Berkeley and Los Angeles: University of California Press.

Ong, Aihwa. 2007. *Neoliberalism as Exception: Mutations in Citizenship and Sovereignty*. Durham, N.C. and London: Duke University Press.

Palley, Thomas. 2005. "From Keynesianism to Neoliberalism: Shifting Paradigms in Economics." In *Neoliberalism: A Critical Reader*, ed. A. Saad-Filho and D. Johnston, pp. 20–29. London: Pluto Press.

Pateman, Carole. 1979. *The Problem of Political Obligation: A Critique of Liberal Theory*. Berkeley: University of California Press.

———. 1988. *The Sexual Contract*. Cambridge, U.K.: Polity.

Patomäki, Heikki. 2008. *The Political Economy of Global Security: War, Future Crisis and Changes in Global Governance.* London and New York: Routledge.

Pollanyi, Karl. 2001. *The Great Transformation: The Political and Economic Origins of Our Time.* Boston: Beacon Press.

Prado, C. G. 2006. *Searle and Foucault on Truth.* Cambridge: Cambridge University Press.

Read, Jason. 2009. "A Genealogy of Homo-Economicus: Neoliberalism and the Production of Subjectivity." *Foucault Studies* 6: 25–36.

Roberts, Julian. 1982. *Walter Benjamin.* London and Basingstoke: Macmillan.

Sandel, Michael. 2012. *What Money Can't Buy: The Moral Limits of Markets.* New York: Farrar, Straus and Giroux.

Sawicki, Jana. 1991. *Disciplining Foucault: Feminism, Power, and the Body.* London and New York: Routledge.

———. 2005. *Abnormal: Lectures at the College de France, 1974–1975. Notre Dame Philosophical Reviews.* http://ndpr.nd.edu/review.cfm?id=1581 (accessed July 29, 2010).

Schear, J. (ed.). 2012. *Mind, Reason and Being-in-the-World: The McDowell-Dreyfus Debate.* London: Routledge.

Scheman, Naomi. 1997. "Queering the Center by Centering the Queer: Reflections of Transsexuals and Secular Jews." In *Feminists Rethink the Self,* ed. Diana Meyers, pp. 124–62. Boulder: Westview.

Schües, Christina. 1997. "The Birth of Difference," *Human Studies 20.* Kluwer Academic Publishers, pp. 243–52.

———. 2000. "Empirical and Transcendental Subjectivity: An Enigmatic Relation?" In *The Empirical and the Transcendental A Fusion of Horizons,* ed. Bina Gupta, pp. 103–17. Lanham, Md.: Rowman & Littlefield.

Schultz, Theodore. 1962. "Reflections on Investment in Man." *Journal of Political Economy* 70, no. 2, Part 2: "Investment in Human Beings": 1–8.

Schultz, Vicki. 1998. "Women 'Before' the Law: Judicial Stories about Women, Work and Sex Segregation on the Job." In *Feminists Theorize the Political,* ed. Butler and J. Scott, pp. 297–341. London: Routledge.

Scott, Joan. 1991. "The Evidence of Experience." *Critical Inquiry* 17, no. 4: 773–97.

———. 1992. "Experience." In *Feminists Theorize the Political,* ed. Judith Butler and Joan W. Scott, pp. 22–40. London: Routledge.

Sellars, Wilfried. 1997. *Empiricism and the Philosophy of Mind.* Cambridge, Mass.: Harvard University Press.

Sider, Theodore, John Hawthorne, and Dean W. Zimmerman (eds.). 2008. *Contemporary Debates in Metaphysics.* Oxford: Blackwell.

Smith, David Woodruff, and Ronald McIntyre. 1982. *Husserl and Intentionality: A Study of Mind, Meaning, and Language.* Dordrecht: D. Reidel.

Soper, Kate. 1993. "Productive Contradictions." In *Up against Foucault,* ed. Caroline Ramazanoglu, pp. 29–50. London and New York: Routledge.

"The State and Quality of Scientific Research in Finland 2012." Publications of the Academy of Finland. http://www.aka.fi/Tiedostot/Tieteentila2012/en/The_State_of_Scientific_Research_in_Finland_2012.pdf

Steinbock, Anthony J. 1995. *Home and Beyond, Generative Phenomenology after Husserl.* Evanston, Ill.: Northwestern University Press.

Taylor, Chloe. 2009. *The Culture of Confession from Augustine to Foucault: A Genealogy of the "Confessing Animal."* New York and London: Routledge.

Valverde, Mariana. 2004. "Experience and Truth Telling in a Post-Humanist World: A Foucauldian Contribution to Feminist Ethical Reflections." In *Feminism and the Final Foucault,* ed. Dianna Taylor and Karen Vintges, pp. 67–90. Urbana and Chicago: University of Illinois Press.

Veyne, Paul. 1997. "Foucault Revolutionizes History." In *Foucault and His Interlocutors,* ed. A. Davidson, pp. 142–82. Chicago and London: University of Chicago Press.

Walby, Sylvia. 2011. *The Future of Feminism.* Cambridge: Polity Press.

Walter, Natasha. 1998/1999. *The New Feminism.* London: Virago Press.

Weiss, Gail. 1999. *Body Images: Embodiment as Intercorporeality.* New York: Routledge.

Young, Iris Marion. 1990. *Throwing Like a Girl and Other Essays in Feminist Philosophy and Social Theory.* Indianapolis: Indiana University Press.

Zahavi, Dan. 2001. *Husserl and Transcendental Intersubjectivity: A Response to the Linguistic-Pragmatic Critique.* Athens: Ohio University Press.

———. 2002a. "Transcendental Subjectivity and Metaphysics." *Human Studies* 25: 103–16.

———. 2002b. "Anonymity and First-Personal Givenness: An Attempt at Reconciliation." In *Subjektivität—Verantwortung—Wahrheit: Neue Aspekte der Phänomenologie Edmund Husserls,* ed. David Carr and Christian Lotz, pp. 75–89. Frankfurt and New York: Peter Lang.

———. 2003. "How to Investigate Subjectivity: Natorp and Heidegger on Reflection." *Continental Philosophy Review* 36, no. 2: 155–76.

———. 2004. "Husserl's Noema and the Internalism-Externalism Debate." *Inquiry* 47, no. 1: 42–66.

Index

abnormality, 59–61, 65, 102, 106
Andrijasevic, Rutvica, 123, 170n14
Alcoff, Linda, 12–13, 53–55, 59–63, 67, 87, 159n6, 162n7, 163nn7, 13, 164nn1–2
Analysen zur passiven Synthesis, 93
a priori, historical, 58
archaeology, 32–33, 94, 139, 159n4

Bartky, Sandra, 14, 47, 111–115, 120, 122, 124, 126
Battersby, Christine, 11, 22–26, 28, 34
Beauvoir, Simone, de, 97, 100, 160n4, 162n26
Becker, Gary, 118, 169n7, 170n8, 172n12
Bedeutung, 78–80
Being and Time, 86, 165n9, 167n1
Benjamin, Walter, 16, 147, 150–154, 156–158, 173nn7–10
birth, 13, 24, 88–93, 95–96, 166nn3–4, 167n10
"Birth of Biopolitics, The," 115–119, 131, 140–141, 172n11
body, 14–15, 22, 28, 39, 63–64, 72–74, 98–99, 105, 111–114, 119–124, 142; and disciplinary technologies, 111–114; lived, 98–99
bracketing, 6–7, 16, 67, 73, 75, 80–82, 86, 97, 99, 103–108, 163n13, 164n1, 165n8, 167n2, 168n8
British empiricism, 117
Brown, Wendy, 15–16, 122, 133, 143–145, 147–150, 156, 171n16, 172n2
Butler, Judith, 15, 23, 51, 128, 135–138, 160n3, 161n19, 164nn1, 2, 166n5, 168nn3, 5, 169n3, 171n8, 172nn2, 102

Cahill, Ann J., 47
capitalism, 119, 123, 127, 131–138, 141–144, 155, 163n12, 172n10

Chapkis, Wendy, 142–143, 172n15
Chicago School, 118, 140, 169n8, 171n3
Cobb-Stevens, Richard, 78
coherentism, 41–42
competition, 119, 140–141
Connolly, William, 133
consciousness-raising, 17, 48–49
contextualism, 161n22
cultural/economic, *see* economic

Dasein, 83, 85–86, 167n1
Dastur, Françoise, 95–96, 167n10
Davidson, Donald, 42
Deleuze, Gilles, 160n7
de/politicization, 7, 11, 23, 32–34, 111, 137, 140, 148; of economics, 136–137, 140
Derrida, Jacques, 10, 16, 27–28, 30, 147, 154–157, 161n17, 167n1, 173n11
discipline, 14, 32, 48–49, 59, 111–120, 124–125, 112–115, 169n1
Discipline and Punish, 31, 111–112
discourse, 10–13, 30, 33, 36–39, 43–45, 48, 50, 53–55, 58–65, 67, 71–72, 74–75, 78, 83, 87, 106, 113, 122, 127, 143, 162nn2, 7, 164n2, 165n4, 172nn10, 18
discursive: experience, *see* experience; practices, *see* practices
Drummond, John, 78

economic: and cultural, 128, 135–139, 141; growth, 131–133, 171; rationality, *see* governmentality, neoliberal; science, 117, 131, 139; subject, *see* subject
economy, political, 131, 136, 139
eidetic: embodiment, *see* embodiment; phenomenology, 88, 96, 99; structures, 102, 106

188